SilverS

Neil Drysdale has been involved in journalism since the mid-1980s and has been praised for the quality of his sport and feature writing. He was an award-winning journalist with *Scotland on Sunday* for fifteen years, prior to working for the likes of the *Herald* and the *Sunday Times*. He is now Chief News Feature Writer with the *Press & Journal*. He is also the author of *Dad's Army*, the book about the Freuchie cricket team winning the National Village Cup in 1985; *COOP*, an acclaimed biography of Davie Cooper; and *Southern Comfort*, which chronicles the history of rugby in the Borders.

He is married and lives in Aberdeen.

SILVERSMITH

The Biography of Walter Smith

Neil Drysdale

This edition first published in 2021 by Arena Sport, an imprint of
Birlinn Limited
West Newington House
10 Newington Road
Edinburgh
EH9 1QS

www.birlinn.co.uk

ISBN: 978 1 91375 907 0
eBook ISBN: 978 0 85790 067 8

British Library Cataloguing-in-Publication Data
A catalogue record for this book is available from the British Library

Typeset by Biblichor Ltd, Edinburgh
Printed and bound by Clays Ltd, Elcograf S.p.A.

CONTENTS

Acknowledgements

I would like to thank Craig Brown, Terry Butcher, Ewan Campbell, Ronnie Esplin, Andy Goram, Jim Guy, Sandy Jardine, Ally McCoist, Robert McElroy, Scott Nisbet, Alan Rough, Stephen Smith, Colin Stein, Sandy Tyrie, the Scottish Football Museum and Chick Young. Thanks are also in order to a number of former Rangers players and supporters, who asked for their contributions to remain anonymous, although since the majority of these respondents were expressing praise for Walter Smith, this shyness was sometimes difficult to understand.

I would also like to thank Neville Moir and Peter Burns at Birlinn and my agent, Mark Stanton, for exuding his usual calmness under pressure. Duggie Middleton worked assiduously in editing the original manuscript with his usual diligence. Finally, my wife, Dianne, had to tolerate me deploying my thumping two-finger typing style, often until 4.30 in the morning, and remained a pillar of support throughout the project, for which I thank her.

Neil Drysdale

INTRODUCTION

There haven't been many occasions in Scottish football when a brief announcement on a social media site has opened the floodgates to a mass outpouring of grief.

But then, there haven't been many characters in the game who have been as well-respected and widely admired as Walter Smith; a figure who straddled the Old Firm divide with the unstinting attitude that he could love Rangers without meaning that he had to hate Celtic.

And, as somebody who managed his country and dragged them back from the abyss when Berti Vogts' ill-starred tenure had reduced the national team to a near laughing stock, Smith became a reassuring presence at the tiller who inspired his compatriots to a famous triumph over France at a passionate, vociferous Hampden Park in October 2006.

Sadly, though, there were different emotions entirely on another October day 15 years later when Rangers FC issued a message informing us that Smith had died of cancer at the age of 73.

Announcing the news, and paying lavish tribute to Smith, chairman Douglas Park said:

'On behalf of the Rangers board of directors, staff and players, I convey my deep condolences to the Smith family.

'Walter leaves behind a wife, children and grandchildren, all of whom are in our thoughts and prayers at this difficult time.

'It is almost impossible to encapsulate what Walter meant to every one of us at Rangers. He embodied everything that a Ranger should be.

'His character and leadership were second to none, and will live long in the memory of everyone he worked with during his two terms as first team manager. I spoke with Walter as recently as last weekend. Even when he was battling illness, he was still able to provide advice and support. For that, I am personally grateful.

'Walter will be sorely missed by all of us at Rangers. Winning ten top-flight titles as manager, five Scottish Cups and six League Cups, as well as leading his club to the UEFA Cup Final in 2008, he will be remembered by the football community across the world.

'However, for Rangers supporters, he was much more than just a football manager. Walter was a friend to many, a leader, an ambassador and, most of all, a legend.'

The word 'legend' is overused in the modern world, but not in this instance. Even the way that the former Dundee United curmudgeon Jim McLean brusquely informed Smith of his deficiencies as a player – 'Let's face it, son, you're shite' – hints at the no-nonsense approach which these fellows from another era adopted to run their clubs and deal with Kipling's twin impostors through a combination of inspiration, intimidation and X-rated language.

The best of them also appreciated that they were dealing with often vulnerable youngsters and, even if it happened off-stage, gradually fostered a camaraderie and a comradeship in their players, forging a bond which could and would never be broken. That much was obvious in the tributes which were paid to Smith in the hours and days after his demise.

Grown men – big tough competitive characters, such as the current Rangers manager, Steven Gerrard – broke down as if they had just lost their best friend. Which, for some of them, was pretty close to the truth. In the case of former Ibrox stalwart, Ally McCoist, the crackle in his voice and sadness in his eyes testified to something which went far behind glib soundbites or expressions of regret.

His words were a eulogy for somebody he loved.

'He was everything to a lot of folk, myself included. He was my boss, he was my coach, he was my second father and then he turned into one of my best friends, to be honest with you. And the loss is absolutely incredible, to tell you the truth.

'I could sit here and tell you 'til the cows come home about Walter Smith, about how good a manager, how good a coach, how good a football man he was. But I think it's only fair to say, I think I can safely say, that he was probably the best husband, the best father, the best friend, everything you would expect in a man.

'And it is a tragic day. We are all devastated, absolutely devastated.'

McCoist is sometimes portrayed as a jovial Jack-the-lad or patter merchant with a microphone, and his involvement in BBC's *A Question of Sport* highlighted his skill with an anecdote or excruciating pun. But I spoke to him after the death of Jim Baxter in 2001 and he was as articulate and affectionate as he was saddened by the passing of Slim Jim.

He was even more expressive in his grief at the premature death of Davie Cooper from a brain haemorrhage, aged just 39 in 1995, and highlighted his belief that his former team mate could have become a terrific manager in due course.

He knew what he was talking about. After all, McCoist had already worked with Smith at Ibrox and grown to recognise the intrinsic decency, intelligence and hinterland of his boss, even when his mentor was exasperated with his time-keeping or lax attitude to training sessions.

They shared a mutual passion not just for football, but for life's idiosyncrasies, for art, rock music and films, and that affinity was replicated when Smith briefly joined forces with Sir Alex Ferguson at Manchester United in 2004.

In the space of a few months, these two granite-hewn Glaswegians – both of whom were in the crowd on the day of the Ibrox Disaster in 1971 and were later enlisted to lead Scotland's 1986 World Cup campaign after Jock Stein's tragic death – demonstrated the qualities which we associate with these working-class sons of the 1940s. Two men who witnessed grinding poverty in their childhood and rose through the sheer force of their personality without ever forgetting their roots.

Understandably, Ferguson was as distraught as everybody else when he heard that Smith had passed away and said:

'He was a great friend of mine for years and years. I had him as my assistant at United in 2004 and he was also my assistant when Scotland went to the World Cup in 1986.

'In all that time, you were dealing with a man with a great moral compass in how he lived his life and the friendship which he offered so many people. His contribution to football with Dundee United, Rangers, Scotland, Everton and Manchester United was immense.

'He was only at United a short time, but he was fantastic. I lost Carlos Queiroz to Real Madrid and I knew I needed an assistant, so I phoned Walter about it and he came for six months and helped us win the FA Cup against Millwall. He had a wonderful connection with people because he was a great listener and that was one of his greatest qualities.

'He listened and showed an interest in people and helped everyone he could. It's such a loss to the game and to everyone that knew him.'

Almost from the outset, even as Smith realised that he was never going to challenge Baxter, Jimmy Johnstone or Denis Law on the pitch, he was working assiduously at learning his trade in coaching and adopting the philosophy that genius lies in an infinite capacity for taking pains.

To his credit, Jim McLean provided the seeds which ensured he flourished in the future, and the former Rangers and Scotland player Derek Johnstone was among the first to witness the methodical fashion in which Smith responded to the challenge of working alongside such an irascible perfectionist as McLean at Tannadice for more than 15 years.

Indeed, Johnstone's maiden encounter with Smith was at Tannadice in 1967 when he was invited to train with United's part-timers while he was still at Linlathen High School in Dundee and, during his month at Tannadice, he saw enough of Smith's coaching ability to realise he was dealing with no ordinary behind-the-scenes apparatchik.

He recalled:

'That spell at Tannadice really opened my eyes. Walter took most of the coaching at United, and he really knew what he was talking about. Everything was geared towards technique, whereas I had been used to everything being geared towards fitness under big Jock Wallace at Ibrox. Right away, I knew that I was experiencing a great coach in the making. Walter treated everyone as individuals and he knew how to bring the best out of players. He was remarkable in that regard.'

But the reality is that football was in Walter Smith's DNA from the early days when he was growing up in the West of Scotland in the 1950s.

Here was a man in thrall to the sport played on hundreds of grass and ash surfaces across Glasgow every day, who was keen as mustard for action wherever there was a match to be savoured and whose whole-hearted commitment and enthusiasm were evident, both on and off the pitch.

His childhood and adolescence were marked by a love for the sport which never deserted him, yet Smith – a lifelong Rangers fan – had an aversion to the sectarianism and religious bigotry which has blighted the Scottish game for decades and – as we have seen even in recent months – has by no means disappeared.

On those Saturdays when there were no fixtures at Ibrox, he would regularly pay his admission money to watch Jock Stein's Celtic parade their skills and happily admitted he was a devotee of the style and panache with which the Lisbon Lions became the first British club to lift the European Cup in 1967.

He was equally delighted when Aberdeen and Dundee United achieved success in different competitions across the Continent in the 1980s and, whatever tribalism might have existed among some of his aficionados in Govan, Smith was his own man with his own strong principles.

He had already gained hero status in the 1990s during Rangers nine-in-a-row title-winning sequence. His stock rose in the 2000s, especially when one considers that his retire-ment – when he was given a standing ovation after Rangers beat Dundee United in his final home match in May 2011 – was a contributory factor in the collapse of the club into liquidation.

But, despite all the turmoil which surrounded Ibrox during that turbulent period in their history, none of it left a stain on Smith, who behaved with unwavering dignity even as some sections of the fan base were up in arms.

In that light, it's no wonder that the tributes were so fulsome – not just from Rangers supporters but from the football world at large. After all, when Celtic stalwart Tommy Burns died of cancer at the age of just 51 in 2008, Smith was one of the pall-bearers at the funeral (as was McCoist) and was clearly distressed at the loss of his friend.

As he said:

'Tommy was one of the best people I ever had the opportunity to work with. Football aside, he was also a terrific man and the more I got to know him, the more I liked him.

'He was a true Celtic man: a supporter as a kid, all the way through to having a really successful career with them. For me, Tommy Burns showed everything that was good about Celtic.'

Many of these values were espoused by Smith himself. As the award-winning writer Michael Grant said in *The Times*:

'When the great trade union leader Jimmy Reid once spoke of the shared characteristics of those towering figures Sir Matt Busby, Bill Shankly, Jock Stein and Sir Alex Ferguson, he said, "Walter Smith is cut from similar cloth. He has a kind of Scottish working-class character. Although they don't make a song and dance about it, they are proud of it and they hold on to it. They are all principled guys and they represent values that the Scottish working class used to hold quite dear."'

It wouldn't do to suggest that Smith was some saintly soul with endless amounts of vitality and virtuous conduct. As this biography makes clear, he didn't suffer fools gladly, was capable of eviscerating his critics with blasts of industrial-strength language straight from the Malcolm Tucker playbook, and there were occasions where he let rip at broadcasters and journalists – just ask the BBC's Chick Young – with the volcanic impact of Vesuvius made flesh.

But, in the case of any human being with lofty standards who finds themselves at the whim of events, and particularly in such a volatile climate as football, there will always be outbursts and spats which are later regretted. Ultimately, Smith was not a serial ranter or a human wrecking ball. He helped many players behind the scenes, including Paul Gascoigne, at the end of his tether as the tabloids circled, with the scent of blood in their nostrils at the prospect of a fresh scandal to cover.

Although they were from very different generations, the response of Steven Gerrard to Smith's death was similar to that of a child losing his father.

The former England and Liverpool stalwart gave tribute in saying:

'Walter was an incredible leader, a very successful manager here at Rangers. I think he epitomised everything that this club stands for and his DNA is all over this club.

'He was and he has been behind me right since day one. I have had many lunches and dinners and coffee and chats and private time with him in my office. So he is obviously going to be a very big loss to a lot of people.

'He's decorated all over the club and he will be forever, because he gave many, many years of his life to this football club which he loved.

'He was honest, he was genuine. And he has made me a better person, so I have got nothing but good words to say about him.'

There were lean years at Everton, where he went with promises ringing in his ears that were never delivered. Somehow, it simply seemed the wrong environment for somebody such as Smith to inhabit. From his twenties, he had prided himself on planning and preparing for every task methodically, and the chaos he encountered at Everton was alien to his nature. Yet, even amidst that bedlam, when there was the possibility of the club being relegated, he propelled them to safety.

That's one of the most enduring features of Smith's life. The ability to make the best of a bad job, whether picking up the detritus left behind by the hapless Vogts with Scotland, or returning to Rangers when they were a shadow of their former selves and driving them forward to domestic glory and a European final in Manchester.

So, let's celebrate a man who never regarded himself as special and who shrugged off suggestions that he deserved to be in the company of the triumvirate Stein, Ferguson and Shankly with the response, 'They were great managers. I've done OK!'

Yet, as McCoist countered:

'When he got the Scotland job, he appointed myself and the late, great Tommy Burns as his assistants and it was a brilliant move on his part. Tam was a great person to be around as well and the biggest Celtic man you would ever meet in your life.

'Well, the appointment grabbed the imagination of the whole country. You had the Celtic man and the Rangers man running the country's football team. These were special times.'

Indeed, they were. But let's go back to where it all started for the fellow nicknamed Sir Walter as we commemorate his extraordinary career.

Neil Drysdale, November 2021

CHAPTER ONE

A MAN IN THE CROWD

'This club is different. This is Rangers Football Club'

Long before there came Heysel or Hillsborough with their relent-lessly grim television images, incongruous floral tributes and uncomprehending vales of tears, there was one Saturday evening in Glasgow on which mothers and fathers, sons and daughters and many friends of friends clung anxiously to the hope that their loved ones would eventually make it home, and confirm that they had escaped the Ibrox Disaster. The majority did come home, and others such as Walter Smith, Alex Ferguson and Andy Roxburgh clambered around the mangled heaps of bodies and stricken souls, the emergency workers and Old Firm volunteers on Stairway 13, and thanked their lucky stars before absorbing the enormity of what had transpired. For 66 other families there was the spectre of a long night's journey into the void, and recognition that the catastrophe which engulfed Ibrox stadium at the end of the New Year match on 2 January 1971, had snatched away their menfolk, and in Margaret Ferguson's case, her daughter.

Decades on, pictures from the newsreels reflect collective mys-tification and bewilderment, accompanied by a sense of futile anger at the casual fashion in which so many lives were sacrificed. But beyond that is a numbness among the grieving families, possibly reflecting their feeling that such hackneyed phrases as 'Time is a great healer' and 'They're in a better place now' are but platitudes for those fortunate enough never to have been obliged

1

to identify relatives with faces blackened and life squeezed out of them. Talk to men such as Smith, Sandy Jardine or John Greig – hard-nosed artisans from an industrial background – and you will not hear easy sentiments, but rather hushed voices and instinctive sympathy for victims who, in other circumstances, could have been their very selves. Then prod them gently on their memories of that ghastly event, and they will relate their accounts of a tragedy which, all too fleetingly, tore through Glasgow's sectarian curtain and saw Orangemen shed tears in the company of priests throughout the west of Scotland and yonder into Edinburgh, before snaking across the Forth Bridge to the Kingdom of Fife and the community of Markinch, where Peter Easton, Richard Morrison, David Patton, Mason Phillips and Bryan Todd, schoolboys who lived within a few hundred yards, perished together on that stairway, which had witnessed an accident in 1961 and near-disasters in 1967 and '69.

Sandy Jardine, one of the celebrated ex-players who still walks the corridors of Rangers FC, describes the terrible events:

'In these days, this was probably the biggest fixture of the season, considering that the Old Firm clubs only met twice a year, but it was dreadfully ironic that what had been a fairly good-natured occasion, with neither trouble on the terraces nor on the pitch, should develop into a waking nightmare for so many people. Everybody knows the circumstances whereby Jimmy Johnstone sent Celtic in front with a minute to go. The ball got centred, we equalised at once [through Colin Stein] and the referee blew full-time immediately. So you had Rangers supporters who thought: "Oh, that's the game over" when Jimmy scored turning to go down the big staircase, then turning back when they heard the huge roar which greeted Colin's strike, and that coincided with a massive number of spectators making their path towards the exit and the subway. Then suddenly somebody fell, and the whole terrible business began.

'The thing is that I was on the ground staff, I had actually swept these stairways, and they were huge, really solid objects, so I could never understand how they could get mangled so badly by any number of human beings. But they were. Just think of it: the pressure of all those bodies cascading over one another and the panic which must have spread . . . Ach, there are no words in the dictionary to describe adequately what happened during those next few minutes. But you have to realise that we as players were completely unaware anything was wrong at that stage. We were in the dressing room fairly happy to have managed a draw, just sharing a few laughs together before getting into the bath. Well, I was one of the last guys to climb out, but as I re-emerged the order came that there had been an accident, and we all had to leave the room as quickly as possible. It could have been a fire alert or anything, but while we started putting our clothes on as fast as we could, the authorities started to bring some of the dead bodies into the place, and as you can probably imagine, everybody turned grey at the sight of them. But even then we had no real idea of the extent of the fatalities.

'As I drove back to my home in the east end of Edinburgh, I heard there were two dead, but soon enough the figures mounted up. It was 12, then 22, then 30, then 44 – I don't know why, but that number sticks in my mind – and finally it climbed to 66 as the news filtered out to all the parents and kith and kin of the folk who had attended the match, and then gone to pubs or restaurants or picture-houses afterwards. I have spoken to hundreds of fans since 1971, and they have told me of how vast crowds assembled at all of the drop-off points for the buses to find out whether their loved ones were okay. The telephone lines were jammed, Glasgow was in turmoil, the hospitals were all packed to overflowing. Anxiety, terror, pain, sadness, horror . . . a blanket of all these emotions was draped over the whole country that night, but there was nothing remotely comforting about it.'

Amid this hellish vista, Willie Waddell, the Rangers manager, somehow offered a semblance of sanity. It was significant that he and Celtic counterpart Jock Stein had observed casualties in other spheres, whether in battle or at the coal-face, and the pair constantly emphasised the desperate need for entrenched communities to pull together, and for religious tribalism to be cast aside. Sadly, but perhaps inevitably given the illogical nature of the positions adopted by extremists on both sides, the so-called healing process proved little more than a nine-day wonder. Yet in the longer term, the calamity yielded some benefits. Waddell, for example, vowed that the scenes he had witnessed would never be repeated at Ibrox, and before his death in 1992 that objective had borne fruit in the creation of a magnificent new stadium. Not that anybody connected with 1971 would forget the condition of the old edifice. 'It's strange what comes into your mind, but when I first went to the top of the steps and gazed down on the pile of bodies, my initial thought was of Belsen, because the corpses were entangled as they had been in the pictures which came out of the concentration camps,' Waddell told *The Scotsman* newspaper's illustrious football correspondent John Rafferty. 'But my God, it was dreadful: there were bodies in the dressing rooms, in the gymnasium and even in the laundry room. My own training staff and the Celtic boys were working flat out at the job of resuscitation, and we were all trying everything possible to bring breath back to those crushed limbs. Honestly, I will never forget the sight of Bob Rooney, the Celtic physiotherapist, with tears in his eyes giving the kiss of life to innumerable victims. He never stopped, nor did the Rangers doctors, nor the nurses and ambulance staff who flocked to join them, and we will never know how many lives were saved in there in that frenzy of activity.'

Nearby, the Southern General Hospital was under siege, their switchboard of only 35 lines, plus a single police short-wave radio, jammed by a crescendo of panic-stricken calls. But by midnight a worse task was in prospect for the likes of Jardine, Waddell, Greig and Colin Stein, who seems troubled to this day by the notion that his goal might have been a catalyst for such carnage: the funerals. And the subsequent protracted search for answers allied to the quest for apportioning responsibility which, despite lengthy inquiries, discovered little beyond the tinder-box of ingredients that would also bring death and destruction to the environs of Heysel and to Bradford and Hillsborough as much as 18 years later.

Inside Ibrox, one fellow had stood intently throughout that Old Firm encounter transfixed by proceedings that were typically pulsating and frenetic. As a registered professional player with Dundee United, Walter Smith would not have been anywhere near Glasgow, let alone Govan, but for his acceptance that he was not good enough to merit inclusion in the Tannadice side's festive plans, and was therefore free to travel to the ground he regarded as his spiritual home, the place where his grandfather had taken him to behold what old Jock had considered the best team in the world. At 22 years of age, Smith strode into Ibrox that afternoon with hardly a care. He was a phlegmatic individual, a young man of substance with a trade as an electrician already acquired, just in case football work proved to be in short supply, and even in those formative days he had started to appreciate that, irrespective of the fact that as a player he would never join the likes of Jim Baxter, Jimmy Johnstone and Billy McNeill in the Scottish Football Association's Hall of Fame, he might have a part to play for his country further down the line. Indeed, Smith's recollection of the Ibrox Disaster epitomises many of the core values that have shone through his ascent to the summit of soccer management:

'I can remember leaving the stadium with my brother at the finish of the match. I was on Dundee United's books at the time, but because of my lack of ability they had omitted to select me for the New Year match, so I travelled to Ibrox on the supporters' club bus, and I remember there being a wall at the side of the staircase which, if it hadn't been there, would have allowed people to spill over. Both of us got out, I thought because the fencing had collapsed, but on the 25th anniversary I looked at a photograph and the fencing was intact. We must have got over the top of other people, although nobody around us was in any danger; the deaths occurred at the bottom of the stairs, but we didn't know that at the time. We got on

5

the bus, which didn't have a radio or anything, and it was only when I arrived home that I remember my mother crying, saying people had died. If we had left two minutes earlier, it would have been us.'

Histrionics are not in Smith's nature, and his composure in discussing the Ibrox Disaster originated from the lessons he had learned growing up in visceral communities, where emotions tended to be best kept in check. In the days after 2 January he absorbed the consequences of the calamity which had befallen so many Scots by diabolical chance, but unlike many young foot-ballers he did not stick his head in the sand or seek refuge in alcohol. Instead, Smith read about the tragic stories of those who had been killed, swiftly recognised that the extended Rangers family had been dealt a devastating blow and pledged that he would do what he could to heal the widespread hurt. At the time he was in no position to swoop to the rescue, but as the years unfolded he never forgot the fundamental experiences of 1971.

The voices of that awful evening still resonate among those who were there, as I discovered when tracking down some of the eye-witnesses. 'I always remember standing in the middle of Stairway 13 and looking at this pile of bodies, some of them black, some of them blue, lying like rag dolls on all sides of me, whilst other fans were desperately grappling on to whatever they could find to avoid falling into the carnage,' recalls Andrew Ewan, a head librarian in Dunoon, who was 23 in 1971. 'I was at the match on my own because my best mate was in Aberdeen with his parents, and with hindsight I believe that one of the reasons why I survived is that I was wearing slip-on shoes, and I lost them as hundreds of supporters were caught up in the crush. I know that might sound strange, but I'm convinced that if I had been wearing shoes with laces, as I normally did, I wouldn't have been able to wriggle out of the morass. But I was tall and skinny in these days, and somehow I escaped.

'Yet in retrospect it always occurs to me that any of us could have been killed, that this was an accident waiting to happen and that you could drive yourself mad trying to rationalise why some survived and others perished. By the time the emergency services reached the scene and started working their guts out to rescue as many of the injured as they could, I was in shock, and I remember a policeman approaching me and saying: "Go home, son. Go home to your loved ones. There's nothing you can do here." That was the helpless feeling which engulfed us all when we woke up the following morning. It brought us all together, Rangers and Celtic fans, united in a common grief. But sadly it didn't last long.'

Craig Smith, a Livingston-based glazier, was not present at Ibrox, but the escalation into tragedy still haunts him. 'My father George was heading off for the Old Firm match, and as he put his coat on I asked if I could go along with him. But he just laughed, and after pointing out that my two older brothers also weren't going with him because it was too big a game, he waved us all goodbye. Well, at about ten to five there was a news-flash on the TV reporting that there had been an accident at Ibrox, but the programme had no details of any injuries. My mother looked worried, and although she wasn't too concerned at the outset, she became increasingly anxious as the time passed, because she and my father had arranged to go to a golf club dance that night. The later it grew you could tell that something was terribly wrong by my mum's expression, and she was constantly on the phone. Then suddenly the doorbell rang. My brother Stephen went to answer it, my mum screamed, then Stephen and my other brother George were standing together with tears streaming down their cheeks, and for a few moments I couldn't understand what on earth was going on.

'Eventually, though, we learned the truth. That while my dad had managed to push his brother John and brother-in-law Alex over the fence, he himself had been swept away with the force of the crowd, and even as John shouted towards him, he saw him die, upright. The very life was squeezed out of him on that terrible, terrible afternoon. At the time we lived in house No. 66 on the 14th floor, although you had to walk down to the living room on the 13th floor. So my father was born on the 14th of August, was killed on the 13th stair, and was one of the 66 killed at Ibrox. I will never forget it.'

In many respects the 1970s still seem within touching distance, but in other ways they belong to a different world. In the distinctly remote possibility of a recurrence of the Ibrox Disaster, television coverage nowadays would be wall-to-wall, obliterating everything else on the schedules. As darkness descended on 2 January 1971, however, Walter Smith, professional footballer, and Craig Smith, pre-school child, were in the dark about the scale of the calamity unfolding at their favourite club. Retired TV executive Bill Malcolm recalls: 'At that time, in my role as the director of the Saturday night football programme *Sportsreel*, we were out of the loop once the Old Firm match finished, whereas when you fast-forward three decades you have Sky, News 24, CNN, Ceefax, the Internet, breaking stories delivered straight to your phone or your iPod . . . all manner of up-to-the-minute news technology. In 1971 we had the *Green Citizen* sports paper reporting that three supporters had died at Ibrox. And that was it.

'Afterwards, some of us at the BBC were criticised for not having pictures of the disaster, but you have to realise that news and sport were entirely separate entities at the time, and there was no blurring of distinctions. All the same, there was never any question of us going ahead with plans to screen highlights of the game, and let's face it, on that evening an awful lot of people decided they would never again describe somebody missing a penalty as a *tragedy*, because the match at Ibrox didn't matter at all in the grand scheme of things. Life couldn't continue as normal in these circumstances.

However, I was involved later in the fatal accident inquiry, and I remember the pressure which was put on my secretary to recall the exact moment when the disaster started. Obviously it was a very painful experience for everyone caught up in the search for answers, and the job of dishing out blame. But, of course, we got off lightly, didn't we? We were still alive to be able to discuss the minutiae of what should and shouldn't have been done on that Saturday. The grieving families had no such get-out.'

❖

From Walter Smith's perspective, nothing would ever be quite the same after the winter of 1971. Born in Lanark in 1948, he had grown up in industrial Glasgow during a period when the metropolis truly fulfilled its reputation as the second city of the British Empire, and he was habitually a man at ease with his roots. By turns introspective, proud and competitive, his demeanour deadpan, sometimes even dour, Smith and Rangers were inextricably linked through his family background and his temperament. Endlessly restive, unsympathetic towards those who indulged in complacency, but fiercely protective of those he considered his friends, even at the age of eight the young Walter would stand up to bullies and was unafraid of the gangs who battled for the ascendancy on their patches of turf across Glasgow in the 1960s and '70s. He quickly found himself drawn towards Rangers with their history, their reputation as giants within the British game, and their cussed refusal to become trendy. Why else, with the advent of the Swinging Sixties and Beatlemania and social revolution effecting a transformation in the ideas of young Scots, would Smith be so fascinated by the Calvinist tradition which permeated Ibrox? That he certainly was. But then it is difficult to picture this individual as anything other than middle-aged, with a tie-rack, trouser-press and Brylcreem, a noted concoction for grooming gentlemen's hair, as essential elements in his bedroom.

None of this should be seen as criticism. After all, if everyone appeared the height of fashion, life would be pretty tedious, but it must be said that Walter Smith was conventional. He played football before starting school in Carmyle, was inducted into the Rangers fraternity by his grandfather, and watched the 1953 team thrash Queen of the South 6-0 with the sort of wonder that many of his contemporaries reserved for the latest science-fiction film. And so began a passionate love affair with the game that has burned more brightly than anything in his existence. And that's it. Smith had three priorities etched in his mind: football, football and football, and his formative years were occupied in watching Rangers, reading about Rangers and discussing club stalwarts such as Eric Caldow and Jimmy Miller with the ubiquitous Jock, whose influence ensured that his grandson never forgot the importance of tradition. The word is central to Smith's philosophy, and can be brought up to date with his commitment to support the Union, an issue which manifested itself in 2007 prior to Holyrood parliamentary elections, when his name appeared in the company of a string of senior footballing figures, including Billy McNeill, Ally McCoist and Sir Alex Ferguson, urging that Scotland remain part of the United Kingdom. That said, Smith has not jumped on any passing political bandwagon. No, he has always believed implicitly in old-fashioned values, whether in sport or in life, but especially in his career at Ibrox, expressed thus:

'Every single thing that happens at the club is related to something that happened here before. There is always someone around the place who will remind you of that. Or there will be someone who says: "Old Bill [former manager Bill Struth] wouldn't have done that." Or: "Deedle [Willie Waddell] would have done it this way." And you listen to that. I know there are those people who say that you cannot operate on history or live in the past, but that is not a view I agree with. When you have a club with a rich tradition, then you examine that tradition and take from it what can still remain important to the club in any era. It's something which is almost tangible when you walk into the foyer at Ibrox, and you live with these feelings every day of your life, and you can learn from the club's history.

'We have always had the tradition at Ibrox, for example, that players have to report for training wearing a collar and tie, and despite recent objections to this, that's the way it will stay. Sure it's a little strange when you first arrive from another club to find that rule in place. But if you think about it, maybe that's why it was there in the first place: to remind each and every player that this is not just any club. This club is different. This is Rangers Football Club, and it works because the players *do* wear collar and tie, and they all understand why that is being done. To wit, that it is another small way in which the club was set apart from other clubs in Scotland when the traditions were first being born.'

Walter Smith can appear a relic of the Struth era or even a soccer-style Mr Pooter, being fastidious to a fault, quietly obsessed with detail and equipped with a boffin's brain for arcane rules and regulations. Yet it is an injustice to portray him as a stuffed shirt. Down the years I have heard a litany of criticisms of Smith, the majority centring on the allegation that he has been a lucky manager who was in the right place at the right time, namely close to David Murray's well-stuffed wallet when Celtic seemed to pursue ever-ascending levels of debt and mediocrity. While there may be a modicum of truth in such complaints, the charges ultimately fail to reflect reality on three counts. Firstly, because Smith was well respected from his managerial exertions at Dundee United before he arrived at Ibrox in 1986. Secondly, because no football club, regardless of the chairman's wealth, can dominate a national championship by winning nine successive titles, as did Rangers from 1989–97, without being blessed with talented direction. And thirdly, because after Berti Vogts' unfortunate spell as Scotland's manager, most of the men who had floundered within his regime performed well for Smith. Are we saying that the man was fortunate once again, that in the few months between Vogts' troops stumbling to ignominy in Moldova and Smith's personnel orchestrating victory over France, a glorious new crop of national heroes emerged? Of course not! For the most part, Smith had to work with the modest resources that had been available to his unfortunate predecessor, and the difference was that the Scot brought purpose, commitment and tactical nous to the international campaign. He deserves credit for his achievements.

Early in his first managerial spell at Rangers, when he co-operated with Graeme Souness, Smith reflected that walking through the Ibrox corridors and inspecting the committee rooms was akin to visiting a museum. Everything was pristine, photographs on the walls were lovingly mounted, and staff from boot room bombardiers to club newspaper employees constantly sported glints in their eyes, as if they had reached the zenith of their ambitions. For some that was probably true, but what was sufficient for the boys of the old brigade was not enough for Smith, despite his devotion to tradition, and certainly not for the ambitious Souness. If they had to implement unpopular decisions and risk offending some sensitivities at Ibrox, so be it. Both recognised that popularity contests have no place in football, especially considering the slough of despond into which Rangers had plummeted during the decade before they took over. Hence the necessity of clearing away the cobwebs and effecting a transformation of an increasingly moribund institution into a streamlined organisation that was fit for modern times. Souness has been accorded most of the praise for persuading a string of England internationalists, including Terry Butcher, Chris Woods and Graham Roberts, to travel to Glasgow to join the Rangers metamorphosis. So too he has garnered accolades for his reputedly brave stance in signing Roman Catholic striker Maurice 'Mo' Johnston from under Celtic's noses in 1989. Nonetheless, the notion that the former Liverpool player was single-handedly responsible for tearing down decades-old barriers of prejudice does not stand up to scrutiny. On the contrary, while Souness was the public face of the Murray-driven bandwagon, excoriating rival players and pressmen alike, whether it be Hibernian's George McCluskey or *Glasgow Herald* journalist James Traynor, and fulfilling his role as hatchet-man of the Thatcher generation, it was Smith who toiled quietly and relentlessly behind the scenes, displaying some of the essential attributes that have made him so admired by Sir Alex Ferguson. In essence, Souness contributed ample sound and fury while Smith supplied the substance, and the divergent paths in their careers since the former departed Ibrox emphasise how his sharp suits and immaculate grooming were no match for his colleague's off-the-peg wisdom.

Indeed, it can be argued that Souness's role in elevating the expectation levels has had potentially ruinous consequences for those who have followed in his wake. Smith continued to be the beneficiary of his chairman's largesse beyond the mid-1990s, but by that stage it had become increasingly difficult to entice European-class talents to Scotland, particularly once the English Premiership structure roared over the horizon. Celtic aficionados can respond with the name of Henrik Larsson, and I would add another couple of characters to accompany the exalted Swede: Lubomir Moravcik and Michael Mols. But the truth is that despite the acquisition of a past-his-peak Paul Gascoigne and a string of high-profile European stars, Smith's stewardship owed more to the virtues of the River Clyde than to the Danube. Quite simply, he was placed in a situation which demanded all his powers of resilience, tenacity and fine-tuning, not least once the crafty Fergus McCann defied the rules of football business by staying true to his word and resuscitating the Celtic cause.

Any fair-minded analysis of Smith's career needs to acknow-ledge the failures on his CV. When he exited Ibrox and signed up with Everton in 1998, some acolytes initially insisted that he could emulate the success achieved by Ferguson, a fellow Glaswegian, at Manchester United. As the months passed and the Goodison Park odyssey developed into a trying adventure for Smith, some of these optimists sought to rewrite history with the declaration that the Merseyside club had made promises to the manager which were not delivered. However, having spoken to a number of passionate Everton supporters who meticulously pointed out the mistakes which marred the Scot's tenure, it is only fair to bear witness to their reservations. 'He was a decent lad, but he bought us a lot of old crap,' observed one, offering the most critical opinion. Another told me: 'Walter Smith looked dead on his feet from the moment he arrived here, and he was knackered by the end of his first season. He didn't need a new challenge; he needed a rest.' A third perspective, provided by a Liverpool-based journalist, may be the most accurate: 'He was the wrong man in the wrong place. Everton had been steadily slipping further behind their city rivals, and there wasn't enough investment from the board to enable the manager to mount a revival. He didn't help his cause, mind you, by trying to shore up his team with old sweats like Duncan Ferguson, David Ginola and a clearly past-it Paul Gascoigne.

The fans tolerated him and liked the guy – there was no problem with him – but when he was sacked in 2002, the new boy, David Moyes quickly proved that he had the youthful ambition which Smith lacked.' Perhaps it is significant that during his four-year period at Goodison, he did not attempt to lay down roots. That might explain why he seemed destined for the chop almost before the conclusion of his inaugural press conference.

A more painful deficiency in Smith's career review has been his lack of success in European competition, not least considering the lavish expenditure at his disposal, as David Murray strove to extend Rangers' dominance beyond domestic terrain. As soon as he assumed the mantle from Souness – after turning down a number of offers from him to move to Anfield – it was obvious to Smith that he required a larger number of Scottish-born personnel, given the limits being placed on foreign players in every squad. Sadly, the abiding memory of Rangers on Champions League duty in the 1990s was witnessing tales of woe, while Andy Goram produced a string of magnificent saves to restrict the damage to 3-0 or 4-0. These outcomes would inevitably prove the prelude to the usual suspects dashing into print to complain that the club had outgrown their origins, and that it was time for the Old Firm to migrate to Europe – a specious argument which nowadays tends to emanate more from Celtic Park, as if England's finest would be so ingenuous as to indulge in favours to rivals.

If the fans were chasing impossible dreams at that time and Smith did his utmost to live up to such grand ambitions, he was thwarted time and again by a queasy combination of superior opponents, tactical naivety, schoolboy howlers from his defenders and, whisper it, a lack of belief that the Ibrox men could seriously trouble the likes of Juventus. Whether this inferiority complex, which is not usually associated with Rangers teams, was the consequence of their relative inexperience in Europe's premier competition or whether Smith, so assured and confident in Scotland, suffered travel sickness when asked to plan strategies abroad, remains a matter of conjecture. I happen to believe that he had difficulties with the concept of assembling a squad who were capable of sustaining a twin-pronged attack. This should not be viewed with an excess of condemnation – Alex Ferguson has been as unconvincing in the role of Scotland manager as he has been magisterial in steering Aberdeen and Manchester United to European triumphs – but it does leave Smith exposed to the sniping of sceptics who pronounce that his domestic bullies wimped out at the highest level in his initial spell as manager.

Perhaps the most glaring manifestation of the tension bubbling constantly beneath the surface was the fundamental fashion in which Smith, usually a polite interviewee, lost his rag while fielding questions from BBC Scotland football journalist Chick Young, and launched into an expletive-laden tirade as the precursor to calling over assistant Archie Knox with the words: "Come and listen to this, Archie. Listen to the shite this wee c***'s coming out with." This clip, which has been screened across the world on the You Tube Internet service, should not be in the least shocking to those who attend football matches, but it is a significant episode for no other reason than that the look on Smith's face, amid his tantrums, reflects an amalgam of anger, frustration and resentment, all vying for primacy. 'People have raised this with me about 100 or 1,000 times now, and I really don't understand what all the fuss is about," says Young, who has laughed off similar spats with most of the high rollers in Scottish football. 'I asked Walter if he felt his players were good enough for Europe, and he took exception to the implication that somebody like Brian Laudrup was having his ability questioned, so there was a bit of industrial-strength language, but it was all done and dusted in the space of a few minutes, and soon enough we sat down and had a good laugh about it. The bottom line is that football is supposed to be a passionate business, and it would be boring if everybody agreed all the time. But I can honestly tell you there was no bad blood, no recriminations. That just isn't Walter Smith's style. The guy is an absolute gentleman, and I wager that you won't hear anything else from every section of the sport in Scotland."

I can testify to such unanimity, having spoken to Scottish

managers of every discernible outlook. Even one such as Tommy Burns, who must have been shell-shocked at the fashion in which the Murray-Souness-Smith triumvirate laid waste to Celtic for much of the 1990s, talks about the Rangers man's honesty, his deep commitment to his country and his love for football with a directness which cannot be feigned. Perhaps the straightforward explanation is that Walter Smith has followed his own path and never sought greatness, but treated it with due respect when it has arrived. He carried out his duties in the wake of Jock Stein's untimely demise in 1985 or when Sir Alex Ferguson summoned him to Old Trafford in 2004, with the impassive relish of a character who fully appreciates that he might easily have ended up repairing electrical pylons if his life had veered a fraction in another direction.

Given which consideration, it is scarcely surprising that when Smith was showered with the accolade of Top Scot for 2006 in the Glenfiddich Spirit of Scotland Awards, he looked, initially at least, taken aback. It's all there in his expression: one fifth's worth of pride, a soupçon of incredulity, a further sprinkling of delight and an extra ingredient or two, of what? The realisation, as he knew well, that thousands of low-paid hospital staff and heroic fire-brigade crews had been saving lives every night across the country, without as much as a moment's thought from the Glenfiddich judging panel? The acknowledgement, however much he might love football and its infinitesimal mysteries, that he was being disproportionately rewarded for a solitary 1-0 success over France on a nerve-shredding afternoon, when the visitors to Glasgow might have been two goals in front in the opening half-hour? In the final analysis, however, Smith's celebratory humility struck the right note.

But then this is a trait that he shares with most of the best managers: an appreciation of the unsung heroes and a relish for those who carry out the regular chores without moaning about their lot. During his playing career Smith was a functional and prosaic performer, but nobody could ever accuse him of not expending 100 per cent of energy and desire. At Dundee United he watched the diverse methods of those on the Tannadice books, and though Smith can be as exhilarated by the flair of a Pele or Maradona as any observer, he is pragmatic enough to know that these players are rare in a Scottish context. Hence the manner in which Smith has praised the unstinting labours of Dundee United's Dougie Smith, a combative centre-half who joined the club in 1958, and who missed only four competitive matches in the next decade:

> 'He was a very quiet, very unassuming boy. He couldn't hold up a bunch of medals or anything like that at the end of his career. But I don't think I've known many people who wanted to win as much as he did. His personality wasn't always what people would hold up as being a winner's, but he definitely had a winning attitude. It was etched in him, this fierce hunger to win. A lot of times players run around kicking people and shouting at referees, and people view that as a desire to win. But Dougie didn't do that. The desire was within him, and it burned very brightly. It taught me that there are guys who maybe don't have a lot of ability who can bring themselves up to a tremendous level in any sport, and though they may just fall short of winning, in their own right they are actually winners, because they have dragged themselves up from being not the most naturally gifted to being amongst the best, and I really admire that. In fact, in some respects, in doing so they may have almost achieved more than some people who win medals. It might not look that way from outside, but a lot of managers in football do a terrific job without getting an end product in terms of trophies or championships.'

Walter Smith's words are significant. They confirm that he has never had patience with those inclined to abuse their talent or to spend greater time at the nightclub than attending to the day job. This is an inevitable reflection of his upbringing, and we have heard the references to how Celtic supporters, asked to choose their club's greatest-ever player, plumped for a prodigiously talented tanner-ba' trickster known as Jimmy Johnstone. The Rangers brethren, by comparison, when presented with the same choice, hummed and hawed at Archie Henderson and Colin Stein, Davie Cooper and Archie Conn before settling for John Greig, an admittedly effective and aggressive defender who possessed all the romance and magic of a knee-trembler in Maryhill. On reflection, while the selection of Greig provoked sarcastic abuse around Celtic Park, he was a genuinely populist choice. Few of the supporters who flocked to Old Firm tussles in the 1960s could possibly have conceived of executing the mesmerising feints and jinks which were Johnstone's trademarks. In contrast, all in the Rangers ranks could easily have imagined themselves lunging at Jinky and kicking him into the middle of Row C. A brutal distinction, admittedly, but Greig was built in the classic Ibrox tradition, namely: if you're looking for frills or fancy-dan stuff, go elsewhere. That robust militarism, the ingrained philosophy of 'Take no prisoners' ensured that while he was nobody's idea of a stylist, the young Walter Smith watched John Greig in action – and cheered.

In that respect, on the long and winding road from Ashfield Juniors to Tannadice and Dumbarton, prior to being instrumental in the Rangers revolution and from there onwards to Everton, and eventually to unemployment, Smith's exploits have all been of the understated variety, and he has never been a man to indulge in trumpet-blowing. Yet for me, the working-class dignity that he has invariably exuded is redolent of the best Scottish values. When the call came from the SFA, when seeking a saviour in the worst days of the Vogts-inspired morass, it would have been the comfortable option to decline their offer and to continue pontificating on the periphery as an occasional pundit, but the easy outcome has rarely appealed. Instead, in his late 50s and safe in the knowledge that he had masterminded 13 trophies in seven seasons at Ibrox, he grabbed the challenge by the scruff of the neck, united myriad factions within the Tartan Army, and galvanised the Scotland side with such basic qualities as discipline, pride in the jersey and organisation. There was no mystery to it, but just as he has done at Rangers since replacing Paul le Guen, Smith has shown that home-spun industry need not be inferior to foreign methods.

Whether he is a good manager with a gifted streak, or a great motivator with a shop steward's ability to motivate the troops, is open to debate. But those who have worked with him and absorbed the lessons he has imparted, are in no doubt as to his status. 'One thing I will say about him is that he is a gentleman, but if you get on the wrong side of him, he will quickly let you know,' notes Charlie Nicholas, an individual one might suppose, as a media-friendly, Celtic-supporting dandy, was everything alien to Smith. 'I worked with him when he was Alex Ferguson's assistant at the 1986 World Cup finals in Mexico, and I had five weeks with him, and he displayed a burning intensity throughout that period. Scotland mattered so, so much to him, and that couldn't help but filter through to the players. When I heard he had taken the Scotland job in 2004, I was mightily relieved, because I knew he wouldn't tolerate a situation where a country with our history was languishing at 77th in the FIFA rankings. And you have to give him credit: he stamped his authority on the team and made a strong impression on the youngsters, and the turnaround was almost immediate. That tells you a lot about the man's ambition.' Typically, Smith is not interested in hogging the limelight, to the extent that even the hapless Vogts escapes his wrath in this summation:

'Let's be fair. It was a very, very difficult time for Berti to take the job. Craig Brown had been in charge of a very settled Scottish squad, but a lot of them were getting older, and those of us who were involved in football in Scotland knew that there were not a lot of guys around who were ready to take their place, so it was never going to be easy. Coming from another country, perhaps Berti didn't quite realise the scale of those difficulties. And there is a different mentality in British football, and I think he maybe found that hard to encompass as well. The thing is, when Scotland had players of the calibre of Denis Law, Billy Bremner, Graeme Souness, Alan Hansen and Kenny Dalglish, the team pretty much picked itself. But when you don't have players of that quality, the mentality of the players you pick comes far more into it, and it helps if you know the personality of the lads you are dealing with. It's maybe why you don't see many foreign managers taking over at places like Coventry and Southampton, where you have to build from the bottom up. When they come to Britain, they tend to come to big clubs with top players.'

Smith has been associated with many notable names in his vocation, and he has thrived in the company of lesser-known individuals, such as Jerry Kelly at Dundee United and the ubiquitous Archie Knox on their peripatetic trail. Though he is not inclined to hero-worship, there is little question which other Glasgow figure he holds in the highest eminence:

'The obvious fact that I know and have worked with Sir Alex maybe makes me a wee bit biased, but when you talk about creating a winning environment, there has been nobody better in my experience. It isn't just what he has done at Manchester United, who are an enormous club, but also at Aberdeen. They are not as powerful a club as Rangers or Celtic, but he still managed to turn them into a side who won a European trophy, who weren't afraid to tackle the Old Firm, and made them a team who were always incredibly difficult to beat. So, probably he more than anybody else is the man I admire and respect in our sport.'

Life has been a tale of ebb-and-flow for Walter Smith since he entered this world on 24 February 1948. His critics too readily condemn his perceived fortune in being privy to David Murray's largesse, and Rangers fans feasted on success so regularly throughout the 1990s that they assumed the regular acquisition of silverware would materialise with or without him in the boiler-room. But as the managerial privations of Paul Le Guen demonstrated, nothing is certain in the world of football, and Smith's return to Ibrox was tinged with the feeling that he might be embracing a poisoned chalice. In the event, he rose to the challenge with the diligence, industry and redoubtable enthusiasm which have been his trademark qualities, and only a fool or a cynic would dismiss these powers. Ultimately, Smith thrives on the gladiatorial nature of life under the microscope in Glasgow, and relishes the positive aspects of the Old Firm's traditional rivalry. But as he showed when his side were striving to chase titles and cups amid a congested fixture pile-up, he realises that defeat is not the end of the world. Indeed, the manner in which he spoke about Celtic's Tommy Burns after his untimely death from cancer at the age of 51, on the very morning following Rangers' disappointment in the UEFA Cup final in May 2008, was a testimony to the shared values of those who can appreciate the distinction between intense rivalry and rabid sectarianism. In sombre tones, intertwined with occasional shafts of laughter at the memory of Burns' sometimes scatter-brained nature, he paid this tribute:

'Tommy was one of the best people I have ever had the opportunity to work with. Football aside, he was also a terrific man, and the more I got to know Tommy, the more I got to enjoy that side about him. From the outside, I had always imagined that Tommy would be a very meticulous manager, but he also had this delightful, harum-scarum side to him. I remember the World Cup qualifier we played against Norway: it was a very important game, and I was in the dressing-room beforehand giving my state-of-the-nation address to the players. There was Tommy, my assistant, in the front row fast asleep. I had to stop because I was laughing so much. Later I said to him: "Was my team talk that good that it sent you to sleep?" He replied: "Oh aye!" That was Tommy. He just had a nice way about him, and there are few people who epitomise a club more than Tommy Burns did Celtic. He was a Celtic man: a supporter as a kid, all the way through to having a successful career with them. For me, Tommy showed everything that was good about Celtic.'

The same words could be applied to Walter Smith's association with Rangers Football Club.

CHAPTER TWO

Growing up in Football
and Life Itself

'He was a good, hard-working Scottish defender'

As Walter Smith is fond of reminding friends, there was a place
for every footballer, irrespective of talent, size or commitment,
among the fraternity of post-war schoolchildren who grew up
addicted to the sport in Glasgow in the 1950s. Move forward to a
new century, and it may seem strange to youngsters that their
Scottish predecessors could have been so easily impressed. While
it would be wrong to paint an overly sentimental picture of a
period when gang warfare was rife and when a criminal dubbed
Bible John was indulging in murderous exploits against women, a
sense of shared community and *esprit de corps* were evident. The
youthful Smith wrapped himself in football to the extent that
every waking moment, when he wasn't at school, he surrounded
himself with comics, match programmes and newspaper features
on his beloved Rangers, and he dared to dream that one day he
might sprint on to the Ibrox greensward. As he came to realise
even before he had reached teenage years, he boasted the commitment, but not the class, the enthusiasm but not the extra
ingredient which marks out the elite from the journeymen, and he
resolved to progress as far as he could without being deluded by
the idea that he was on a par with John Greig or Colin Stein.

There was no shame in that acceptance. The opposite, because Glasgow at that time was fixated with three things: football, heavy industry and religion. Smith could do nothing about two of those factors, but the sport was another matter. In common with thousands of his contemporaries, he was hooked.

As he related recently, the die was cast from his first fleeting experiences. Every Saturday and Sunday, wherever he and his mates could find pitches, the sole thought was to organise matches of six-a-side, 11-a-side or 22-a-side. Who cared, so long as there was the opportunity to break the monotony with a trip to dreamland? The weather, the state of the facilities and prospect of exams were rendered irrelevant, and though Smith was no class-room dullard – he shared with Alex Ferguson the capacity to soak up general knowledge like blotting paper – he was content to be captivated by his favourite game, as Glasgow lived up to its billing as the first city of football. It was, quite simply, another world, a vanished sphere of rudimentary pleasures. Many youngsters in the 21st century appear lost without mobile phones, PlayStations and other sophisticated devices, but the ground rules were much more straightforward in the formative Smith years. If it snowed and then froze, as it frequently did, he and his comrades would use sand to mark out impromptu pitches; if it rained, they would clamber over walls and sneak into car parks and school premises, and kick lumps out of one another on concrete or tarmac. Luxuries extended to the occasional Christmas present of a spanking new strip or a leather ball, and this down-to-earth upbringing was evident in the home: for much of the 1950s people were considered pretty posh if they owned a television and had a telephone. As for other items which we now take for granted – microwave ovens, video recorders, refrigerators and washing machines – Smith and his childhood contemporaries would have thought the Martians had landed if they had stumbled across any of these contraptions in the east end of Glasgow.

Even if it was a basic upbringing, Smith revelled in it. 'I was as keen as anybody else when I was a kid, and I went where the games were,' he recalls. 'It's the same with everyone, isn't it? You want a game, you are desperate to play, and you follow the rest of the lads in your group just to make sure that you are playing football somewhere.' At the outset, this entailed the two best performers convening the others and picking their best pals, whereupon they would move down the line until just a couple of duffers were left. In some respects this was a cruel process of elimination, but it was effective, and lest anyone forget, Smith grew up in a halcyon period for Scottish football, an era when the Old Firm, Hibernian, Heart of Midlothian and Dundee all celebrated rousing European adventures, and posted some momentous wins against the best on the Continent. Across the country, but most notably in Glasgow, every tiny strip of land was a home to wannabe Jimmy Johnstones and John Greigs, and as Craig Brown, the former Scotland manager, recollects, the competition for places at every level, from juvenile and junior to amateur and professional, was relentless: 'In these days, you could travel round Glasgow at weekends, and on every street corner there were laddies chasing a ball for dear life, while the parks, whether they were blaes or grass or ash, were always packed out.' Brown offers the noteworthy observation that Scottish children in those days received 10 sessions of physical education, hence the avoidance of the chronic obesity which has crept into our vocabulary in the past 20 years. 'Most of us who love football know that we will never see a situation such as that again – there are too many other distractions for kids and a lot of the old playing fields have been swallowed up by developers – but although there was no shortage of problems in Scotland 50–60 years ago, there was also something heart-warming about being in an environment where football was king.'

Less admirable was the bitter sectarian divide which existed in the west of Scotland, and guaranteed that most of Smith's generation strolled unquestioningly into the blue or green camp, often without recognising the more nefarious elements that inhabited such a culture. Even with hindsight, it seems extraordinary that so many lives should have been wasted on this issue, let alone that an appalling degree of ignorance often lies at the heart of the most deep-rooted bigotry. In the years when I grew up in West Lothian, on the edge of the Harthill Triangle which veered into the fastnesses of Lanarkshire, I noticed the graffiti on the walls between Whitburn and the Polkemmet Estate:

'Kaflix are Skum,' declared one legend. 'Protistants are Kunts,' was one response.

Along the road at regular intervals the letters 'FTP' had been spray-painted with finesse sufficient to stimulate thoughts that the perpetrator might do well on an art course, rather than wasting the talent on insulting the man in charge at the Vatican. Once, while walking from the estate to the relative civilisation of my home town, I was stopped by a couple of wild-eyed men who pinned me against a wall and demanded to know my religion. 'Protestant,' I blurted out, which was apparently the correct answer, since they did not beat me to a pulp. Earlier, as a primary-school laddie I was in the act of buying my *Victor* comic from the newsagent's on what happened to be the day of the famous European Cup final involving Celtic and Inter Milan. The shop owner, Jim Hamilton, a rubicund chap sporting blue-nose and red-nose propensities, and with an unnerving ability to snivel and shout at the same time, adopted the role of chief interrogator and defender of the faith:

'So what team are you supporting?'
'Er, well I want Celtic to win.'
'Why's that?'
'Because they are Scottish, Mr Hamilton.'
'Aye, but they are Catholics, son.'
'Yes, but aren't the other team Catholics as well?'
'That disnae matter – they are *foreign* Catholics! Now that'll be thruppence, please.'

This was perhaps bigotry of a minor character, but almost 20 years later one of my occasional Catholic football-playing colleagues fatally stabbed one of his Protestant workmates in a drunken brawl that was precipitated by an argument over the Old Firm, and he found himself behind bars for the rest of his active life. All of which testifies to my belief that, long after drawing-room pontificators have lost interest in the subject, sectarianism will continue to be a blight on Scotland and the west of the nation, in particular, perhaps not around Ibrox and Celtic Park, where security and policing have eliminated most of the trouble, but more probably through random outbreaks of violence and hostilities, sparking agony for communities in Ayrshire, Lanarkshire and West Lothian. Within these areas I know of families who won't allow their children to dress in green, or even use a crayon of that colour. Similarly, I am acquainted with one or two Celtic followers who casually make jokes about the Ibrox Disaster or strive to defend the Enniskillen bombings during the troubles in Northern Ireland, while striving to refute my argument that Aiden McGeady, who was born and bred in Scotland to Scottish parents and who established his reputation by playing for a Scottish club, should be honoured to represent Scotland, instead of trotting out words such as history and tradition to justify his decision to aspire to international honours with the Republic of Ireland.

In circumstances which inspire such enigmatic episodes, it would be unsurprising if Walter Smith had not been dragged into the ritual bigotry which used to tarnish Glasgow on Old Firm derby afternoons, and which was brilliantly depicted in Peter MacDougall's *Just Another Saturday*. Yet to his credit, he has managed to transcend tribal conflict by adopting the mantra: 'Treat people as you find them'. Even as a teenager, when he turned out for Chapelhall Youth Club while studying for an apprenticeship at Coatbridge Tech, Smith was blessed with the knack of being able to make friends on gut feeling, not after checking what educational establishment or church his new ally had attended. Time and again his only priority lay in being part of a team, whether at Chapelhall or the Albert Youth Club in Springburn, or after joining Bishopbriggs Amateurs at the age of 17. Smith soon stepped up to the junior ranks at Ashfield in the company of team-mates Jim Cameron and Gerry Hernon. Suddenly he was in demand, and though there was no sign of scouts from Rangers, Smith was astonishingly pragmatic for one of his age. He ignored the idea that football might offer him full-time employment, and bolstered by his father he chose to conclude his apprenticeship before contemplating his next stage in life. He devoted himself to his five-year stint, first at Dalmarnock Power Station for the South of Scotland Electricity Board, and one former co-employee told me: 'Walter was intense. He was anxious to pick up as much as he could, and I wager he would still know what to do if he suffered a power cut at home. He would come into work and talk about football over a cup of tea. But once that was finished and his shift had begun, he was only interested in doing his job.' Those words epitomise the Smith philosophy. Ally McCoist once jested that his gaffer had walked into Ibrox with the hair of Sacha Distel, and had departed with that of Steve Martin, such was the stress he had experienced within the goldfish bowl. But Smith has always been naturally meticulous, intense and disinclined to laziness, all of which makes him awkward company for time-wasters. Craig Brown, a friend for more than 30 years, sums him up:

'Walter was one of the most driven and enthusiastic people you could hope to meet, right from the early days. It was as if he knew that while he might not reach the top of the tree as a player, there was no reason why he couldn't use his intelligence and his football knowledge to make an impression as a leader, a coach, a manager. What you have to appreciate is that while Walter, and to some extent Sir Alex Ferguson, might give the impression that they are pretty gruff individuals, the truth is they are very droll characters, who can deliver a punch-line perfectly when the mood takes them.

Another factor in their success is the fact that both are incredibly competitive characters – they hate losing, utterly detest it, and we're not talking here about matches, but games of Trivial Pursuit on the bus!

'Whenever we were on Scotland duty together, the pair of them would start their quizzes, and I suppose it boils down to the old Scottish notion of the lad o' pairts. So if Fergie was able to name every member of the cast of *The Magnificent Seven*, then Walter would come back at him with the list of actors in *The Great Escape*. They have been like that for as long as I can remember: ultra-competitive men, fiercely-passionate folk who enjoy their successes, but suffer their defeats as much as any fan. And they share the notion that genius is an infinite capacity for taking pains.'

By the stage that Smith had joined Ashfield Juniors in August 1966, he had demonstrated that what he lacked in class as a defender was compensated for by lashings of sinew and purpose. Such was the impact that he made at Saracen Park, the home of his new junior colleagues, that within a couple of months he had been recruited by Dundee United's stalwart manager, Jerry Kerr, on the old provisional signing forms. Smith spent most of that subsequent season alternating between fulfilling his commitments to Ashfield, turning out in reserve matches for the Tannadice club and completing his trade apprenticeship at the Dundee-based company, Loudon Brothers, where he worked full-time while embarking on gruelling training sessions in the evening. It sounds an anachronistic means of pursuing a football career, and many were the nights when Smith was dead-beat even before entering the changing rooms, but he recalls that he was young, fit and ambitious, and the alternative was an anonymous existence surrounded by crossed wires and short circuits. And yet the question hangs in the air: if Smith was able to secure a deal as a teenager with Dundee United, could he have been as lacklustre a performer as he claims? 'I was ordinary, very ordinary. And I am not being in the least modest when I tell you that,' he retorts. 'Over the period I played for Dundee United, I like to think that I developed into a good pro, and I did look after my fitness, but in truth almost from the start I knew that, much as I loved the game, I was never going to be any great shakes as a player.' Craig Brown offers a different assessment of his colleague: 'Walter was much better than what you might believe from hearing him dismiss his career. He was a good centre-half, he read the game well, expended lots of energy, and he tackled for keeps. If he had a failing, it lay in his lack of mobility, and obviously once he began picking up injuries, that didn't help him at the highest level. But it is plain wrong to describe him as some sort of donkey; more accurate to conclude that he was a good, hard-working Scottish defender, who coped well in the domestic leagues without aiming any higher.'

What is not in doubt is that Smith's migration to Tayside was the best move he could have made. Away from his roots he thrived under the influence of Jerry Kerr, a sharp-suited, pipe-smoking polymath who seemed to belong in another age. When Smith arrived, he witnessed the swansong of the Swede, Lennart Wing, and he recognised that the club, buoyed by such tireless servants as Tommy Millar, Denis Gillespie and his icon Doug Smith, were set to supplant near-neighbours Dundee as the No1 team in the city, not least because the wily Kerr was a past master at snapping up veterans with one or two more prolific seasons still in them. All of which ensured that Smith was quickly enjoying experiences that he could only have dreamt about back in Carmyle and Springburn. At the end of his first season in 1968, Dundee United travelled to the United States with a clutch of other representatives from Scotland and England, in a concerted attempt to sell round ball football to an obdurate American public. The Brits were unsuccessful in that objective, but Smith was in his element while turning out for the Dallas Tornados and settling down comfortably in the Texan city, relishing the lifestyle that was lavished on the British missionaries. This experience did not last, but Smith prospered briefly in the United States, returning to Scotland with the notion that anything was possible and enthused by the fashion in which Kerr rebuilt his side to meet their rising aspirations. He was bolstered by the advice and comradeship of Millar, who had witnessed almost every idiosyncrasy which football can deliver, and he learned important lessons from Gillespie and Alan Gordon, who had signed from Hibs, thanks to the trademark eye for a main chance which characterised Kerr. Smith wrote in 1994:

'Things were different back then, and Jerry was probably the last of the old-fashioned managers. I say that in the nicest possible way, because Jerry was a remarkable manager for Dundee United. Indeed, it's almost impossible to criticise him after what he did for the Tannadice club. He built the main stand, he took them into the top league, and he kept them there during his time as boss [1959–71]. And he took them into Europe, where they beat Barcelona, frightened the life out of Juventus, and made United known outside their country for the first time in their history.

'But his style of management was from an era which was dying out when I went to United as a professional. The age of the track-suited manager was in its infancy in Scotland, and Jerry was completely untouched by it. He ran the club, he picked the team and he bought the players, and then he allowed them to get on with the tactics by themselves. He never took training, and was always dressed in a collar and tie and usually a suit, but the bottom line is that he was successful, and he deserves credit for that.'

Kerr's achievements reflect the wind of change that swept through Tannadice as the 1960s progressed. A product of Armadale in West Lothian, his playing career included spells at Motherwell, Alloa Athletic, Edinburgh club St Bernard's and Dundee United before he briefly turned out for Rangers after the Second World War, but it was in the sphere of management that his radical ideas bore fruit. Equipped with the theory that the bigger the club the worse their talent-spotting, he insisted on a full-time structure at United, was adamant there should be a properly constituted reserve side, and abandoned the policy of relying on parochial, probably over-the-hill talent. Instead, with Morton FC's Hal Stewart he tapped into the flourishing Scandinavian football scene, and purchased a string of cultured performers at affordable prices: Mogens Berg, Lennart Wing and Orjan Persson were among those who provided sterling service for Scottish employers. Kerr, though, was not one whose life revolved around football exclusively, and he relished cricket with equal enthusiasm. He had watched with curiosity as Warwickshire County Cricket Club raised thousands of pounds for rebuilding their Edgbaston ground in Birmingham by establishing their own pools structure. Kerr, a bright man who was always happy to seek advice, engaged with county secretary Les Deakin, and the consequence was the creation of Taypools, which proved an instant success and brought significant sums of money into Dundee United's coffers by the end of the decade. Given the dynamism and bristling sense of purpose which this livewire engendered, few Taysiders were surprised when he marched his Tangerine warriors into Europe for the first time in 1966, and they swept to an astonishing 4-1 aggregate victory over Barcelona, including a 2-1 triumph at the Nou Camp. This was the environment into which the youthful Walter Smith had advanced, and during the next decade he soaked up loads of inspiration to good effect. Little wonder that when Jerry Kerr died in 1999 aged 87, Smith was among the first to pay tribute to the methods and mystique of a hero whose achievements remained largely unsung.

CHAPTER THREE

A COACH IN THE MAKING

'Wattie was the guy who kept the spirits up'

One of Walter Smith's great joys is the camaraderie of the training ground, which is central to the crucial transformation of a group of young men from a collection of disparate individuals into a solid fighting unit. Every squad will possess their gregarious types and their loners, those who enjoy their alcohol too fondly and who fret that they don't belong, and those who feel homesick and perhaps suspect that they are not part of the manager's plans. In fostering harmony, the leaders of such men must quell restless spirits without dampening their fire, combine equal proportions of comedy, common sense and cantankerousness, and be able to persuade each man, from first-team superstar to grafter, that they have a unique role to act out in a championship challenge. Smith has long appreciated that there is no magic formula to the process. After signing with Dundee United in 1966 and gradually earning respect from Jerry Kerr, he struggled to command a regular first-team position, a situation which he accepted with the knowledge that the manager had assembled a fine ensemble of performers, and that if he had to settle for bit-part status, so be it. One of the rewards of charting Smith's rise to the highest level, though, is recognising the fortitude that he displayed while lingering around the periphery on so many weekends, apparently consigned to the substitutes' bench. In parallel with what appears often to have been a thankless exercise, he took the opportunity to sharpen his tactical acumen and to embrace the positives.

Had he been a wastrel who was disposed to slip away from training or a prima donna who was disinclined to carry out reserve duty, surely Smith would not have flourished when Kerr handed over the reins of Dundee United to Jim McLean in 1971. But he did. And McLean, no matter those facets of his personality which could be described as thrawn, impatient, unreasonable or plain grumpy, achieved more in his 22-year spell as manager than any individual before or after. From the outset, as a bustling and redoubtable 34-year-old who had been in charge at Dundee FC, and was damned sure he would not cross the barricades only to come a cropper, the not-so-sunny Jim barked out instructions with a relentless beat, but his tactics had the desired result. The club's fitness regime was intensified, training grew ever more organised with longer sessions and an evident emphasis on strategy, and Smith, who was already considering a future in football after he retired from the playing arena, was immediately impressed by the new boss. This was in contrast to several United stalwarts, who actively resisted the changes and argued that Mr Kerr's notions suited them better – and were rapidly destined for the Tannadice exit.

As it happened, Smith decided to move on in 1975, for a spell with Dumbarton, and the decision owed much to McLean's determination to construct a new young team, which he could mould in his own image. For all that he admired the unstinting work ethic and resilience exhibited by Smith, a worthy defender was by now excess to requirements. There was nothing untoward about the temporary split, and the two men were reunited at Tannadice in 1977, by which time Smith's playing career was winding down on account of a pelvic injury, though he did not make his 250th, and final, senior appearance for United until 1980.

This proved to be a pivotal period in the history of the Scottish game. At the start of the 1970s, the Old Firm continued to dominate their Scottish rivals and Celtic reached their second European Cup final, only to be surprisingly vanquished by Feyenoord, while Rangers triumphed in the 1972 European Cup-Winners' Cup. Despite the processional fashion in which Jock Stein's Celtic accumulated nine consecutive titles and their Glasgow rivals clung on to end the stranglehold in 1975, changes were afoot in the shape of novel ideas and the unearthing of a new generation of aspirational managers. In some respects, figures such as Alex Ferguson, Craig Brown, Andy Roxburgh, Jim McLean, and eventually Walter Smith, were assisted by the deficiencies within Scottish football at the highest echelons, a malaise confirmed by grim recollections of World Cup campaigns, which were laced with embarrassment and amateurism. Much has been made of the 1978 finals fiasco in Argentina, where manager Ally MacLeod failed properly to analyse his squad's opponents, and a national hangover of monumental proportions followed. But if the opprobrium heaped upon MacLeod was merited, the SFA were exposed as a bunch of mediocrities, who seemed to many observers to be more concerned with checking themselves and their wives into high-class accommodation, while the poor bloody infantry of players were consigned to lodgings that were much inferior. Looking further back to the 1974 World Cup, Willie Ormond, a likeable and engaging chap with an enormous soccer talent but with limited managerial skills, had found himself out of his depth, while the SFA seemed satisfied that their team had excelled by merely reaching the tournament finals.

Beyond such trials and tribulations, Smith was offered a platform to hone his tactical skills, and he grabbed the opportunity. After his return to Dundee United, Jim McLean eased him into a coaching role in which he worked with S-form youngsters for a few hours every week, and examination of the list of youngsters that he instructed, including Davie Dodds, John Clark, Dave Beaumont and Maurice Malpas, confirms the quality that was emerging at the grass-roots. Not only was he demonstrating his worth at Tannadice: he had gained employment with the Scottish youth team, who would go on to conquer Europe. From the age of 25, Smith had ventured to the SFA's coaching courses at Largs, sitting exams and gaining certificates with as much resolve as he had entered into tackles on the pitch. Craig Brown, who was instrumental in presenting the courses with Willie McLean and Peter Rice, pinpoints that dedication:

'Walter was one of the best students you could imagine. He listened, he learned, he asked questions, and if there was something he didn't understand, he would come to us later and find out what he wanted to know. It was a fantastic time to be involved, as we moved into the 1980s. The Old Firm's aura of invincibility had been shattered by the emergence of so many good players at Aberdeen and Dundee United, and you sensed that life was going to be exciting in the future. At youth level, there was a rich seam of guys making their mark, people of the calibre of Ally McCoist, Charlie Nicholas, Eric Black, Pat Nevin, Brian McClair, Jim McInally, Dave Bowman . . . The list goes on, and all these boys were determined to reach the top of their profession – it was no longer just a game for these lads – so there was no problem with motivating them. As soon as Walter entered the scene, his eyes lit up and he recognised that there could be big things in store with this amount of raw potential at his disposal. And true to form, he pressed the buttons and clicked the right gears.'

Irrespective of the opposition, Jim McLean's teams learned to prosper, and they displayed a good deal of panache and derring-do in doing so, the product of endless hours of coaxing and cajoling by the manager. In December 1979 he guided the club to a Scottish League Cup triumph, and retained the trophy the following year. Meanwhile, United were amassing a sequence of wins against European sides, among them AS Monaco, PSV Eindhoven, Anderlecht, Werder Bremen and Borussia Moenchengladbach, whose cumulative effect ensured that continental coaches and players started to fear a date with the men from

Tayside. As for Walter Smith, who had slipped seamlessly into the No. 2 job at Tannadice, there was no mystery about the club's surge, which saw them secure the Scottish championship in 1983:

'Jim was one of the most thorough managers you could ever meet. And I mean anywhere. I don't care where you go. It would be hard to find anyone who put more into planning for games and for training sessions than he did. That was always one of his great secrets, namely that he would leave nothing to chance. His tactics when going into specific games were worked out to the very last detail. And his own discipline, and the discipline which he imposed on other people, was very tough to live up to. But he demanded that, and he always led by example.'

In tandem with Andy Roxburgh, Smith had adapted well to the requirements of coaching his young charges at Scotland level, and the distillation of their labours was a great victory in the European Youth Championship in 1982 in Finland, where they saw off the challenges of England, the Netherlands, Czechoslovakia, Poland, Turkey and Albania with a mix of traditional values, which included robust defence, wholehearted commitment and playing for the jersey. This was combined with a high-tempo, attacking style which perplexed many of their rivals, but constituted no surprise to those who had studied the emergence of Dundee United under McLean, and Aberdeen under Alex Ferguson. One of Smith's few regrets in looking back at the event was the realisation that only three members of a gifted Scottish squad, Paul McStay, Pat Nevin and Gary Mackay, went on to gain full international honours. If that failure to translate teenage flair into adult fruition remains a dilemma for Scotland, it was no fault of Smith, whose stature in the game rose significantly after the triumph of his youthful charges. Mackay recalls:

'Andy was in charge, but Wattie was the guy who kept the spirits up and organised all the activities which you need when you are away from home for ten days. He was second-in-command, but he kept the players bright and alert and positive about themselves. He had been involved in the build-up and had helped develop the squad over the course of the season, and it was a particularly strong group of players, with guys like McStay, Nevin, Ally Dick and Neale Cooper, although Neale missed the finals because he was involved with Aberdeen. But the bottom line is that you can have a collection of good players, but unless they are drilled properly and trained properly and they care about one another, they won't amount to much, and that is where Wattie came into his own. He and Andy both stressed the importance of the team ethic, but they also allowed individual exuberance to flourish, and getting the blend right was one of the reasons why we won the tournament. I will always remember what Wattie said on the Saturday night before the final. England had just beaten Scotland 1-0 in the Home International Championship at Hampden Park, and he told us this wasn't just a chance for us to make a name for ourselves, but also an opportunity to dispel the disappointment of the whole nation. He was passionate, his eyes were burning, but he was really inspiring, and that fired us all up for the job.'

Smith was a mere 34, but most of the qualities which would earn him a plethora of plaudits later in his career had manifested themselves. As he surveyed the Scots dismantle the Czechs 3-1 in the final, with goals from Mackay, Nevin and Stirling Albion's John Philliben, the click of his jaw and leap in the air at the climax told its own story of a joyful campaign. He came over as a calm, stoical presence on the touchline, but disagreeing with him could set off volcanic responses, and the intensity of Smith's wrath left hardened men quaking. While several former players told me of how he had allegedly challenged them to put their fists up or shut up, none would speak on the record, not least because as one explained: 'Walter was right. I was being a prick, and I needed a slap. He only lost the rag if he thought you were letting the side or yourself down. And I was able to laugh about it with him the next day. But believe me, when he felt he had to crack the whip, he was bloody fearsome.'

Away from Tannadice, seismic cracks were beginning to appear in Glasgow, which would eventually have major repercussions for Smith and Scottish football. With Dundee United securing the league title and Aberdeen subsequently recording a magnificent 2-1 victory over Real Madrid on a sodden night in Gothenburg to collect the European Cup-Winners' Cup, the balance of power had shifted markedly away from the Old Firm and at Rangers, as their supporters showed their disaffection in a flood of fickleness and an embarrassment of empty seats, manager John Greig left his office in the autumn to the unfamiliar sound of booing from those who had once saluted him (and indeed would acclaim him as their hero again in the future). Alex Ferguson was sounded out to replace Greig, but the redoubtable Glaswegian declined, principally on the grounds that he had witnessed at first hand the pernicious effects of sectarianism, and considered it anathema that Rangers, publicly at least, adhered to their policy of refusing to sign Roman Catholic players. Several had turned out for the club, including John Spencer, but discrimination hung in the air, and Ferguson, despite being made an offer that many individuals could not have refused, remained at Pittodrie. Next up Jim McLean was invited to speak to the Rangers board, and in the course of the initial meeting informed the directors that he intended to bring Smith with him to Ibrox. There was no discussion between the men, McLean assuming correctly that his No. 2 would be cock-a-hoop at the prospect of a move to the club that he had supported from childhood. The deal seemed cut and dried, but no sooner had newspapers started to debate how best the new management team could extricate Rangers from the mire, than McLean, normally such a purposeful character, slipped into procrastination. He asked Smith for his opinion, receiving an unequivocal response: 'Let's go for it.' He decided to sleep on the matter for a night, followed by another, and despite keeping his counsel, it was obvious that McLean was harbouring misgivings. At the beginning of the following week, with one or two Rangers officials furious at how the affair was unravelling, he announced forcefully to Smith that they were definitely going to Ibrox: he had communicated that message to the Dundee United chairman, Johnstone Grant. Yet it proved another false dawn. On Friday morning a board meeting was held at Tannadice at 10 a.m. rather than the usual midday, and as a small group of players sat in the dressing room just before noon, a senior director, George Fox, marched in to confirm that McLean was staying where he was, as was his No. 2.

It was a crushing blow for Smith. He could not comprehend why there had been so much hesitation from a man he had always held in the highest regard; there was no explanation from his colleague why he had blown hot and cold over the move; and by proxy, Smith had spurned his beloved club, and surely could forget any notion of being handed another chance in future. His reaction to Fox's announcement was carried through on auto-pilot. Have a shower. Get dressed. Bite lip forcibly. Jump into car and drive away as quickly as possible. Ignore the press. Draw a veil over the business, and continue to be professional. After all, he was still in employment with the Scottish champions. In the intervening period, little clarification has come to light to explain McLean's ultimate reticence. One theory is that he felt he could not be seen to embrace Rangers' non-Catholic signing policy, which he considered an anachronism, especially as he had signed many talented Catholics for Dundee United. A less credible proposition is that McLean believed that he should have been in the frame for the Rangers job ahead of the less experienced Ferguson. There again, as one who had regularly voiced his concerns over the excessive influence that the Old Firm held over Scottish football, perhaps he indulged in private intrigue at Rangers' expense. Or more cynically, McLean, who had always commanded a Napoleonic sway in Dundee, perhaps could not tolerate the idea of having to delegate power or deal with genuine superstars, who would not be content to be treated as chattels on six-year contracts or risk having wages docked after winning a match 6-0 because they had relaxed in the final 20 minutes, as happened at United. Whatever the reason – and it may be that McLean simply decided that he and his family were perfectly happy with life in the environs of Broughty Ferry – he has not voiced any regrets. But then there *is* life beyond the Old Firm.

Smith and his manager remained friends, but the relationship had altered perceptibly from avuncular to merely amiable. One long-serving Rangers official says: 'All through his career, Walter Smith has done his best to avoid fall-outs with other people, and has largely succeeded. That's not to say he is a soft touch, far from it, but there is a sentimental streak beneath the gruffness: he really wants to think the best of folk, and if he is disappointed in that judgment, he is really disappointed. So I can imagine that he would have been devastated by what happened with Jim McLean, but he wasn't going to spill his guts to the press or go looking for confrontation. That's not him at all.' As it was, Smith and McLean were travelling towards a fork in the road, and the younger man had resolved that if he received an offer from a leading club he would not stick around in someone's shadow. He had all but relinquished hope that Rangers would come calling anew, but then life is full of surprises, some of them tragic.

CHAPTER FOUR

Intriguing Duo Answer
Call to Ibrox

'He was a perfect foil for Graeme Souness'

After years of striving hard behind the scenes, Walter Smith suddenly burst into the public eye at the end of 1985. The circumstances were not as he would have wished, and Scots and followers of football across the globe were left numbed when Jock Stein collapsed and died at the end of Scotland's World Cup qualifying match against Wales in Cardiff. The tearful scenes that followed the demise of the national team's charismatic manager ensured that Scotland's bid to make the finals in Mexico became even more charged, as they faced a play-off over two legs against Australia. The SFA installed Alex Ferguson as stand-in manager with Smith as his deputy, accompanied by a coaching staff of Archie Knox, Andy Roxburgh and Craig Brown. A routine 2-0 Scottish victory brought goals from Davie Cooper and Frank McAvennie in the first leg, though the team's failure to secure a decisive third strike rankled with a few supporters. But on the night of 20 November most of the Tartan Army were too wrapped up in the emotion of the occasion to care that much. Many were still in mourning for the Big Man, and Ferguson, who was normally so masterful when dealing with an Aberdeen team that he had nurtured for much of the previous decade, fretted over tinkering with his predecessor's squad. Indeed, when the Scots travelled to Australia, some of the players spoke of the air of unreality which pervaded their mission, epitomised by Ferguson's decision to depart the squad to visit a relative, and it was as if they all wished they could all be somewhere else. Smith, though, took charge of the players with an assurance which demonstrated the techniques that he had assimilated from his stimulating association with Scotland's youths. Recognising that the worst thing he could do, in the sweltering temperatures of Melbourne, was to adopt a heavy-handed approach by enforcing an excess of training sessions, he granted the tour party a day off, and the players were offered the opportunity of a round of golf or heading to the races. Former international goalkeeper Alan Rough fills in the fascinating details of a golf story and its aftermath:

'The only proviso was that we had to be back in our hotel by teatime, because we had been invited to attend a function by a group of local expatriates, and the management had lent their blessing to the proposal. So it was that Graeme Sharp, David Speedie and I popped off to a nearby golf course, and the thought that we might suffer in the heat hardly crossed our minds. Our round started at 11 a.m. with 100 degrees already showing on the thermometer, and it climbed by another 10 degrees as our game progressed, but we continued with the stiff upper lip, for which the British are renowned. The golf finished with the scores level, so we organised an impromptu "skins" event, and we were just knuckling down to that challenge when wee David blurted out: "Oh boy, oh boy" – and promptly passed out from sunstroke. He had collapsed in a heap and was obviously struggling, so we took him back to the hotel, and told him to grab a few hours' sleep. He was looking really peaky and had turned lobster-pink, so, as the senior member in the Scotland ranks, I decided I would let him stay in bed and relax for the whole evening. However, by 6 p.m. he maintained that he had recovered, said there were no ill-effects and told me straight: "I am absolutely fine, there is no problem, so let's go out and have a party." There was just no stopping him.

'He was soon staggering around drunk as a lord, and barely capable of standing on his own. I glanced at the lad and thought to myself: "God, I wish I had persuaded him not to come." Then suddenly in walked Walter Smith with a grim look on his face, and he asked me: "Where's Speedie?" I was a bit flustered and mumbled: "Erm, he's just about to pass out on the couch over there, so there's no point trying to talk to him. He's plastered." At which point Smith, who was clearly furious, responded with all the affection of a speak-your-weight machine. "Right, this is a balls-up. You two were put in charge of him, and you had better get a grip of him, because he has been booked to appear live on *Grandstand* this evening. Take him back to the hotel, and sober him up smartish."

'Well, we were both flummoxed, but that was Walter. His attitude was that we had to accept personal responsibility for our actions: we were grown men, and we shouldn't have got ourselves in that mess in the first place. And he was right. The problem was that the BBC had requested an interview with David as part of their build-up to the second leg, and we had to do our best. So I took one of David's arms and Graeme held the other, and the pair of us dragged him to the studio link between Melbourne and London. By now he was babbling interminable nonsense, shouting: "How's it hangin', big man?" to strangers in the elevator, and I said to Sharp: "If we pull this off, it will be a miracle."

'Well, we didn't, and it wasn't. Bob Wilson [former Scotland goalkeeper turned sports anchorman] was on the line, and the plan was that he would lob a few easy questions over to Speedie. You have to remember that while it was around midday in Britain, it was really late on Saturday night in Melbourne. We tried to prop David up, between passing him orange juice and mineral water. But it was futile. He was sozzled. Eventually Bob began by asking: "Hello there, David, how are you enjoying yourself over there, and how is the Scottish squad acclimatising?" Whereupon our team-

mate replied: "Ach, f***ing nae problem, big man, how's yourself?" At that moment, we heard the producer screaming into the
microphone: "Get him off the f***ing line this instant!"

'And there was a brief announcement that the satellite had
malfunctioned . . .'

The episode provided a rare note of levity in an otherwise insipid
trip Down Under. Australia's coach Frank Arok had promised
that the visitors would face a cauldron above and in front of them,
but as it transpired Jim Leighton was in immaculate form in goals,
and the match resulted in a no-scoring draw. Scotland, with their
customary huffing and puffing, had reached their fourth consecutive World Cup finals, and the SFA swiftly confirmed that the
Ferguson–Smith partnership would remain in charge for the 1986
campaign. What most people did not know was that the wheels
were in motion for one of the most dramatic developments in
Scottish football. After New Year, Smith began to hear murmur-
ings of discontent from within Ibrox, where another league
campaign had fallen flat with Rangers languishing far behind
Hearts and eventual champions Celtic. Rangers started a process
of restructuring with Lawrence Marlborough taking control and
appointing David Holmes as his chairman. They searched for a
high-profile figure with the clout to embark on a radical new
policy for the organisation, and chose Graeme Souness, the
Edinburgh-born firebrand who had starred at Liverpool and
Sampdoria, and was a Scottish internationalist of repute. Holmes
contacted Smith and they met at the Pond Hotel in Glasgow,
where mutual admiration was palpable. The conversation
touched on multifarious subjects without the question of money
being broached. The next step was for Souness and Smith to sit
down and discuss their respective ideas for the regeneration of
Rangers to discover whether they could establish a viable partnership, and they met in the build-up to Scotland's friendly fixture
with Romania, shortly before the World Cup finals. On the
surface, they were starkly contrasting personalities. Souness

was a well-heeled and well-groomed cosmopolitan character, who had even featured in a walk-on appearance in the television series *The Boys from the Black Stuff,* whereas Smith was an unassuming creature of habit with no airs and graces, who was rather akin to a Clydeside shop steward of yesteryear. Yet from the first moment of their encounter, Souness realised that he was in the presence of a true football man, and Smith recognised that his colleague-to-be harboured bold plans for Ibrox. The chemistry was right between the men and the die was cast, despite Jim McLean's reluctance to release his No. 2 from duties at Dundee United. When the news broke, he accused Rangers of poaching Smith, a charge which might have merited more serious consideration but for the dilatory fashion in which McLean had behaved three years earlier when presented with the opportunity to move to Ibrox. Even when Holmes submitted an official request to talk to Smith, and United agreed reluctantly to sanction the meeting, they refused to release their employee from his contract, and demanded significant compensation of £50,000. On this occasion Rangers refused to be dragged into any nonsense, and the energetic Holmes telephoned George Fox, asked the United director for an address to which he could dispatch the £50,000, wrote out the cheque in Smith's presence and summoned a courier. The cheque was delivered to Fox's Carnoustie residence that evening.

The subsequent period yielded a giddy whirl for Souness, Smith and for the institution that they had resolved to restore to glowing health. Stark evidence of the need for strong medicine in the wake of the regimes of Greig, and latterly Jock Wallace, was forthcoming when Smith finally fulfilled his boyhood dream by entering Ibrox as an employee in April 1986, aged 38. As he remembers, a swirl of thoughts enveloped his mind, and it would have been understandable had he indulged in some self-congratulation, but when the lifelong supporter signed his contract at Rangers, the team had just been defeated 2-1 by bottom-of-the-table Clydebank at Kilbowie. The torpid performance confirmed that too many of the senior personnel were inadequate. Nor were matters significantly better during the first game under Smith's oversight, when an industrious St Mirren beat Rangers at Love Street by the same score-line of 2-1. The prospect of European qualification seemed to be disappearing, particularly given that one of their two remaining matches was at Pittodrie, a venue which in recent times had developed into a northern fortress. 'The St Mirren defeat handed Graeme and I our first Ibrox crisis,' Smith reflects wryly. 'I'd been at the club less than a week, and Graeme hadn't even joined up yet!' Yet Smith's skills of organisation and motivation paid off when a Ted McMinn goal earned a 1-1 draw in Aberdeen, then Motherwell were defeated 2-0 with goals from Dave McPherson and Ally McCoist. Much of the play in these fixtures was unconvincing for fans accustomed to confident displays by their team, but at least the first objective of entry to Europe had been attained, albeit by a whisker.

Off the pitch, Smith was under no illusions. Indeed, the manner in which he trawled through the Ibrox corridors and surveyed the amenities and day-to-day running of the club merely emphasised the notion that glorious tradition alone does not guarantee continued success. On the pitch, the Rangers squad were long on perspiration, but painfully short of individuals to bring a spark of pizzazz to major European occasions. Though he ruled out snap judgments, his reports to Souness were couched in urgent terms, and the gauntlet was handed on to Holmes. There could be no quick solution without serious investment, and if that meant chasing major signings in England and Europe and breaking transfer records, there was no alternative.

Smith and Souness had been provided with an opportunity to engage in some detailed planning, but sadly such conditions were scarcely available for Scotland's World Cup campaign in Mexico, where a low-key exit followed a lacklustre tournament for Alex Ferguson's men. According to reports from several of the squad, the team were riven with factions with Ferguson and Souness constantly at odds, when Scottish fans might have assumed that the priority was tackling Denmark, West Germany and Uruguay. It was suggested by some that the explanation for the breakdown in the relationship was that Ferguson had coveted the Rangers job, which is implausible when it is recalled that he had knocked it back in 1983, and anyway he was poised to decamp to take charge of Manchester United. Whatever the reason for the schism, Smith had to use all his diplomatic skills to keep the channels of communication open. Alan Rough, a non-playing member of the squad on this occasion, again provides telling insight on squabbling that he witnessed:

'The SFA had decided that Scotland players should only be permitted one three-minute telephone call home twice a week, which was pretty pathetic for those guys with wives and young children, especially when you considered the wads of cash which were swilling around in the governing body's coffers. Well, as soon as he heard about the phone restrictions, Graeme Souness went ballistic and told the rest of us: "This is f***ing ridiculous," and elected to fight our corner. It developed into a really big argument between him and Alex with the pair bawling at each other, but that wasn't out of the ordinary in Mexico. On the contrary, at nearly every meeting the players held with Alex – and Graeme was the head of the players' committee, so there were plenty – they seemed to become embroiled in shouting matches, frequently over the most trivial of matters, and it was hardly conducive to fostering a climate of unity. To be fair, Walter did his best to act as mediator, but since everybody knew he was linking up at Rangers with Graeme as soon as the World Cup was over, that hardly improved the atmosphere.'

Internal divisions had emerged prior to the tournament, when Souness and a group of the perceived party animals within the Scotland ensemble, including Frank McAvennie, Mo Johnston and Graeme Sharp, drove into Los Angeles in a chauffeur-driven limousine for a meal with Rod Stewart, at the superstar's behest, and dined on oysters, caviare and champagne at a plush restaurant on Sunset Boulevard. For Ferguson, who had nurtured his outstanding Aberdeen side on the virtues of temperance and staying out of the limelight away from football, this was the kind of reckless behaviour which might have been specifically designed to attract hordes of paparazzi. Smith, while hardly lax on the disciplinary front, looked far more benevolently upon the players' soirée with Stewart: after all, the singer acted as an unofficial ambassador for the Tartan Army. This should not be misinterpreted as suggesting that Ferguson and Smith were involved in some sort of petty stand-off, but the focus of both men, and Souness too, seemed to be a few thousand miles away. An illustration of this comes in a conversation with Rough, in which Souness outlined the magnitude of vision for his forthcoming role at Rangers. Rough remembers:

'We shared a couple of beers outside his hotel room, and he spoke of how David Holmes was prepared to bankroll a revolution at Ibrox by recruiting some genuinely international-class performers. I was sceptical at first, and inquired: "Who exactly are we talking about here?" Then calm as you please, Souness replied: "Well, I have been studying all the good sides in recent years, and their success has been based round a spine of a top-notch keeper, an inspirational centre-half, a midfield supremo and a prolific striker, and that is why I am doing my best to bring people of the calibre of Chris Woods, Terry Butcher and Trevor Steven to Glasgow. What we need is a total transformation of Scottish football, and if Rangers are ever to become a truly leading European club, we have to broaden our horizons and change our attitude to everything from diet and nutrition to creating soccer academies and introducing the kids to good habits." It was strong stuff, and I have to admit that while I believe the subsequent influx of foreign players has been detrimental to Scottish football, Souness was a genuine visionary, and his arguments made a lot of sense.'

Given this backdrop, the Scots' World Cup road meandered to nowhere in Mexico. They lost 1-0 to the Danes, courtesy of Preben Elkjaer-Larsen's 58th-minute goal, then succumbed 2-1 to the Germans, Rudi Voller cancelling out Gordon Strachan's excellent early strike before Klaus Allofs secured a deserved victory. Controversy subsequently surfaced when Ferguson dropped Souness from the squad for the final match against Uruguay, which still offered a chance of progression to the later stages. It was a baffling selection from the usually astute Ferguson, with Paul McStay introduced to the fray for the first time in the competition with Arthur Albiston, Paul Sturrock and, to his immense surprise, Graeme Sharp. The line was peddled by the management that Souness was suffering from dehydration after his notable industry in the defeat by the Germans, but few within the camp believed this, and it was impossible to avoid the suspicion that his omission was due to a personality clash. For his part, Smith was in constant contact with Souness as they made a string of international calls to a raft of potential Rangers signings. Ferguson, no stranger to banner headlines, declined to comment on the ditching of Souness, apart from sticking to the party line. Some players, who were bored to distraction in their sub-standard accommodation, actually began to wonder whether elimination might not be preferable to being asked to tackle a rampaging Argentina team in the quarter-finals, and it was scarcely a surprise when the Scots served up one of their most innocuous performances in slipping to a goal-less draw versus Uruguay, whose Jose Batista was sent off in the first minute of the proceedings for a horrible challenge on Strachan. Even with a long-term numerical advantage, Ferguson's men barely engineered a clear-cut opening as the Uruguayans put up the shutters. The Tartan Army barely had the strength to vent their disapproval in the heat that engulfed them.

❖

At this point speculation over Souness and Smith's impact on Rangers was rewarded with some genuine news, and if any of the ranks of Ibrox fans had been sceptical over some of the names linked with their club, the events of the summer of 1986 countered their misgivings to a large extent. The imposing Terry Butcher joined on 1 August and Chris Woods, the sort of high-class goalkeeper that the club had required for years, also began looking at plots of land in the Dunblane area, clearly convinced that he was destined for a lengthy stay in Scotland. Souness laid out his vision to a reverential media, and it was evident that substance matched the hype. He had been appointed as Rangers' player-manager, though, and he had no experience of coaching at any level, which meant that Smith's role was crucial. As Butcher explains, he rose to the challenge superbly well:

'Walter was very knowledgeable about tactics and what makes people tick, and we had some great times at Rangers between 1986 and 1990. My quote when he was eventually installed in the Scotland job [in 2004] was that he was a great manager, because he likes heavy-metal music and red wine – a couple of assets that any decent manager should possess. But being serious, Walter was the one who organised things like set-pieces, and he would walk and talk things through with you, like who you were up against and what their qualities were. He was a different character to Graeme: more methodical, more technical, more interested in hard graft than pretty stuff, and that made him a perfect foil for Souness. He had a terrific manner about him, an aura which inspired confidence, and if anybody can promote a feel-good factor, and get the best from players, it is him.'

Rangers' supporters realised soon enough that while Souness would command centre-stage and doubtless generate lashings of trenchant raw material for sports journalists, Smith was every bit as significant to the club's future. Long-term supporter and author Alex Anderson provides this interpretation:

'A man who cut as measured and modest a public figure as Souness appeared glamorous and confrontational, Smith was a quietly hard man, whose calm demeanour was wrought from steel. Though no one would have guessed it from his on-camera persona, Walter was not averse to inviting training-ground mutineers into the privacy of the dressing room, locking the door and offering them the first punch. He was the studied personality who had studied the Scottish football scene his entire life. Alex Totten and John Hagart departed Ibrox along with Jock Wallace, and Smith was a change in the right direction in terms of coaching staff. However, mere change was not enough to retrieve Rangers from the embarrassment they had become to the heavyweights of British football they would soon be: what was required was a tectonic shift. That could only manifest itself through a singularly chaotic, destructive force of nature. Smith was, if you like, the method behind the Souness madness.'

As the Souness era commenced, some predicted grimly that he would eventually bankrupt Scottish football. What should not be forgotten, though, is that Butcher and Woods, respectively the England captain and the deputy goalkeeper to Peter Shilton, cost the club £1.2m which, seen from a distance, seems like the bargain of the century. And despite the further recruitment of striker Colin West, David Holmes was not endowed with the financial resources which David Murray would bring to Rangers upon his arrival in 1988. Once the two English players had staked their future at Ibrox, no more money was available in the transfer market, as Smith publicly confirmed. 'We were told that we could not afford to bring in another class player. Although we were to spend far more money in the years ahead, we had reached our limit with these first signings. That was why it was so important to Graeme and me, as well as to the club, that the signings we made were the right signings, and it turned out they were the men for the job.' No immediate indication of a glorious renaissance was in evidence, though,

51

when Rangers commenced their Scottish league campaign against Hibs at Easter Road. Quite the contrary, because Souness marked his playing debut for Rangers by scything into opposing centre-forward George McCluskey, and he was red-carded. That precipitated a mass brawl, though Hibs' goalkeeper Alan Rough was not involved. He had been booked, and did not wish to risk joining Souness in the dressing room. Butcher describes the match and the follow-up:

'It was neither the best of sights, nor the best of starts: Ally McCoist scored from the penalty spot, but we lost 2-1. I ended up getting a yellow card in my first game, and afterwards the SFA decreed that everybody who was involved in the fracas would receive two penalty points, so with my other booking I managed to pick up four disciplinary points on my league debut. A nice quiet start to life in Scotland. After the match, Souness was a nightmare. We went out in Edinburgh that evening to drown our sorrows, but he almost finished up in a fight in a bar. A guy was trying to be smart and clever and I tried to placate him, but Graeme got fed up with his attitude and told him to f*** off. It was time to catch a taxi back to the Norton House Hotel, and some sort of sanity, before something worse happened to cloud a pretty bad day.'

Butcher's testimony explains why Walter Smith had to navigate through choppy waters on many occasions. At his best, Souness was a dominant, wonderfully aggressive threat to any opponents, blessed with skill, vision and an instinct which had been refined at Liverpool. On the debit side, he had a long history of lunging into wild challenges when the red mist descended, and in these instances he was often a liability to those around him. At these moments, it was incumbent on Smith to dictate matters from the sidelines, and almost to ignore his nominal boss. Treading this tightrope requires calmness and tact, but Smith had learned the balancing act in his association with Jim McLean, who also tended to operate on a short fuse. A member of the team that lost to Hibs that day reveals: 'He didn't make a big fuss about it, but Walter was worried that there might be a breakdown in communication because of Graeme's decision to play on. And you have to believe it: there were tensions and a lot of pressure on both men in the build-up to that match, and the worst possible thing that could have happened did happen, with Souness losing the plot. But I spoke to Walter at the end, and he said to me: "Better it all goes off today than later in the season." He couldn't have been more in check of his emotions, and he was more disappointed with the result than the fight. It tells you something about the guy. Yes, he's a decent bloke, but he is as tough as old boots.'

That was just as well, because there was no disguising the fact that, in the early stages of the season, Rangers were still punching below their weight. The Hibs reverse might have been shrugged off, but when Souness's men toiled to beat Falkirk at Ibrox in their next match and then surrendered a two-goal half-time lead at the same venue in losing 3-2 to Dundee United, they were languishing in seventh place in the championship table, and anxious followers sensed that something was amiss. The pre-match regimen which had been introduced by Souness was one of the most obvious sources of discontent, since the new manager, who was determined to do things his way, had decreed that the players would train on Friday mornings, then spend the next 24 hours at the Grosvenor Hotel in Glasgow. Alas, most of the young men who had been dragged away from families and friends in a futile attempt at team-building, were bored witless. A sound rationale, no doubt, lurked behind the ploy by Souness, which may have worked in Italy where Serie A clubs can be separated by long distances, but it seemed absurd for players to be shunted off to the confines of a hotel when they were due to face Falkirk, Hamilton or Celtic the following afternoon. Soon enough, after Butcher and McCoist had broached the subject with Walter Smith, he persuaded his colleague to ring the changes, and he duly obliged. It was not the only time that diplomatic intervention would be required to ensure that the managerial partnership flourished.

Rangers began building momentum as August progressed, and the process was helped greatly by the first Old Firm match of season 1986–87, played at Ibrox. For Smith, who had grown up to relish these occasions, this was the first significant test of his qualities and capabilities, and he admitted later that it was one of the most memorable afternoons of his life. To be sure, it was a fairly humdrum encounter enlivened only by a trademark spark of genius from Davie Cooper, whose reverse pass pierced the Celtic defence and allowed Ian Durrant to whack the ball past Pat Bonnar. But when that goal was scored a crescendo of noise enveloped the ground, as fans who had been starved of success for too long rejoiced. Smith and every person associated with the club were treated to a huge surge of adrenaline, and lingering apprehension that this was another false dawn ebbed away as Rangers produced an impressive sequence of six victories in their next eight fixtures to start climbing the league table.

As successes were chalked up, the mood was transformed not merely within the club's support, but among those who worked for the organisation, as one former employee told me, with an Anglo-Saxon flourish:

'By the mid-1980s, we had reached the stage of thinking that we might have to dwell on the glories of the past. Some of my mates had even stopped going to matches, preferring to spend their time at junior games on Saturday, where they didn't have to listen to anybody talking about Celtic or f***ing Aberdeen. That was one of the key areas where Souness made a difference: he walked in the door big and strong and proud, and obviously didn't give a f*** what anybody else thought, and told the board: "Right, you used to do things this way, but now you are going to do it my way." When you look back at what Graeme actually did, it wasn't rocket science. I mean, why on earth Rangers hadn't been interested in players such as Butcher and Woods before he arrived was a mystery to me. Let's face it, if you go to clubs like Coventry and Norwich and tell world-class players: "Here's the chance to play in front of 50,000 supporters on a regular basis, as well as a higher profile than you will ever get in England," why wouldn't they want to come to Scotland? Especially if you remember that the English clubs were banned from European competition [after the fatal rioting at the 1985 European Cup final at Heysel]. But Souness was a showman, and he lifted up our spirits in the space of a few weeks. Even when he was doing mental things like getting sent off at Hibs, it just showed he was never going to take a backward step.'

That belief intensified on 27 October when Souness and Smith collected their first item of silverware after Rangers defeated Celtic 2-1 in the Skol Cup final, goals from Ian Durrant and Davie Cooper sealing a significant triumph for the club. The result was a testimony to the new-found confidence which the management team had instilled in their players, and the afternoon demonstrated the bond that had been forged between the duo and the mercurial Cooper, who was destined to become one of the tragic figures of Scottish football. For years, the elusive and instinctively unpredictable winger had danced to his own tune, transcending the mediocrity of many around him, which justified the assertion of Dutch master Ruud Gullit that he was the best player he had come up against. With Souness in charge, Coop was allowed licence to parade his panache with an increasingly gifted squad. Throughout his career, Cooper had suffered, somewhat like Kenny Dalglish, from possessing too much vision. He would, for instance, dispatch a glorious 50-yard pass, only to be let down by the failure of a team mate to capitalise on the situation. But his talents were certainly appreciated by Souness: 'Coop was special'; by Butcher: 'One of the best I have ever played with', and by Smith: 'Coop could have featured in any team you care to name. He was a magnificent footballer.' As Rangers battled their way to glory in the League Cup, their strengths were greatly admired by the watching Graham Roberts and Chris Waddle, who spoke later about the fantastic atmosphere which the game had generated. It was not long before Roberts, a fractious and aggressive individual who provided a fearful prospect for rival strikers, was signing on the dotted line and pledging his future to a club which, up to 1986, had been in danger of slipping into a sad state of disrepair. It is simplistic to downgrade the Souness achievements with the rejoinder that he has not achieved anything in football without recourse to investment in lavish signings, but so far as Smith was concerned, this was the start of a beautiful friendship, his view expressed succinctly:

> 'He was the catalyst for change. He turned the dream into reality. He brought it alive. Without him, it wouldn't have happened. He knew these players; they knew him. And they recognised that if Graeme Souness was going to continue his career in Scotland, then it was worthwhile joining him.'

By the end of the year, Rangers were on the march once more. They had beaten Celtic in their two most recent meetings, had collected a trophy for a fan base long starved of reasons to be cheerful, and had sailed into the UEFA Cup with an assurance which suggested that Souness's knowledge of European football might be invaluable in the years ahead. The campaign commenced with a potentially fraught tussle against Finnish club Ilves Tampere, but Cooper, who was ubiquitous during this period, was in sublime form in the first leg at Ibrox, and helped to orchestrate a 4-0 win. Robert Fleck scored a hat-trick, and Ally McCoist applied the *coup de grâce*. It was game, set and match, which was just as well, for in the return leg – without the services of Souness, who was injured, Ted McMinn and Derek Ferguson – Rangers were ragged and unconvincing in slipping to a 2-0 defeat with goals from Aro Hjelm and Arto Uimonen. Souness, watching from the sidelines with his usual saturnine stare, declared: 'We played like a pub team.' Progress had been secured and embarrassment averted nonetheless, and in the next round Rangers were paired with Boavista of Portugal. This proved to be a more daunting task, as expected, and the Ibrox support were stunned when Toninho broke the deadlock on the half-hour. Dave

McPherson levelled matters within three minutes, and as half-time beckoned Butcher fed the ball to McCoist, and the prolific striker finished the attack decisively. It was a narrow advantage, particularly considering that the Scots had conceded an away goal, but Smith checked out Boavista at home, and he and Souness retained the faith that their personnel would secure the tie. This they did with a display which was as professional and masterful as their second outing against Ilves Tampere had been shoddy. Thanks to a nerveless display from Woods, the hosts grew increasingly desperate, and Derek Ferguson was the beneficiary of Cooper's inch-perfect lay-off, scoring the solitary goal in the 70th minute. It sparked feverish celebrations from the band of travelling fans, for this was the first instance that Rangers had advanced to round three since the giddy success in Barcelona 14 years previously.

Few were deluded into proclaiming that Rangers were now capable of troubling the super-heavyweights of the European scene, certainly no one from the Souness-Smith school of pragmatic assessment, or any supporter who examined the playing squad and noticed individuals such as Bobby Russell, Jimmy Nicholl, Cammy Fraser and Stuart Munro still commanding regular slots. By the stage of their third-round meeting with Borussia Moenchengladbach in late November and early December, Rangers were in the process of signing Roberts from Tottenham Hotspur for £450,000 – which proved to be another outstanding piece of business – but he would obviously have no part to play in what developed into an old-fashioned scrap between two fiercely committed teams. The Scots had the opportunity to build an advantage, but despite thrilling their fans with an early goal from McCoist following a superbly constructed build-up, they created a string of excellent chances only to be punished with a sucker-punch equaliser after 30 minutes when Uwe Rahn latched on to Andre Winkhold's cross, and headed past Woods. That was it at Ibrox, but Rangers had triumphed abroad on their previous mission, and remained positive for the re-match in Germany. They had good reason to feel they were well in contention, given the belligerence with which they roared into action at the Bokelborg Stadion, but McCoist struck the bar, Butcher was denied a stonewall penalty, and as the match raged on the Germans seemed content to cling on for a goalless draw. Rangers suffered another blow when Munro was dismissed after a clash with Winkhold. It would have demoralised most sides, but the visitors were unstinting in their labours, eventually to no avail. In what seemed an absurd conclusion, Cooper was booked for comments made as he was poised to take a free-kick in the 87th minute. Referee Alex Ponnet suddenly remembered that he had already cautioned the player, hence a red card for a second Rangers player.

This occasion perhaps could be regarded as a microcosm of Rangers in Europe under Graeme Souness. There was no shortage of passion, tenacity or craft, but too often the essential touch of class would emerge from rivals, or they would find themselves the victims of botched officialdom. By the death, as Borussia clung on for a scarcely merited draw, Butcher was in tears, though the big fellow and his comrades paid tribute to the 3,500 supporters who had followed them to the Continent. It would be no consolation that Moenchengladbach were knocked out in the semi-finals of the tournament 2-0 on aggregate . . . by Dundee United.

CHAPTER FIVE

TROPHIES, TRIALS AND TRIBULATIONS

'The guilty pair shook their heads in disbelief'

When one considers Rangers' experiences under Graeme Souness and Walter Smith during 1987 and '88, it is possible to detect a battle between benign and malign influences for the soul of the club, the occasional lurch into insanity and the regular straining of the credulity of thousands of fans. Freak results were in the mix, too.

Hence a team packed with superstars were knocked out of the Scottish Cup by Hamilton Academical months after many of the same players had performed wonders in beating the mighty Dynamo Kiev, and an eruption of violence during an Old Firm tussle led to Terry Butcher being vilified by the tabloids, one infamous headline proclaiming: 'Goldilocks and the Three Bears', a description which is explained later in the chapter. Then there was the puzzling case of Robert Fleck.

Early in the new regime at Ibrox, Souness had decided, in the no-nonsense style which made him unpopular with some sections of the Scottish public, that Fleck was not up to the standards he required in skill or keeping his discipline, which some thought a bit rich coming from a fiery character such as the manager. He and Walter Smith discussed the matter, and concluded that the player would be better off leaving. Smith phoned his mate Jocky Scott, who was in charge of Dundee FC at that point and urgently required a striker. Scott told Smith that he would be interested in acquiring Fleck, but that the cash-flow situation was desperate. Smith returned to Souness with this information, and they agreed to reduce the player's transfer to £20,000 – this for a footballer who subsequently won four Scotland caps – but even that asking price was still too much, and the prospective deal fell through. Yet, within months of Fleck languishing in the reserves, he bounced back into contention with a series of fine performances for Rangers' senior team. Lo and behold, Norwich were sufficiently impressed to make a bid for him, amounting to £580,000, which led to his moving to Carrow Road, and eventually to Chelsea for the sum of £2.1m.

Thus as 1987 appeared on the horizon, the suspicion was that Souness's Jekyll-and-Hyde personality would leave his players and supporters wondering on a regular basis whether they stood on the verge of a windfall or a catastrophe. In the Ne'erday Old Firm clash came resounding affirmation of how Celtic's grip on their title was being loosened, but even here life could have been so different for player/manager Souness. He piled into the Celtic captain Roy Aitken early in the game with a cynical challenge which earned him a yellow card, but also had the effect of knocking the stuffing out of his opponent for the rest of the encounter. Had the card been red, Souness would have had no excuse, but his ploy worked as McCoist and Fleck established a comfortable cushion for the hosts, and that proved the catalyst for Souness to taunt the opposition with a succession of back-heels and flicks, as if emphasising his team's superiority over the old enemy. The Edinburgh man had clearly decided that he could not care less whether Celtic's support burned effigies of him later: he had laid down the battle lines and issued a resounding declaration of intent. Which is fine, until fate intervenes.

Rangers entertained lowly Hamilton on 31 January reflecting the sort of arrogance which comes from those who anticipate a mis-match, though this was the 20th anniversary of their notorious exit in the cup competition at the hands of unsung Berwick

Rangers. On paper it should have been a rout, but Scottish Cup ties offer no guarantees, and after Adrian Sprott had sent the underdogs in front, the 1,200–1,500 Hamilton fans basked in what they assumed was to be a brief spell in the spotlight. Gerry Collins almost made it 2-0, however, and the likes of Souness and Roberts were clearly discomfited by the lung-bursting efforts of their rivals. Rangers mounted a sustained onslaught, but Hamilton's defence held firm, thanks to a rash of frantic goal-line clearances and desperate hacks to safety, while the crowd grew ever more hostile towards the wee team. Robert Paterson was one of the visiting supporters who savoured the cup shock, but his recollections demonstrate some of the more noisome aspects of Rangers during the Souness era:

'It was a great day, but it was also pretty scary. When we got to the ground, as usual wearing our scarves, there was the usual patronising stuff from their fans, asking us to enjoy life in a big stadium, because it would be the only thing we enjoyed that afternoon. You can cope with that, it comes with the territory, but once the game started and Sprotty scored, it was as if we had broken some law or other. There was this old guy in an expensive suit and tie – he looked as if he might be an accountant or a lawyer – but he was hurling this non-stop stream of sectarian abuse at the guys in the Hamilton team, who he regarded as being Catholics, and it was just sickening listening to this endless torrent of F words and C words; and the C didn't stand for Catholic, by the way. In the final 20 minutes, somebody flung a few coins at me, and I was advised by a couple of stewards to take off my scarf "for yer ain health". But what the hell was that about?

'Then, when I walked out of the stadium at the end, a group of the more inebriated Rangers fans milled around me and my mate and began pushing and shoving us, hoping we would retaliate and get in a ruck. We didn't respond, so they eventually started calling us "f***ing poofs" and other such insults, and that went on for the best part of 10 or 15 minutes. And the worst thing was that a couple of Strathclyde Police officers were only standing a few yards away from us, and they never batted an eyelid, almost as if they were saying to the Rangers guys: "Go on, tell them to f*** off. That's what they deserve for knocking the mighty Rangers out of the cup."

'Put it like this: we were happy to get back to Hamilton, but that episode showed me that Rangers were developing this mentality again, where you weren't allowed to beat them. They had kind of lost that during the previous decade, because they were pretty crap and Aberdeen and Dundee United had climbed above them, but when Souness came to Ibrox, he had clearly got the message rammed home that they needed a siege mentality. "Nobody likes us, and we don't care" . . . that sort of thing, which was a bit pathetic. I'm not saying they should have cheered our victory, but would it really have hurt them to have let us enjoy one of our best-ever results?'

The short answer, from the perspective of Souness and Smith, was a resounding yes. For them, embarking on a crusade which had to be swift and brutal, there was simply no room for sentiment, particularly in light of the manner in which chief executive Holmes had irritated sections of the Rangers support by his apparent lack of interest in helping them cheer on their heroes while in European action. Club historian Robert McElroy commented: 'The relatively small number of Light Blue followers who wanted to travel to Finland [for the Ilves Tampere game] found their best efforts obstructed by the club, with chief executive David Holmes and his sidekick, the former Mars Bar salesman Freddie Fletcher, regarding supporters as an intrusion and an encumbrance rather than customers.' It was a volatile period in football in general, but an exaggerated tension afflicted Ibrox which Smith, as courteous and civilised as he was, could not ease, and certainly not as Souness's men powered their way towards the championship with a philosophy that owed more to industry than inspiration. Nor did the ceaseless niggle do anything to dissuade sceptics that Souness's grand plan basically amounted to assembling a squad that reflected his bombastic and bullying approach, and to hell with outdated notions of the beautiful game. When Rangers were finally beaten by Celtic towards the end of the season, by 3-1 at Parkhead, even the likes of Butcher, newly recruited to the Ibrox scene, got caught up in the sectarian strife: he reacted to the green walls and Celtic crest in the bathroom by taking a couple of pictures of the Queen into the Rangers dressing room and placing them at each end. Butcher, who is an intelligent man and who has since become involved with the anti-bigotry group Nil By Mouth, seems mystified nowadays about how he could have been captivated by factors that he did not fully understand. But if there was a serious sectarian problem, few were intent on facing up to it in 1987.

After victories over Dundee, Clydebank and Hearts, Rangers journeyed to Aberdeen on 2 May with a chance of securing the title, but only if Celtic came unstuck against Falkirk. It was another in the list of controversial occasions for Souness, who was given a torrid time by the home side's sprightly Brian Irvine, before responding with a nasty challenge, which earned him another red card. As for the match itself, Butcher opened the scoring when he latched on to a Cooper free-kick, only for Irvine to equalise at the end of the first half. It was fraught and frenetic with too many fouls and not enough football, but Butcher and Roberts mopped up the pressure, and news filtered through to the players that Celtic had lost. And so, with Pittodrie festooned in red, white and blue, the Souness era had seized significant spoils – with the ultimate assistance of Celtic. For Smith, there was satisfaction that his club had won their first league title for nine seasons, but certainly no triumphalism on his part, given that he recognised as much as anybody that their success had been only fitfully convincing, and that greater challenges lay ahead. However, having been involved in the capture of two trophies after such a barren spell for Rangers, Smith knew that at least the management had the fans on their side for the foreseeable future, an important factor considering the intrinsic fickleness of Ibrox supporters en masse.

In some respects, the months ahead proved frustrating for the Souness/Smith duopoly. Football writers fuelled speculation that a string of high-profile signings, on a level with Butcher and Woods, were poised to put pen to paper, but frequently such tales were inspired by chit-chat in the pub or in the confines of a supporters' club, such is the fashion in which rumours and reality become intertwined in Glasgow gossip about the Old Firm. In the event, once some of the more fanciful notions had been laid to rest, Souness had to settle for a bargain-basement collection, recruiting Avi Cohen, a former team-mate at Liverpool, Trevor Francis, an old colleague at Sampdoria, and Watford's Marc Falco. These were hard-working professionals, especially Francis, but not the dynamic young talents that the club required, particularly since Souness was winding down his long and impressive playing career, and was becoming increasingly prone to injury and provoking the wrath of referees for mistimed tackles. Unsurprisingly, he perceived the latter phenomenon as a conspiracy, and if one trait epitomised the Souness years with Rangers, it was conflict. Officialdom, rival managers, the press and broadcasters were regularly at loggerheads with the temperamental Scot, and while his outbursts provided rich fare for red-top papers in particular, they merely acted as fodder for those who held grievances against Rangers. Perhaps Souness enjoyed the incessant spats. Few others did.

Back in the engine-room, where Smith was in his element, the club prepared for the 1987–88 campaign, and the No. 2 sensed that this would present a far stiffer test than their maiden season. Celtic were heading into their centenary year, and there was a renewed frisson of purpose and solidarity in their camp, even if the biscuit-tin approach to buying and selling had left their resources looking limited. Though the performances of Terry Butcher since his induction to Scottish football had been typically industrious, he was such a wholehearted warrior that there was always the risk he might incur a serious injury. In the midst of a fractious meeting with Aberdeen at Ibrox in November, that scenario materialised, the big Englishman suffering a leg break after a collision with Alex McLeish, which forced him to accept that he would play no further part in the renewed championship bid. Before that blow, Souness could afford a brief spell of basking in glory when Dynamo Kiev, opponents of high quality, were beaten over two nerve-shredding European Cup encounters in September, not least because at the Republic Stadium his team produced a resilient and controlled display in front of 100,000 spectators. Though Rangers eventually conceded a goal after 72 minutes, when Alexei Mikhailichenko converted a penalty award, they and their band of supporters, who had braved labyrinths of red tape in fulfilling travel plans, returned to Scotland with the feeling that the tie was there to be won. Such thoughts were justified, but not without ritual controversy. When the Soviet champions trained in Glasgow on the night before the return leg, they readied themselves for battle on a normal-sized Ibrox pitch. However, 24 hours later, at the behest of Souness, the touchlines had been narrowed on both wings in a bid to negate the width and pace of Kiev's skilful wingers Vasily Rats and Oleg Blokhin. Whether this was within the spirit of the game was debatable, but the legality of Rangers' actions was not in question according to the UEFA regulations. The ploy certainly unsettled the Russians to the extent that they gifted their adversaries the lead with a howler from goalkeeper Victor Chanov, whose abortive clearance struck Sergei Baltacha on the backside, teeing the ball up for Ally McCoist, who fed on to Falco to score in the 25th minute. On such nights, with the Ibrox throng in full voice, the stadium can resemble a revivalist meeting, and as the din swelled with Rangers controlling most of the play, a Francis cross was headed on by Falco to McCoist, who guided the ball into the corner of the net. Kiev flung everything they could muster at their hosts for the last half-hour, a period which seemed to drag on, and on, but there was to be no denying Souness's team a famous victory. He rushed out towards his side, and one might have imagined that they had won the cup itself. Not too many occasions in the months ahead would link the words smile and Souness.

The events of 17 October 1987 and thereafter seem almost farcical when viewed from this distance. Celtic, who were desperate to restore their winning ways, had signed the redoubtable trio of Andy Walker, Frank McAvennie and Mick McCarthy, and after losing the season's first Old Firm tussle by 2-0, despite Souness being sent off yet again, they recognised that they could not afford any more slip-ups. Consequently, when Rangers and Celtic next met in the league, on a bad-natured afternoon, strewn with petty vindictiveness, the Ibrox men lost the plot in spectacular fashion. McAvennie crashed into Chris Woods on three occasions in the early stages, bundling him into his net on the second and boxing his ears on the third. Woods grabbed his assailant round the throat with one hand, McAvennie sought to slap him away, then Butcher charged over and pushed his opponent in the chest. Graham Roberts was next into the frame, contact was made between him and the Celtic striker, who collapsed in a heap. The referee produced red cards for Woods and McAvennie, but if official sanctions were meant to restore relative calm, they failed dismally. Butcher then scored an embarrassing own-goal, lofting the ball over stand-in keeper Roberts as Celtic established a 2-0 interval advantage. When the action resumed, Butcher next became involved in a collision with rival goalkeeper Alan McKnight, aimed a little kick at the Celtic man, and was promptly shown a second yellow, and a red card. As he sat in the Ibrox dressing room disconsolately, McCoist and Richard Gough managed to salvage a 2-2 draw for their team in the unlikeliest of circumstances, but for all the headlines that this encounter provoked, they were as nothing to the mounting resentment which was accruing against Rangers, for their alleged over-physicality.

In this respect Souness and Smith were as one. Earlier in the

1980s, Rangers' line-ups had started to look frail when placed under pressure, and Alex Ferguson's Aberdeen had grown renowned for successfully challenging their hated Glasgow rivals. For a club who had long prided themselves on never contemplating a backward step, this was humiliating, and the new management determined that they would not countenance fielding any individual who was not prepared to respond to muscle with more of the same. 'All I ask of my players is that they offer me 100 per cent, and walk off the pitch feeling as if they have nothing more to give,' said Smith. 'If somebody gets stuck in and chases the ball endlessly, I shouldn't criticise him for that, I should be thankful that he is bothered enough to get involved. What do you want me to do: look for guys who aren't bothered, people who don't care?' While one can understand Smith's reasoning, there is a certain naivety in his argument, if for no other reason than that the team were under increasing scrutiny as the 1980s unfolded. Butcher, for instance, was asked to report to Govan police station after the acrimonious Old Firm tussle, and he was joined by Rangers' operations officer Alistair Hood and solicitor Len Murray, as a prelude to being informed that he was being charged with behaviour likely to cause a breach of the peace. This struck him like a bolt from the blue, and the affair attracted wide press coverage and many conspiracy theories on football phone-in programmes, before it emerged that Butcher, Woods, Roberts and McAvennie were all facing charges. Despite some sporting observers deploying the facile argument that the courts were no place for footballers' misdeamours, a trial date was fixed for 12 April 1988.

Readers should understand the culture of mutual loathing that existed between the two sides of the Old Firm divide at that time. McAvennie, a character who was later lampooned as a leering Lothario intent on merry-making with the nearest maiden in TV programmes such as *Only an Excuse*, was actually a rumbustious player who was well acquainted in the dark arts of soccer. Roberts, by comparison, was a surly individual whose life has not been short of unsavoury scraps, while Woods and Butcher were among English footballers who were not simply sucked into the Old Firm vortex when they signed for Rangers, but seemed to feel that they had to behave even worse than the Scots on the pitch, as if to justify their inflated salaries. None of this should be regarded as a vindication of what materialised at Ibrox on that mad October day, but having examined all the relevant evidence, the outcome of the proceedings at Glasgow Sheriff Court still strikes me as incomprehensible. The four accused, who had been dubbed 'Goldilocks and the Three Bears' in tabloid style, sat together, but none of the Rangers trio spoke a word to McAvennie, who was regarded by them as the agent provocateur, which he was. Evidence was presented about crowd incitement and the referee's report was discussed at length, and as the trial progressed it appeared that the outcome would be nothing more serious than judicial slaps on the wrist for the footballers. Such predictions proved ill-founded. McAvennie was found not guilty; Roberts breathed a sigh of relief when the case against him was found not proven; Butcher was pronounced guilty and fined £250; Woods was also convicted, but a £500 fine was imposed. The guilty pair shook their heads in disbelief. Even at this juncture, Butcher claims that he cannot fathom the thought processes behind that week spent in court, though he clearly believes that the trial was whipped up by political expediency, and that it had less to do with the Scottish justice system than government posturing. His view:

'Prime Minister Margaret Thatcher hated football, hated its reputation, and loathed the way that its hooligans had tarnished Britain's image abroad. This was only three years after the Heysel tragedy, remember, and English clubs were still banned from Europe. And to this day I have a strong feeling that Woodsy and me, as high-profile players, were used as an example. Just consider the events on the pitch at Easter Road during my first league game for Rangers [when Souness was sent off for the George

McCluskey challenge] . . . that was much more likely, I would have thought, to cause a riot than the brief flashpoint in what was, after all, an Old Firm derby. What would they have done in a similar political climate after the more recent Manchester United and Arsenal melees? Put them away for life? I had done worse things on a football pitch, and not found myself standing in court. So why did it happen this time?'

Twenty years on, such an incident might be dismissed as another storm in the pint glass of Scottish football, but it heightened the perception that the two Glasgow institutions were being treated in contrasting fashions. As the perpetrator, 'Goldilocks' McAvennie should have suffered at least the fate as his two Rangers counterparts, but the disparity in verdicts simply reinforced the suspicion, prevalent at Ibrox that everybody was against the Bears, even the judiciary and the police. Celtic, by comparison, were constantly depicted as downtrodden victims who benefited from a saccharine media spin, which allowed them to present themselves as good-natured jesters who were interested only in aesthetic football, while the much-reviled 'Huns' were miserable Calvinists on the hunt for a scrap. It should be added that much of the rampant paranoia at both clubs was a by-product of sad little conspiracy theorists, but the tensions boiled over with increasing regularity on Souness's watch. Smith, a more insightful customer by comparison, is notable for resembling the dog in the Sherlock Holmes story *Silver Blaze*. He didn't bark.

With Butcher out injured, Richard Gough returned from Tottenham Hotspur, but there was no doubt that Rangers stuttered badly in that second season. They retained the Scottish League Cup in a pulsating final with Aberdeen, the match finishing 3-3 and being settled by a 5-3 advantage in the penalty shoot-out. They beat Dynamo Kiev, a meritorious achievement, and they eliminated the Poles of Gornik Zabrze 4-2 on aggregate in the next round, McCoist once more to the fore with a brace of goals, one in each leg. But reality could not be ignored. 'Basically we were not nearly as good as we wanted to be. The standard of player at the club did drop in that second season, and we went back almost to square one,' Smith observes. 'What that second year showed us early on was that things won't just happen for you – you have to get out there and make them happen. And it demonstrated to me that there was never any time for relaxation when you are part of a club such as Rangers. That's why we began the push for new players towards the turn of the year, and why we told the directors that more money had to be spent. We lost the league, in fact we were third [behind Celtic and Hearts], but we had a growing belief in the squad of players we were bringing together.'

Graham Roberts was destined for the exit door, in an episode highlighting the solidarity that existed between Souness and Smith. They were prepared to accept criticism of their strategies within the sanctity of the dressing room, but certainly not if a player threatened to spark anarchy at the workplace or, worse still, go public in the press about his dissatisfaction. The row erupted after a poor display from Rangers in going down to Aberdeen and after Smith, very matter-of-fact according to an individual who was there, questioned Roberts' culpability in conceding one of Aberdeen's goals. It started like any post-mortem, but the Englishman refused point-blank to accept that he might have been responsible, and as the language deterio-rated and tempers flared Souness walked in and asked what the f*** Roberts was complaining about, backing his assistant immediately. Reports claimed that Roberts and Souness traded punches – the truth, according to my source, is that they had to be pulled apart by other players or they would have brawled – but the result was that the men at the helm of Rangers glanced at each other, and in that instant and without any words needed, Roberts' fate was sealed. He did not help his cause by talking to the papers about the affair, then on the following Saturday at the final league game of the season against Falkirk, taking his seat in the stand among a large group of Rangers supporters, who cheered him to the rafters, and barracked Souness and Smith in the dugout. This was mutiny, and it was not as if Roberts was a 21-year-old ingenue, who might have been excused his intemperate behaviour on the grounds of immaturity. From Smith's perspective, if discipline broke down, everything else would collapse. His unflinching view of the business was:

> 'Managers cannot afford to walk away from difficult or unpopular judgments. Often things happen away from the public gaze which determine the direction you take, but if you bottle a tough disciplinary matter once, then you can lose *all* the players, and not just the one who brought the trouble to a head.'

Roberts was thrust on to the transfer market, and suffered professional humiliation for his trangressions. During the pre-season tour in the summer of 1988, Rangers' first-team squad travelled to Italy, but he was dispatched with the reserves on a low-key sojourn around the Highlands, instructions having been posted to the coaching staff that he was to strip as a substitute, but not be used in any of the matches. It was a stark reminder to him that no person was bigger than the club. It was also an indication that his bosses were growing more confident about the strength of the resources they had at their disposal. Ray Wilkins arrived from Paris for a cut-price £150,000, and developed into one of the best signings of that era, his positive attitude and never-say-die mentality instantly endearing him to the Ibrox faithful. At New Year Mark Walters joined the ranks: he was another classy performer who would grow in stature throughout his time in Glasgow, not solely as a player, but as a man, given the racial abuse that he was forced to endure on travels across Scotland. Other useful performers pledged their allegiance to Souness: John Brown, a bullocking threat to those who dared impede his progress, a similar character in Ian Ferguson, England regular Gary Stevens, and Kevin Drinkell, who complemented an already potent attacking line-up. While none at Ibrox ever enjoyed a Celtic title celebration, there was a sense that the Bhoys had better savour their party, because the balance was shifting decisively away from Parkhead. As it transpired, seven years would elapse before Celtic again finished in the top two, let alone harboured serious pretensions of lifting the league championship. With the arrival of entrepreneur David Murray at the climax of 1988, the final pieces were efficiently fitted into a grand scheme which would delight Rangers followers, and depress those of Celtic.

CHAPTER SIX

MURRAY AND MO

'I never thought that in my wildest dreams they would sign him'

Many words have been spouted about David Murray in the past two decades, laudatory and critical, reflecting contradictions in the businessman's personality. A committed individual who has transcended personal and family tragedy – his legs were amputated after a car crash, and he lost his wife to cancer – the Ayrshireman can be hugely protective of those he employs and respects; he can be surprisingly sentimental for someone whose concern is the balance sheet; and he can surprise even bitter opponents with his tireless innovation, industry and refusal to accept that any cause is lost. Alternatively, Murray can be a spiteful enemy, a man who bears grudges and spends an excessive amount of time checking out the backgrounds of those who dare to besmirch his name. He can also be pettily protectionist and ostrich-like, exemplified by his failure to tackle the scourge of sectarianism head-on when it was obvious that a section of the Ibrox support were bringing their club into disrepute as the 1990s progressed. But over the course of his stewardship as Rangers chairman – he bought the club from Lawrence Marlborough for £6m, and was unveiled in his new role on 23 October 1988 – precious few supporters have had genuine grounds for grievance. The now Sir David Murray may be found wanting if we scrutinise his words: 'Judge me on Europe', and there is little question that a

73

man with such foresight in other areas should have created a youth academy sooner, but whatever his failings, Murray's arrival coincided with a golden era unfolding for Rangers.

From the start of the 1988–9 league campaign, prior to Murray's appointment, it had become clear that Celtic's achievement in winning the double in their centenary season had provided the dying gasps of a once-mighty organisation. From as early as the third game of the season, when Celtic travelled to Ibrox and were hammered 5-1, the gulf between the sides could not be disputed. This was Rangers' biggest winning margin in an Old Firm fixture for 28 years, testifying to the quality of the personnel who had now signed up. A couple of goals from Ally McCoist, a venomous volley from Ray Wilkins and strikes from Mark Walters and Kevin Drinkell highlighted their potency, and reduced Frank McAvennie's opening goal to a meaningless act of defiance. As soon as Terry Butcher looked over towards Celtic goalkeeper Ian Andrews before kick-off, and noted his glazed eyes, he fancied that a rout might be on. Similarly, former Scotland keeper Alan Rough, who had signed for Celtic during the summer, watched and marvelled at the spirit generated within the Rangers camp:

> 'Even the visitors had to grudgingly admit the power of the light-blue tidal wave which engulfed poor Andrews that day. Their ranks oozed with class and virtuosity, from Terry Butcher and Richard Gough in defence through to Wilkins, Ian Durrant and Ian Ferguson as the midfield enforcers, and McCoist, Walters and Drinkell up front, all of whom posed constant problems for Celtic. By comparison, Celtic weren't a great side. They were more workmanlike than inspired, and although they tried hard to stem the tide, they were never at the races. So it was an important afternoon, because there was just no arguing with the evidence that the balance was tilting decisively towards Rangers.'

By this stage the relationship between Graeme Souness and Walter Smith was operating like a well-oiled machine. Both knew their roles and where they had to be, knuckled down to their areas of expertise, and the symbiosis was sufficiently strong that they could go days without speaking, yet still know what the other was thinking. Their duties were subject to clear demarcation lines: so far as organisation at the grass-roots was concerned, Smith was the master of detail, accepting responsibility for much of the work which rarely earns recognition, but without which no club could hope to function smoothly. Within the training set-up, whether deploying various regimes so that players would not grow bored, Smith was in his element. He built a rapport with the playing staff and backroom employees which left the more aloof Souness free to concentrate on targeting signings, plotting tactical master-strokes and generally acting as Cock of the North. This suited them. Smith did not believe in the notion of joint managers, and his colleague had bigger ambitions than worrying about how the plastic cones should be arranged at practice sessions. While Smith was content to handle the chores, he was far more integral to Rangers' success than his self-effacing manner might have suggested. Both men were ultimately accountable for the success or otherwise of a team backed by substantial finance, and therefore every team selection and transfer signing involved a collaborative effort. Souness would enjoy the last say, but on most occasions he listened attentively to the contribution from his older partner.

All of which ensured that Rangers, who were developing the consistency which had eluded them in the previous two seasons, stretched away from their rivals in the championship race. They defeated Celtic in three of their four league encounters, including a first triumph at Parkhead in nine years, and after the arrival of David Murray set out on a rampant streak which brought them 14 wins in their last 16 matches, including nine consecutive victories. As if to emphasise the fashion in which the star-sprinkled team were primed to make grandiose statements, they lifted the domestic league trophy by a six-point margin over Aberdeen, totalling a record of 56 points and suffering just six defeats in 36 matches: this was in the days before three points were awarded for a win.

As Murray and Souness regularly made clear in their pronouncements, Europe was a massive priority, and when the team entered the UEFA Cup in the autumn of 1988, an auspicious challenge was anticipated. Rangers were pitted against GKS Katowice, and though a Mark Walters goal gave them only a slender lead before their journey to Poland, confidence within the squad remained high. The second leg was played at the Slaski Stadion in Chorzow, venue for an earlier European defeat to Gornik in 1969, and initially it seemed that Scottish optimism might be misplaced when Jan Furtok opened the scoring for GKS in the fourth minute with a curling free-kick. That merely served to galvanise Rangers, who mounted a sustained riposte and came close three times before Terry Butcher equalised with a fine header from a Walters corner in the 13th minute, and a Wilkins free-kick gained the lead four minutes later. Woods had to be in sublime form to thwart excellent efforts from Miroslaw Kubiztal and Krzysztof Walczak, and the hosts gained a temporary lifeline when the dangerous Kubiztal levelled matters shortly after the hour. But this was simply the precursor to Rangers finishing in barnstorming style, well-worked goals from Durrant and Ian Ferguson cementing a 5-2 aggregate success, and ensuring a relatively smooth passage into the second round, where they were drawn against familiar opponents in FC Koln. Rangers had met the German team three times before in their European history, and such a draw should have offered an alluring prospect, the chance to wipe the slate clean for their European Cup quarter-final defeat at the hands of these opponents in 1979. For the first time, however, Rangers were forced to realise that participating simultaneously in several tournaments carried drawbacks. Three days before their first-leg trip to the Stadion Mungersdorfer, Souness's troops joined battle with Aberdeen in the Scottish League Cup final, and though they clinched the trophy with a 3-2 win in a thrilling dénouement at Hampden Park, they paid for their exertions in the closing stages of a fraught tussle in Germany. Until the last 15 minutes the visitors were exemplary in terms of discipline and attacking intent, but the normally dependable McCoist squandered an opening. Legs grew weary as the clock ticked on, with the consequence that Olaf Janssen and Thomas Allofs found the net to leave Rangers facing an almighty struggle, a plight that was exacerbated when McCoist was ordered off in the dying seconds.

This match in some ways served as a template for many of Rangers' later European disappointments. The early promise, the signs of composure persuading fans to suppose that a goal would arrive if they remained patient . . . then the anti-climactic shattering of these hopes as the tide turned through self-inflicted error or a spark of world-class ability from an opponent. It was not as if FC Koln were anything more than a well-coached, modestly talented side with no great pretensions to featuring among the continental elite, but when they travelled to Glasgow with their significant lead, they found Rangers seriously weakened by the suspension of McCoist and Wilkins and injuries to Durrant and Brown. This should not have presented an insuperable obstacle to the team in clawing their way back into contention, but striking profligacy again cost them dear, and they were not helped when Walters crashed a 46th minute free-kick off the crossbar and Richard Gough hit the post with a 65th minute header. It was starting to develop into a wearily predictable pattern for Rangers, and though Drinkell broke the deadlock with a goal 15 minutes from the end, there was nothing else in the locker. Except, that is, from FC Koln, who sealed victory with a belated goal from the prolific Janssen. It was a deflating conclusion to an impressive display from Rangers for possibly 140 of the 180 minutes over two games, but there was nothing to be gained from seeking excuses about how the fixture list affected the club. After all, Dundee United had reached the UEFA Cup final in 1987 with a similar heavy schedule, and the Rangers' management duo had to accept responsibility for their refusal to countenance building two separate teams: one for domestic activity where the pace of every game was intense, the other designed for European action with skilful, multi-layered personnel in the mould of Brian Laudrup and Paul Gascoigne, who would eventually turn out for the club. Such a policy would have required a huge level of investment from Murray and his board, but the money was there at the end of the 1980s, and was never quite utilised to its full potential on the wider stage. All of which meant that Smith had to resort to using an uncharacteristically porous argument in striving to defend Rangers' problems in Europe:

> 'The players are being asked to do too much, it's as simple as that. At a club like Rangers the burdens are heavier, because we are enjoying a period of success which has seen us in League Cup finals and Scottish Cup finals as well as playing in Europe. We also have a fair number of international players, so you finish up with lads being asked to play 60 or 70 matches a season, and you soon discover that you cannot ask them to train too much during the week. It's impossible to do so. Asking players to do too much eventually damages them. It leads to more and more stress injuries, and it also damages them mentally.'

Some of this would have sounded a bit more convincing, but for the reality that Rangers seemed to want favours from clubs that they were stripping of their best players, at a stage in their history when most factors were in their favour. Celtic were on the wane, though they still managed to deny their traditional foes the treble by winning the Scottish Cup final 1-0, courtesy of a controversial goal when Roy Aitken took what should have been a Rangers throw-in and Joe Miller nipped in to score. Aberdeen, while still showing glimpses of their glory days under Alex Ferguson, were also not quite the force of old. As for Hearts and Hibs, more drama was being enacted off the pitch than on where the Edinburgh clubs were concerned. Rangers, in short, were sailing away into the distance in Scotland. Their policy was spend, spend, spend; they had a voluble manager, a multi-millionaire chairman, a swelling infrastructure and huge swathes of the west of Scotland where they could have charged almost anything in season ticket prices, just so long as Celtic were crushed. But Europe continued to be a baffling area, and one cannot escape the feeling that the club fell awkwardly between two stools when a more single-minded approach might have reaped dividends. The trouble was, and is, that European victories are not sufficient if Celtic, Hibs and Aberdeen are not being beaten on a regular basis. Souness did not square that circle.

What Graeme Souness did succeed in doing was stirring up a hornets' nest in July of 1989 when, greeted by banner headlines normally reserved for presidential assassinations and royal deaths, Maurice Johnston, the controversial striker who had once head-butted the Ibrox team's Stuart Munro, confirmed that he was crossing the great divide by signing for Rangers. It was sensational stuff, for the self-styled Mojo was a Roman Catholic who had been pictured in May sporting a Celtic jersey as he stood beside manager Billy McNeill, and had proclaimed to reporters: 'It is a dream. I never thought they would want me back. I had offers from the Continent and England, but I wanted to wear the green and white again. Deep down, I have always wanted to be back at Celtic.' In cold print that seemed pretty conclusive, but the issue has become one of the most contentious incidents in the recent history of the Old Firm. At the heart of it was a bold step by Souness to erase at a stroke the traditional Rangers policy of not signing Catholic players. Why should the club be handicapped, he inquired early in his tenure, by being denied the opportunity to pick x or y simply because of their religion? Behind the scenes one or two Catholic players, such as John Spencer, were starting to emerge, but Souness recognised that he could inflict a double whammy by shattering the old taboo and embarrassing those in charge at Celtic Park, if he could entice Johnston to the club. The player had written in his autobiography: 'Let me just spell out where I stand here. I am a Celtic man through and through, and so dislike Rangers because they are a force in Scottish football and a threat to the club I love. But more than that, I hate the religious policy which they still maintain. Why won't they sign a Roman Catholic? I hate religious bigotry, and the Rangers fans always tried to single me out [for special abuse] in Old Firm games.' As usual with the two Glasgow clubs, outlandish notions exist as to how the deal came about. But the most likely chain of events is that Souness had made contact with his target before Johnston was paraded by Celtic, which suggests that that occasion was little more than a disastrous PR stunt, which backfired. Terry Butcher, who had locked horns with Johnston during the Scotland v England match won 1-0 by his team, suggests that Mo wasn't exactly shy about his plans:

'At one point, I asked: "So you're coming back to Scotland next season?"

'"Yeah," he replied. "I will be with you next season."

'"I responded: "Yes, and I am looking forward to giving you a good kicking."

'"But he looked at me a little quizzically, and answered: "No, I will be playing with you."

'Had I been really sharp, I would have picked it up, yet I dismissed it as the usual ramblings of a centre-forward trying to put me off my game. But it was true.'

It is understandable why Celtic responded so badly, and with such sustained lack of grace, to the manner in which one of their former heroes had slipped through their grasp. But that still does not undermine the stance adopted by Souness, who had previously striven to bring Ray Houghton to Ibrox without success, and who was painfully aware that Johnston's signing would create ructions. Hence the plethora of meetings involving Souness, Smith and Murray as they discussed all the possible ramifications of the deal coming to fruition. As Smith explained, all three were in favour of proceeding with the move, but they were not so naïve as to pretend that it would not cause shock waves within Scottish football and beyond. They had to wonder how the player himself might react to sectarian outbursts from the worst elements in both enclaves. As they weighed up the considerations, none of them was concerned about how Celtic might react, and why should they have been? In plain terms, the player had been to Celtic Park for talks, had maintained that he would sign, and he had posed for the media wearing a Celtic jersey. Ultimately he had not signed any forms and he was not a Celtic player, though if chairman Jack McGinn had conducted the formalities appropriately, he might well have secured his man. As it stands, there is sufficient evidence to support the notion that Souness had sounded out Johnston prior to the media occasion at Celtic Park, and that when McGinn & Co procrastinated, it was the last straw. Celtic had been gazumped.

The most predictable response to this taboo-shattering story hitting the headlines was the sound of fury, which ultimately did not signify that much, but was indicative of the deep passions which lurked in normally sober people when the natural order of their world was turned upside down. David Miller, general secretary of the Rangers Supporters' Association, offered this opinion: 'I never thought in my wildest dreams that they would sign him. Why sign him above all others? There will be a lot of people handing back their season tickets. I don't want to see a Roman Catholic at Ibrox. Rangers have always stood for one thing, and the biggest majority of fans have been brought up with a true-blue team.'

Meanwhile, as a staff writer on the recently launched newspaper *Scotland on Sunday*, I visited my birthplace of Whitburn, West Lothian, and sought a variety of views on the Johnston business, with alarmingly depressing consequences. Bobbie R [who refused to give his surname] said that 'hell would freeze over' before he would ever return to Ibrox and 'put money into that wee Fenian bastard's back pocket'. Peter Brown, a 29-year-old joiner who described himself as being 'not interested in religion', changed tack somewhat when MoJo was mentioned: 'That wee c*** is a money grabbing piece of s***, and he should f*** off back to the Tims, because we dinnae want him at Rangers.' My third interviewee, 64-year-old Margaret Crawford, hummed and hawed prior to confiding that she couldn't care less about football. But her views on the bold Maurice were, in certain respects, even creepier: "He's just no' one of us, know what I mean? He's a Pape, he thinks differently from us, and we are Protestants for a reason, you know. That mob didnae even support us in the Second World War; they went bleating off to the enemy, and I've never forgiven the Fenians for that.' Later, in the Cross Tavern, I heard that a man had strolled up to another at the bar, punched him in the face and shouted: 'That's for f***ing Mo Johnston. Then he walked out, and the barman explained: 'Och, that's just Archie.'

Vitriol manifested itself throughout the west of Scotland and beyond, but gradually it became clear that Souness, Smith and Murray had calculated correctly that they could live without a few bigots who might tear up their season tickets – just one book was returned – and that plenty of opportunities would arise for Johnston to silence his critics where it genuinely mattered. In essence, a few burned scarves and a collection of expletive-laden letters to Ibrox should not be allowed to halt the march of progress any more than the death threats to Johnston which were made to newspaper offices – mostly from pubs, one suspects. Granted, there was the absurd spectacle of Rangers' kit man Jimmy Bell refusing to acknowledge his existence, while at meal-times a number of the Scottish players preferred not to sit with Johnston. When the club attempted to hold a press conference on their pre-season tour of Italy, to endorse his arrival, there was no problem with such as Wilkins, Woods and Walters, whereas most of the Scots in the squad declined to attend. But Souness was utterly unflinching in his resolve. It was his finest hour at Ibrox.

❖

Amid the fuss, Rangers had to concentrate on launching a league title defence, and they began in stuttering fashion by losing to St Mirren and Hibs in their opening fixtures as the prelude to pitching up at Parkhead, where those affable characters inhabiting the old Jungle section of the ground screamed out relentless abuse at Johnston for a full hour-and-a-half. This was complemented by some hissing and booing from a section of the Rangers support, which did not relent even after Butcher sent the visitors ahead. But credit where credit is due: there was no shortage of courage in Johnston's handling of the experience, explaining why more discerning observers swiftly reached the conclusion that they might never be able to fall in love with MoJo, but they could respect his ability, appreciate that he had shown guts by crossing the line, and cheer politely. As frequently happens in sporting endeavours, within a couple of months of being pilloried, Johnston survived and prospered. His goal helped Rangers to defeat close challengers Aberdeen, his scoring sequence continued against Hearts, Dundee United, St Mirren and Hibs, and even the most taciturn traditionalists could be heard to mutter in their beer variations on the theme of: 'Aye, he's a Pape, but he's our f***ing Pape, and the Celts are no' getting their hands on him.' Irrational of course, but so much of sport cannot be defined in logical terms, and it seemed almost inevitable that Johnston would score against his former team when Celtic arrived at Ibrox for the second Old Firm derby of the 1989–90 campaign, the first having finished 1-1. He did just that! His intervention came with the deadlock unbroken, and as both sets of fans were starting to settle for another share of the spoils. Johnston latched on to a loose clearance at the edge of the Copland Road penalty-area, and dispatched a powerful right-foot shot into the corner of the net. In an instant he rushed towards the crowd, and he was mobbed by a congregation of euphoric Rangers hailing him as their hero. The goal helped to accelerate Rangers towards another title, and made a massive dent in whatever optimism remained in Celtic hearts. Rangers continued to strengthen the team with the likes of Trevor

Steven and Nigel Spackman, who clinched victory at Celtic Park in their first New Year victory at the ground since 1964. The Ibrox club could even afford a mini-slump in March, when they went five matches without a victory, without letting it disturb their equilibrium. It was typical of the contrasting fortunes being experienced by the Glasgow clubs that Rangers restored their poise with a 3-0 win of such a comprehensive nature against Celtic that the date, April Fools' Day, seemed fitting for the vanquished. A Butcher cross struck Anton Rogan's hand and Walters hit the penalty home; Johnston added a second, and McCoist completed the demolition. Wrapping up the title was a formality, and the job was concluded briskly at Tannadice on 21 April with a Trevor Steven goal as the catalyst for the partying to commence. Sadly, it was not sufficient that Rangers had been thoroughly professional in their campaign, the hour of triumph was clouded by contoversy. With their guard down, the champions were foolish enough to partake of a few alcoholic beverages while still ensconced in the Dundee United changing rooms, and subsequently decided to let rip with a collection of Rangers songs, including *The Sash*, a popular anthem among Orangemen. Predictably, a BBC television crew were on hand to relay pictures to an unimpressed nation, which must have been infuriating to Souness, in particular, considering his attempts to exorcise such demons from his side.

Other problems proved just as obdurate, most notably the club's failure to make an impression on European ventures. They were drawn against the formidable Bayern Munich in September 1989, and though the first leg was at Ibrox, that did not faze the German maestros. With an accomplished and clinical showing, they effectively killed off the tie in Glasgow, recovering from losing an early goal, a Walters penalty, before Ludwig Kogl equalised after half-an-hour and the Bavarians produced a resplendent second-half display with goals from Olaf Thon and Klaus Agenthaler, which left Rangers 3-1 down. It was a disappointing performance, admittedly against opponents of fine quality, but doubly frustrating was Rangers securing a goalless draw in the return leg, which would have been a creditable achievement had they not relinquished the initiative so emphatically in front of their own fans. In the build-up to these major European occasions, tension gripped the Souness demeanour, which suggested that he realised the club could stack up as many domestic prizes as they wished, but would be judged only on the wider stage. Walter Smith sympathised with this predicament, yet as one who was close to the Rangers fans, he appreciated that no excuses or alibis would be accepted by followers with the attitude: we have triumphed in Europe in the past without the resources we have now, so we should be capable of succeeding these days. No matter that the management could justifiably claim that many of the best European sides had transformed themselves totally between 1972 and '90, the supporters were entitled to their opinion.

Quite apart from Souness acquiring the knack of being able to turn a kerfuffle into a full-scale row, having fallen out with among others Ally McCoist (whom he stuck on the bench and tried to offload to Sunderland), Scottish Television, Terry Butcher (who moved on to Coventry) the SFA and even the tea lady at St Johnstone, the manager must have recognised that he was no longer the exciting new kid on the block by the time his side were drawn against the powerful Red Star Belgrade in the second round of the 1990-91 European Cup. It was a treacherous proposition given the pedigree of the opposition, and though Mark Hateley had joined Rangers from Monaco in a £1m transfer, the scale of the task was illustrated when Smith, who had travelled to watch Red Star in action, returned to Glasgow and uttered just one word, of the four-letter variety, to Souness. Unsurprisingly, considerable apprehension was noted among players and fans as they embarked on the flight to the Balkans, and one follower on the journey, Rangers' historian Robert McElroy, was suitably impressed by the hosts:

85

'Smith's feelings of foreboding were well founded. In the first leg, Red Star tore the visitors apart with their class and pace, watched by 82,500 packing the sprawling bowl that is their very own "Maracana" stadium. Souness's team selection puzzled many onlookers, two wingers having been included, namely Mark Walters and Pieter Huistra, in the absence of Hateley. The nightmare began in just the eighth minute, when the pace of Dusko Radinovic tore the left flank of Rangers' defence asunder, his low cross being diverted into his own net by John Brown.

'The Light Blues were being overrun by the Slavs, with the class and speed of Robert Prosinecki, Dragisa Binic and Darko Pancev showing them to be a class apart. Somehow, by dint of good fortune and outstanding goalkeeping on the part of Chris Woods, Rangers survived without further loss as the clock ticked past the hour mark. Indeed, Rangers seemed to be gaining a foothold in the game when a superb free-kick by Prosinecki found the net, via an upright, after 65 minutes, with serious questions being asked about the discipline of the wall and the positioning of the goalkeeper. Seven minutes later, Huistra should have secured a priceless away goal, heading wide when it seemed easier to score, and in their very next attack Red Star surged up the park for Pancev to take clinical advantage of hesitation on the part of Gough.'

This was a 3-0 defeat which could have been 6-0 or 7-1, and there was nothing to do but applaud the mastery of the victors. Souness, who was normally an upbeat and robust individual, looked close to being crushed, lamenting to journalists at Belgrade Airport: 'How can I possibly win the European Cup with 11 Scots in the team?' It was a feeble comment to offer, considering that the side he had sent out to tackle Red Star contained six non-Scots in the guise of five English players and Huistra, and that Souness had been at Ibrox for more than four years and, given his foreign contacts, could surely have bolstered his squad with French, Italian or German players. But the weariness of his remark was an indication that no individual can rage against the world forever without hitting a wall. Souness and his team managed minor redemption in the second leg when they restricted Red Star to a 1-1 draw, the goals springing from Pancev and McCoist, but there was no disguising the truth that this was a watershed. It was the beginning of the end for Souness.

CHAPTER SEVEN

A Dream Come True

'He couldn't have made a better choice'

As Graeme Souness discovered during his spell in Scottish football, garnering respect, even grudging, can be a difficult task. The Ibrox throng could admire him for resuscitating their beloved club, but that did not mean they were prepared to take him to their hearts or to like him particularly, whereas Walter Smith was swiftly acknowledged as the true heartbeat of the Rangers empire. Ewan Prentice, a long-time Rangers supporter, wrote to me when he learned that I was writing this book, and his words on the disparate nature of the two management figures reflect sound common sense. He homes in on Smith in the first instance:

'He was one of us. We watched him at matches, and he went through the hundred little agonies which we did in the stands when a player misses a sitter or makes a bad challenge or gets smacked, off the ball, by an opponent, and that was one of the biggest differences between Walter and Souness. With the latter, there was always the sense of a volcano about to blow its stack, but not to anything specific – he was just an angry bugger with a bad temper and a huge ego who thought every referee and linesman was against him. We didn't mind when Souness first began bringing the big names to Glasgow. We would have been daft to have rejected the opportunity to have big Terry [Butcher] and Chrissy [Woods] at Ibrox, but I don't know how much success he would have had without Smith working away behind the scenes.

'Certainly, you never got the impression when you listened to Souness that he was wasting too much time studying videos or chalking up tactical formations on blackboards. It was as if he was more interested in the strut and leading with the chin, than actually getting his hands dirty. We tolerated that, of course, because Rangers won trophies again under his command, but me and my mates weren't fooled by all the bullshit. Losing [Graham] Roberts needn't have happened, but we thought: "Oh well, we have plenty of other options." Then when Terry fell out with Souness as well, we started to think to ourselves: "Hang on, everybody else can't always be wrong in these disputes." And that scepticism built up, month by month, especially when we heard that Souness didn't fancy McCoist and wanted to get rid of him as well. I mean, McCoist! Super Ally! He was a bloody talisman for us, and anybody who didn't appreciate that fact simply had no real understanding of Rangers FC.'

The antipathy between Souness and McCoist could not have been more glaring, at least on the management side. Quite simply, every time he marched into the dressing room and noted the easy charm which McCoist possessed in abundance, it was like a red rag, the more so because when he had initially arrived at Ibrox, Souness was determined that every major signing, every high-profile recruit, everybody who was anybody within the club, would dance to the same tune. Dissent was not tolerated. Anyone who stood up to him was sent packing, if not to another club, then to the bench or the reserves, where any talented footballer hates languishing. In the early days the manager had the power and the authority to make these rules stick, but the longer he remained in office the more obvious it became to players and fans that Souness had drive and desire, but could not be described as lovable. Not even remotely. McCoist, on the other hand, was the sort of personality who had a twinkle in his eye and could even induce a smile in a Celtic supporter, and that infuriated Souness almost as much as the fact that *'Super Ally!'* soon turned into a familiar chant at matches. Richard Gough often saw player and manager at close quarters in situations where Walter Smith would be forced into the role of conciliator and peacemaker. After a 2-0 defeat at Celtic Park on 2 January 1988, the full extent of Souness's dismissive attitude towards his striker erupted: he regarded him as not fit to lace Kenny Dalglish's boots, and McCoist does not dispute the point. Gough provides the details:

'That was my first game at Celtic, and they were playing well at the time and we were struggling a bit. Our side was changing week in, week out and Graeme picked himself and said: "I'll take care of Paul McStay, no problem." I loved it when he said that, but McStay was magnificent in that match; he ran the show and we were beaten comfortably. Anyway, as soon as the game finished, Graeme tore into the dressing room and went through every one of us like a dose of salts. He said to Chris Woods: "You're the f***ing England goalkeeper? You're a *girl*." Then he slaughtered Gary Stevens, and killed me. No one was spared. He said we were all a bunch of women, we had no heart, or nothing. Then he got to McCoist, who was hurting badly enough in any case, because he had had one of his quieter games. Souness turned to him and bawled out: "You were a dud at St Johnstone, you were a dud with Sunderland reserves, and you're a dud here. There were 22 players out there, and you were the f***ing worst of the lot of them."

'Coisty was shivering with emotion, nearly crying, and eventually he shot up to his feet and shouted: "I wasn't the worst. *You* were!" Then all hell broke loose, and Graeme had Ally round the throat until we all dived in and separated them. Then we climbed on to a very quiet team bus. It was like a morgue on that journey.'

Eighteen months into his tenure, Souness could behave in this fashion without incurring any penalty. But as Smith sought out

McCoist to reassure him that he had at least one fan in the managerial ranks, similar instances of needless machismo and negative publicity kept filtering out to the paying customers, whose early praise for Souness altered into carping about his endlessly confrontational style. This meant little to the man at the centre of the issue, but Smith heard the whispers of discontent on the periphery, and eventually negotiated a path off the bench for McCoist, whose goals started to stack up again. Their relationship, which blossomed as the years passed, is based on three factors: a shared love affair for Rangers and everything connected with the club; an appreciation that football serves up a variety of experiences ensuring good and bad days, the trick being not to let travails supersede the triumphs; and that there is no shame in not succeeding if you have gone into an adventure with 100 per cent courage, commitment and camaraderie. It's a straightforward philosophy, perhaps based on the men's working-class roots, but it also revolves around feeling blessed to be able to enjoy a career in football and that, whatever might transpire, this is no environment for po-faced mercenaries. Hence the deliberate delivery that Smith employs for banter, an instance of which came on a morning that McCoist turned up late for a training session (again): 'This is simply not good enough, Ally. You'll miss your own funeral at this rate. If everybody else can be here on the dot, why can't you?' McCoist made a show of consulting his watch, interrupted Smith in mid-flow, and responded loftily: 'I think you'll find, boss, that this is the *earliest* I've ever been late.' No answer to that.

By 1991 it was apparent that Souness had achieved as much as he could at Rangers. The club had whimpered out of Europe at the hands of Red Star Belgrade, and despite a regular influx of expensive new signings, including the acquisition of Mark Hateley from AC Milan for £1m, their league form was more juggernaut than Rolls-Royce, closer to a prosaic score-one-and-win mantra than the free-flowing football which supporters craved. Souness was orchestrating his exit strategy, en route to the familiar surroundings of Anfield. On a fog-laden February Tuesday in Glasgow, he and Smith met in the Bellahouston Hotel for a sauna, a couple of soft drinks and a chat about life in general. Conversation switched abruptly into serious mode when Souness announced that he had been offered the Liverpool management job, following the resignation of Kenny Dalglish. Smith was taken aback, not so much by the revelation as by the fact that his colleague, who was normally so confident in his abilities, sounded slightly apprehensive about whether he should accept the job. The obvious questions came: 'Walter, what do you think? Should I stay or should I go?' Smith, who could have regarded this issue as an irrelevance or as an opportunity to encourage Souness to quit Rangers in the expectation that he would take over the top job, went home, thought carefully about the situation, and arranged to catch up with Souness the next day. He then responded with a cogent, well-researched argument that Souness should decline the Anfield post. His reasons were persuasive: Liverpool had slipped into decline from the mighty force they had been in the early- and mid-1980s, some of their more exalted players were close to being over the hill, and not a lot of money was available to replace them. Nor would the supporters tolerate any kind of expanded rebuilding programme over five or even three years.

Once Souness had listened patiently, he appeared to have grasped the message that this job had all the potential of a poisoned chalice. Within a few days he let Smith know that he had turned down Liverpool, and that it was business as usual at Rangers. Whether either really believed this is open to question, and one of the 1991 team told me that most of the Rangers squad were praying that Souness would go:

'The Red Star defeat was pretty devastating. It wasn't as if we should have gone into that match afraid of the opposition, but we were all over the place tactically, and they showed that we were a long way behind the best European teams in terms of pace or vision, or even being able to move the ball quickly out of defence.

Afterwards Souness had the look of a man who knew basically that he was f***ed. He had been given a fantastic chance by Rangers, but he had also been told by David Murray that it wasn't enough for the Gers to be strong in Scotland; they had to be a major force on the Continent as well, and I don't think he had a clue as to how to make that happen. The thing was that if we had become a fabulously entertaining team on the domestic circuit and we had been knocking five, six, seven goals past Hearts, Hibs and Celtic every week, the supporters might just have been satisfied to be kings of their own jungle, because I knew from talking to guys at the supporters' clubs that they weren't obsessed with climbing to the top in Europe. If you gave these lads a choice of four wins a season against Celtic or a European Cup final appearance, I know which the majority of them would have chosen. So they had their priorities, and whether they were right or wrong, at least they stuck to them. Souness, on the other hand, seemed to be all over the place by 1991.'

The man was certainly not intent on loitering long in Glasgow. Although his initial rejection of Liverpool's approach was made public to notably mixed reviews, newspapers north and south of the Border continued to speculate that he was simply negotiating an enhanced deal, and Merseyside radio stations reported on his movements as if he had signed the new contract. Three weeks after his initial conversation with Smith and with Rangers now having become embroiled in a fraught battle for the Scottish League title with Aberdeen, the two were flying to London to check out a couple of prospective signings when Souness confirmed that Liverpool had made a second bid for his services. With no trace of the indecisiveness which had marked his previous reaction, he told Smith that he had taken the job, and he would leave Rangers as soon as convenient. This provoked conflicting emotions in his companion, but further information provided a jolt for Smith. As they flew over Heathrow Airport, Souness announced: 'I have big plans for Liverpool, Walter. And I want you to come down with me to

Anfield, and be my assistant.' Smith was tempted . . . for roughly half-a-second. The money would have been good, as always with Souness, but significant considerations outweighed a bounteous bank balance. Everything that Smith held dear, namely his family, friends and football club, were in Glasgow. He belonged there, the city was in his blood, and the reservations that he had expressed about Liverpool to Souness still applied. Smith could envisage problems for a football figure heading to Anfield as an assistant, and being asked to transform the hierarchy of the fabled Boot Room. If he was being honest with himself, Walter Smith was also fed up being second-in-command. That might have suited him at Dundee United and in his introduction to employment at Ibrox, but he was now 43 and had built up more than 15 years in a variety of coaching positions. He did not have to make excuses to anyone, hence his reflection on his decisive response to decline the Souness invitation:

> 'No matter how much I had enjoyed the roller-coaster years of working with him, I just didn't want to leave Rangers. My heart was at Ibrox. It had been since the first time I ever walked through the gates as a wee boy, and that was incredibly important to me. Graeme understood my point of view, and although he was disappointed, we both knew what we had to do.'

Despite weeks of intrigue, Souness had neglected to inform David Murray of his imminent intention to decamp to Anfield, but then the Glasgow rumour mill is never stilled or silent. One Friday evening prior to a match Smith received a phone call from the chairman, who asked directly: "Do you know about Graeme going to Liverpool?" The question could have placed Smith in an invidious position. If he answered honestly, Murray might suspect him of plotting behind his back, and if he was less than truthful, that could rebound on him. As was his wont, Smith plumped for candour, and replied: 'Yes, he has talked to me about it.' Murray, who had suspected as much, then displayed no-nonsense leadership qualities, while Souness attempted to cling on at Ibrox until the end of the season, to collect another trophy. That scenario might well have suited the outgoing manager, but it definitely did not sit well with Murray. He was a close friend who was entitled to feel if not betrayed, then disgruntled at the covert manner in which discussions had been progressing for the best part of a month. There could be no more dithering, no more media speculation, hence his decision to inform Souness that he should clear his desk and vacate his post with immediate effect. No matter that the story hit the headlines at an inopportune moment for Rangers – the club were stricken with a lengthening injury list, and coming under increasing pressure from Aberdeen – Murray's reasoning was that once a man had committed himself to another club, particularly one such as Liverpool that required instant remedial treatment, it did no one any favours to have him lingering for a week, even a few days. In April 1991, just as had occurred when Souness arrived at Ibrox and also when Mo Johnston was unveiled in a Rangers jersey, the club were suddenly propelled into a whirlwind of hype and hysteria. It was to their advantage that during the more extravagant flights of fancy, one man remained stubbornly down to earth, and Murray realised that Smith ticked all the right boxes. He was talented, astute, receptive to new ideas but a traditionalist at heart, a warm and engaging presence for the youngsters in the squad, who termed him Uncle Walter. A big brother for the older lads, he could engage with them in droll patter or full-strength industrial invective, whatever was required, and his loyalty to Rangers was paramount.

Other names were mentioned, and for a few days after Souness's peremptory exit Kenny Dalglish was front-runner at 4-1, with Smith down the list at 7-1 behind Alex Ferguson at 5-1, who had yet to make magic at Manchester United. What most of the punters did not realise was that Murray had spent all of 24 hours mulling over a replacement before engaging with Smith after a match at Ibrox, and presenting the simple message: 'If you want the job, you can have it.' It may not seem the most enthusiastic offer, but what both personalities knew was that some questions can be answered only in the affirmative, and this was assuredly one of them. Smith certainly did not have to concern himself with people quibbling over his selection, and he was acclaimed as the natural choice by most observers. The response of the man himself:

'Anybody who has stood in the crowd at Ibrox as a six-year-old, and felt like I was in heaven, will know what was going through my mind. It felt like a dream come true. But of course there were other things to worry about as well.'

John Greig's reaction:

'When David Murray told me he was appointing Walter to take over from Graeme, I told him he couldn't have made a better choice. Walter had worked closely with the players during his time in charge, and he had earned their respect – but he was smart enough to recognise that all good teams need to keep evolving.'

Craig Brown, at that stage the Scotland assistant manager, recalls similarly effusive feelings:

'Sometimes, after a period when there is a lot of unrest and you have gone through a revolution, you need somebody to bring stability to the table, and Walter was one of the calmest people in a crisis you could ever imagine. I recall meeting him a few weeks after he had been appointed Rangers boss, and he was bristling with purpose, and he looked as if he couldn't wait to get down to business with his team, his methods. That was no slur on Graeme, but rather that when you are the No. 2, there are always those who wonder if you can make it as a No. 1. He soon showed them.'

Walter Smith thrived in testing circumstances when a combination of managerial turmoil and a weakened squad might easily have allowed Aberdeen to break the Old Firm's recent stranglehold on the title. Smith's first match in charge was against St Mirren in Paisley, and despite an error-strewn performance from the visitors, Sandy Robertson's goal was sufficient to seal victory. Dundee United were defeated at Ibrox, but as that success was being celebrated, Richard Gough went down with hepatitis, and the scale of injury and illness was such that Smith confessed: 'For a couple of days we were genuinely struggling to put a team together.' Critics would maintain that the club were to blame as they should have had ample resources at their disposal, but all Smith could do was drag out the sticking plaster, ask the physios about best- and worst-case prognoses, and cast his eye over the reserves in case a teenager or two could be pressed into service in the final two matches of the championship. Aberdeen must still be kicking themselves at their profligacy, when it might have been simpler for them to wrap up a title triumph which few could honestly have begrudged them. In the lead up to the showdown between the main rivals, Smith's men were trounced 3-0 by Motherwell at Fir Park, while the Dons stretched their 12-match unbeaten sequence with a win over St Johnstone, which installed them at the top of the table, and guaranteed that a draw would suffice when they came calling at Ibrox the following weekend. This was the closest finish to a campaign since the dramatic events of 1986, when Hearts delivered the trophy into Celtic's grasp, and as Smith plotted in the short term, he recruited an assistant from Manchester United, the familiar figure of Archie Knox, the coup creating a temporary chill in relations with Alex Ferguson, who was less than impressed at losing his invaluable colleague while preparing for the European Cup-Winners' Cup final against Barcelona in Rotterdam. Smith was as surprised as anyone that Knox took the bait, after he had sounded out Ray Wilkins without success, but these two characters were hewn from granite, would never waste their breath on flowery language when straightforward signals would do the trick, and they worked instinctively from the outset. The empathy, which had to be witnessed to be believed, meant that each could end the other's sentences, and that Smith could walk away from a conversation and return a few minutes later, and pick up on the thread that Knox had sewn. A terrific party trick if the football work dried up!

What was immediately evident to these wily operators was the need to make changes during the summer break, but the priority was striving to clinch Rangers' third consecutive league title. It might have been a tall order in other circumstances, but Aberdeen were no longer as confident on their travels to Glasgow as they had been under the maestro Fergie, and though they carved out a substantial number of chances, lack of composure and a killer instinct cost them dear. Mark Hateley, who had been written off prematurely by some when he toiled to adapt to the pace of the Scottish game during early outings, had established himself as a potent attacking threat in the air or at close quarters, and Aberdeen were left cursing the Englishman's name, and mourning their loss of a wonderful chance of the championship, as he twice pounced to secure a 2-0 victory for Rangers. It was an afternoon of conflicting emotions for Smith. He accepted the applause, but ultimately understood that this was not his team: 'I didn't look on it as my first trophy as a manager, because I didn't feel I could do that when it was clear that I had only been in charge for the last few matches of the season. Mind you, I knew deep down that if we had lost against Aberdeen that day, then it would have been looked on as the first trophy I had lost as a manager.'

Relief pervaded Ibrox as much as any emotion. By now Celtic were in such a poor state that their supporters' humour tended to be of the gallows variety. As for Aberdeen, who had provided such a stubborn and sustained challenge on a budget a tenth or so of that available to Rangers, they would not provide such a potent threat again for many years. Over in Edinburgh Hearts and Hibs were at each other's throats over Wallace Mercer's controversial proposal to create one capital side, which would have had the unfortunate effect of consigning the Easter Road club to oblivion. Given these circumstances, Rangers had the scope for expansion that had never quite materialised under Souness, and Smith was already planning for future challenges, even if there was one final communiqué to his former Ibrox associate, which he could relish:

'The dust had barely settled on the Aberdeen victory, when Graeme phoned me in the manager's office after the game to congratulate me and the players on the victory. When I told him the team that had finished the match that afternoon, he wouldn't believe me, because we had so many people operating out of position, and yet we still held on for the title. It gave me the basis for the changes which I knew I had to make the following season, but it also proved to me that there was a vibrancy and a resilience about this particular Rangers squad, which would see them through thick and thin.'

Many taxing episodes were in store for Smith and Knox, not least in tackling the conundrum of how to prosper in Europe and to continue to dominate domestic matters. Smith clocked up hundreds of miles on scouting assignments, speaking to a raft of agents about players who might bring something special to the Rangers cause. He also demonstrated that while he was nowhere near as in-your-face as Souness, his hunger for football prizes was acute, and his words emphasise also that he has not strayed far from his origins:

'It has just always been there, the desire to win, and the bringing together of a collection of individuals into a successful team, and that was my main task at Rangers. My desire to be the best doesn't just stop at football. If I am involved in anything competitive, I like to win, and it's actually winning that keeps me going and allows me to keep working. Not too many other people are in that position, and I count my blessings. A lot of my pals in football haven't been quite as fortunate as me, and I learned a long time ago exactly how hard they had to work to achieve anything in the game. As football managers, we are lucky because of the rewards and benefits we receive that are denied people in this country – who are unemployed, for instance.'

CHAPTER EIGHT

A Canny Path from
Tradition to Transition

'He fostered a shared purpose among all the guys'

When he succeeded Graeme Souness in the major role at Rangers FC, Walter Smith could not have been accused of letting the grass grow under his feet. He had scrutinised the squad and assessed resources barely before celebrations had finished to mark a third league title in a row, and he reached the conclusion that he would need to inject some fresh blood and increase the number of Scots-born personnel, given a new UEFA clampdown on teams deploying foreign mercenaries rather than promoting home-grown talent. Since Souness's policy of enticing a string of English players had become counter-productive – Mark Hateley had been forced to watch from the stand on a number of instances during the previous European Cup campaign – a shift in emphasis was clearly required, and Smith wasted no time. For those who had perceived the manager as being a cautious individual, his foray into the transfer market offered a pleasant surprise. The first, most important, piece of business was completed when Andy Goram was acquired from Hibernian for £1m, and Smith snapped up David Robertson from Aberdeen and Stuart McCall from Everton. As the revolving door whirled, Trevor Steven, Terry Hurlock and Nigel Spackman exited, and Alexei

Mikhailichenko and Dale Gordon entered. Smith's attitude was that he saw players he valued, he offered them terms and a deal was negotiated if these were mutually acceptable. No fuss. Smith and Knox also spelled out the message that the reserve team had to be viewed as a priority, considering the urgency of developing young Scots into first-team performers. The boss also insisted that oil paintings of eight predecessors – William Winton, Bill Struth, Scot Symon, Davie White, Willie Waddell, Jock Wallace, John Greig and Graeme Souness – should be hung in his oak-panelled office. 'They were scattered all over the stadium, and I thought it would be nice to have them all hanging together to remind me of the men who had shaped the club's history from the very early days. Was it intimidating? Naw. It was inspiring, more like.'

The recruitment of Goram was a shrewd move. The gifted goalkeeper had proved repeatedly that he was of international class during his travails at cash-strapped Hibs. Though never far from controversy before or after his arrival at Ibrox, or in subsequent years when his name became a common feature on the front and back pages of the tabloids, Goram provided the dependable last line in an already robust defence. Smith was also bolstered by a resurgent Ally McCoist, who had been one of the beneficiaries of Souness's return to Anfield. From being stuck on the bench so often that he was nicknamed The Judge, the striker was informed by Smith before the league kick-off that he would be a pivotal member of the starting line-up every week. That news was the catalyst for McCoist to contribute a flurry of opportunistic goals, and beaming smiles, which tantalised opponents. He was the very devil to contain when he was in his element, yet any individual inclined to dismiss him as a cheeky Jack-the-lad with a superficial gloss would discover in his company that he is a thoughtful individual, and he was genuinely undermined by being forced to languish on the periphery at Ibrox. It is hardly surprising that McCoist should wax lyrical about the manner in which he was offered redemption by his mentor Smith. He told me:

'Walter knows a lot about football, but he also knows an awful lot about what makes human beings tick, and I was eternally grateful to him for bringing me back into the fold, because no footballer likes being sidelined, and I was as frustrated as the next man. As it was, life at Ibrox under Walter was one of the most enjoyable periods of my life. Sure, it helped that we won trophies and were generally successful, but there was much more to it than that: he fostered a shared purpose among all the guys, he knew when to shout and when to crack a joke, and it was brilliant going into the ground every morning and knowing that we were all joining forces again.

'Nothing beats it. Nothing. That sensation of waking up on Saturdays and getting myself psyched up for three o'clock – and the banter, the ribbing and the wind-ups which are part and parcel of the daily training routines – and then hearing the mighty roar when you step out of the dressing room.

'At Rangers, under Walter, everybody was pulling in the one direction, and you forge bonds which are never broken when you live like that with a group of people for any length of time. Yes it was hard, we were constantly under pressure to perform at a high level, and the gaffer was spot-on when he remarked that you are never more than two defeats away from a crisis at Ibrox. But he was a fantastic motivator, partly because he had so much passion for the club that it filtered down to everybody else, even the guys who joined us from abroad, who might only have a fleeting knowledge of Rangers.'

Some difficult adjustments were required as Smith fine-tuned his new squad, not least because of another continental disappointment for the club. The basic format of the European Cup had been altered, with the last eight being formed into two groups of four, as UEFA gradually advanced towards the creation of the Champions League. There seemed no reason for Rangers to be fearful when they were pitted against Sparta Prague in the first round, though the collapse of communist regimes had sparked a surge in nationalistic fervour throughout those countries that were no longer under the yoke. They were drawn away in the first leg, and a considerable number of supporters travelled to the old Eastern Bloc confident that their team could only improve on their display a decade earlier, when they had been trounced 3-0 by Dukla Prague. Their optimism proved ill-founded as Rangers served up a stuttering showing, which exposed them at regular intervals. The Scots were mighty fortunate to be only 1-0 down at the end, the goal arriving courtesy of Jiri Nemec's dipping cross, which unusually was misjudged by the despairing Goram. On another night with a different referee, Rangers could have conceded two or three penalties for a string of rash challenges as they fought to stem the tide, but despite the wretched nature of the performance, they were probably still entitled to regard themselves as favourites in the home leg. Once again early promise, passion and pace that promoted a swirl of noise from the stands at Ibrox came to naught. Rangers had moved into the lead in the tie with two goals from McCall, and were obliged only to maintain their discipline and shape, but the Czechs, deservedly over the two games, were gifted victory deep in extra time when Goram fumbled a deflected Horst Siegl back-heel. It was an inauspicious European baptism for the new keeper, but The Goalie would more than atone for the blunders in months and years ahead. Not that that offered him, or Smith, any consolation in the immediate aftermath.

The manager now had to concentrate on preserving domestic supremacy and striving for new levels of consistency, plus satisfying rising numbers of supporters cramming into Ibrox. Critics of the Souness regime might suggest that Rangers simply bought success, but that policy has never stopped people joining the crowd when it works, and Smith's job proved to be a delicate balance between eking out victories against teams who came to Glasgow in search of a draw, and serving up entertaining football whatever the negative tactics of the opposition. Rangers were not always successful, but statistics tell a stirring tale: in 1986–7 the average attendance was just over 20,000, by 1988 it had advanced to 30,000, and as the club progressed into the 1990s the figure had risen beyond 40,000. Even if one accepts that many of these spectators were formerly disillusioned fans or fair-weather friends, the crowds remain a testimony to the zeal with which Smith propelled his team forward. He was growing used to dealing in the multi-million-pound transfer market, a process for which life at Dundee United had left him ill-equipped. This was one of the domains where Smith, as a pragmatic, hard-headed operator, was occasionally left floundering by some sharp-suited agents, who could talk a better game than some of their clients played it. Yet the manager persuaded some truly international class talent to journey to Ibrox, and if he was guilty of the occasional mistake, no boss is faultless when it comes to hiring and firing staff. His signing philosophy, alluded to pre-viously, was based on four tenets: Will the player be good for Rangers on the pitch? Will he generate positive vibes in the dressing room? Will I have to spend an excessive amount of time worrying about what the player is up to when he isn't at Ibrox? Can I rely on this player to dig me out of a hole when the going gets tough, as undoubtedly it will, at certain times during the campaign? These priorities might have differed in their order, according to whether x or y was coming from within Scotland or abroad, but they exemplified the message that Smith was not looking for strutting showmen who would respond to the adula-tion of a packed Ibrox with feats of trickery and sleight-of-foot. He required footballers to exude the same level of commitment and desire on mid-week games played out in miserable wintry conditions, whether at East End Park, Broomfield or elsewhere.

It was evident that few would offer any sympathy if he messed up, and given the residual bitterness which supporters of other clubs harboured towards the Old Firm, he approached his task with a single-mindedness that was passed on to his foot soldiers, ensuring a scorched-earth policy in the sporting sense for the next two seasons. Rangers opened their 1991–2 league itinerary with a 6-0 rout of St Johnstone, Mark Hateley collecting a hat-trick.

He added another two as Celtic were brushed aside 2-0: the disparate parts of Smith's ensemble were knitting together. As the weeks passed, the massed ranks of Rangers fans lapped up the familiar sight of McCoist hurtling away from another stricken defence, arms aloft in jubilation, while on the other side of the Old Firm, the efforts of the Celtic board to extricate themselves from a financial mire merely deepened the sense of gloom among their support. Rangers continued with a remorseless surge. Aberdeen, who remained a threat, were defeated 3-2 at Pittodrie in December as the prelude to Celtic being overcome by 3-1 at New Year, and even when Hearts sought to initiate some sort of sustained title challenge, the ubiquitous McCoist snuffed out their hopes with the only goal of the game at Tynecastle in February. Generally it was as comprehensive an exhibition of collective responsibility as could have been requested, and while Smith was determined to downplay his achievements and refused to get carried away by it all, he privately acknowledged that his side had reacted pretty well to his insistence on 90-minute displays.

For neutrals some of these displays were a joy to behold, but impartial souls tend to be thin on the ground in the west of Scotland, in particular, and it was around the start of 1992 that Celtic fans started seriously to peddle the conviction that Rangers were nothing more than an efficient bunch of hired assassins, and that they could not be compared in any way with the Lisbon Lions and the vintage of the late 1960s and early '70s, who had won nine consecutive titles. It was as if some of these individuals could not foresee a quick end to their suffering, and were therefore intent on stressing that Celtic had embarked on their trophy gathering with a clutch of Scots who were born within a limited geographical radius. Smith gave this argument short shrift. He would confess to feeling admiration for that earlier Celtic side, but he would make no apologies for hiring the people that he believed were best for his purposes, and anyway it was futile to indulge in comparisons between teams of different generations. What could be deduced was that any Old Firm side would have benefited from a strike partnership such as Hateley and McCoist, but though most of my Celtic-supporting colleagues were generous enough to grant that Rangers had taken strides forward from the rather sterile showings that were commonplace under Souness's stewardship, they stuck to the view that the only true test of the Ibrox club's credentials would be if Celtic were capable of launching a riposte.

On the run-in to a fourth league championship in succession, which had amounted to little more than a procession, Smith and his men greeted St Mirren at Ibrox on 19 April in the knowledge that victory would seal the prize. It was typical of Rangers that they offered a stirring exhibition with no shortage of skill. McCoist, as unquenchable as he had been for the rest of the campaign, opened the scoring early on, and as the visitors' ramparts were increasingly battered, second-half goals from Gary Stevens, McCoist and Pieter Huistra wrapped up the title. More than 40,000 of the faithful hailed the old-stagers and the newcomers, and sang themselves hoarse as Smith waved to all parts of the stadium. In the final analysis, they posted all kind of milestones during a season of rampant achievement. They scored more than a century of goals for the first time since 1939, and lost just five matches in 44 fixtures: if the current structure had been in place with three points for a win, Rangers would have amassed 105 points. McCoist, perhaps inevitably, was the leading marksman with 34 goals, every one a reminder of Graeme Souness's faulty judgment, but also a tribute to the striker's ability to bounce back from adversity.

Nor was there any slackening of the Rangers' commitment when they ran on to the pitch at Hampden Park for the Scottish Cup final against Airdrie on 10 May. Much had been made in advance of their poor record in this competition, and how they had flattered to deceive even in the Souness years. Smith noted patiently the stream of largely tabloid-inspired fodder, which was designed to whip up interest in a match that might otherwise have looked less than a contest, but he did admit that his side's Scottish

Cup form had been fairly unimpressive. On the only previous occasion in which he had been involved in a final, Celtic's Joe Miller had secured the trophy in 1989, and Rangers had experienced embarrassment against Hamilton and Dunfermline, so some observers wondered if pawky, industrious Airdrie might just inflict a fresh surprise on their famous opponents. Smith told the press it was a game in which his team had to score first. As had been the case for much of the season, he gained his wish when Hateley opened the account after half-an-hour, then McCoist struck on the edge on the interval to deflate the underdogs. The Airdrie players rolled up their sleeves and pulled a goal back through Andy Smith, which precipitated a fraught climax, but Rangers held on to attain their first league and cup double for 14 years. All this had been immensely rewarding for Smith, but in lifting a glass of wine to toast the twin achievements, thoughts would be turned to the future, and especially that thorny issue of European competition.

CHAPTER NINE

Amazing Adventures in Europe

'Let's fire this in, and see what happens'

There is no other way to describe the 1992–3 season for Rangers except in the language of victory and triumph. Heady performances were enacted in front of packed crowds, who rose to acclaim a sequence of redoubtable team displays and outstanding individual exploits that were imbued with a sense that anything was possible. It was gallus, to use a distinctly Scottish description; it was Glaswegian swagger, and the campaign twisted and turned in unexpected directions. Indeed Rangers might well have triumphed in the European Cup, but for enough corruption and underhand behaviour from opponents to delight conspiracy theorists. It was unquestionably one of the club's greatest seasons, overseen by a man apparently endowed with a doctorate in football alchemy. That certainly seems to be the feeling of several of those who appeared in the treble-winning year. Trevor Steven, who had returned to Ibrox from Olympique Marseille, summed up the mood around the camp:

'Everything just clicked, and there was this shared feeling that we could go out and offer anybody in Europe a decent match. It wasn't over-confidence, but Walter Smith had done a magnificent job in building up team morale and getting the boys to pull together, and everything went well – the training sessions, the pre-season, the nights out, the works – so that we were as fit as we had ever been, and of course the lads had built up so much momentum as the previous year had progressed that it was like pressing a switch when Walter sent us out for battle again. We weren't taking anything for granted, but he made us confident, we all knew our jobs, what we were supposed to be doing, and were all fighting fit. You can't underestimate the buzz which goes through a dressing room when that happens.'

Another of the team told me that Smith assembled the Rangers squad at an opulent hotel away from Glasgow, and methodically conveyed his wishes and plans in advance of the Scottish league schedule.

'He relayed the message to us that we had to be utterly ruthless and focus on nothing else but giving 100 per cent for Rangers, and that if we did that, he would stand by us all. He told us that the league was still extremely important and that our supporters wouldn't tolerate us becoming sidetracked by Europe, but it was clear the latter was very, very important to him. I heard that he had met with [David] Murray, and that the chairman had promised Walter significant amounts of cash if the Champions League went well for the club. So he was making it clear to us that we had to be ultra-professional in every match, that we hadn't done ourselves justice in Europe in the last two years, and that it was time to set the record straight and show we could go where Aberdeen had gone [in winning the European Cup-Winners' Cup]. He really hammered home that point, that if a club of Aberdeen's stature could beat Real Madrid and enjoy such a marvellous success in that company, that there was no reason for Rangers to be apprehensive about tackling anybody, if we showed the right attitude and had the belief in our own abilities. It was a pretty inspiring speech. Walter sometimes gets described as a bit dour and down-in-the-mouth, but when he was talking to us that day his eyes were sparkling, he was animated about the challenges ahead, and it was riveting stuff. We went away thinking: "Well, if the gaffer reckons that we have the potential to lift the European Cup, why don't we prove him right?"'

Having scrutinised the players at his disposal, Smith was amply justified in his optimism. McCoist and Hateley had already knitted together superbly during their alliance, and had demonstrated their avaricious appetite for goals, and the presence in midfield of such stalwarts as Ian Durrant, Trevor Steven, Ian Ferguson and John Brown meant that Rangers would be nobody's pushovers. Add the likes of Richard Gough, Dave McPherson, Andy Goram, Steven Pressley, Pieter Huistra and Gary McSwegan to the mix, and they made up an ensemble that would probably have beaten the Scotland side in 1992–3. They were too strong for any of their club opponents as the weeks and months passed, and what had always threatened to be a one-sided championship quickly turned into a stroll in the park. True, Rangers were tested during a 1-1 draw with Celtic at Ibrox in August, an outcome which persuaded some of the more optimistic Hoops followers to proclaim that their side could launch a sustained title fight, but Rangers embarked on an unbeaten sequence of the type that drives opponents to distraction. It extended for seven months and encapsulated a total of 44 matches in all competitions, and featured myriad instances of striking trickery from McCoist and Hateley, encouraging even the most cautious of Ibrox fans to acknowledge that their team were something special.

The league was wrapped up efficiently, the battle more or less won, when Rangers, who had already moved five points clear of Aberdeen, travelled to Pittodrie and emerged with a 1-0 victory. The climax came on 2 May 1993, in the unprepossessing setting of Broomfield Park, where Airdrie attempted vainly to halt the blue juggernaut. Smith had lost the services of his talisman McCoist, who had suffered a broken leg, and it was left to deputy McSwegan to score the only goal of the afternoon after 46 minutes in an encounter characterised by numerous scoring opportunities for the visitors, which were not accepted. If that profligacy annoyed the manager, the fact remained that Rangers had accrued 97 goals in 44 league matches, 34 springing from McCoist. The Dons finished second in the table on 64 points to the champions' 73.

Domestic cup competitions brought similar exhibitions of clinical professionalism and hungry execution. In the League Cup dénouement on 25 October 1992, Smith's men arrived at the stand-in venue of Celtic Park feeling the strain of a midweek meeting in Europe with Leeds United, and were soon locked in a thrilling tussle with Aberdeen, which marked the fourth occasion in six years in which the clubs had met in the final. It had promised to be a tense affair considering the fractious history between the teams, and once again Smith asked for an early goal, Stuart McCall obliging in 14 minutes after Theo Snelders was involved in a mix-up with David Winnie. The setback did not faze the men from Pittodrie, and as the contest ebbed and flowed, Duncan Shearer levelled the score in the second half to force extra-time. Smith confessed that he had been worried – 'The concern for us was how the players would be able to cope with another 30 minutes after their exertions against Leeds' – but befitting the discipline, control and relentless energy which had become their trademark, Rangers dominated the match the longer it progressed, and eventually defender Gary Smith put the ball into his own net when under pressure from Hateley. The victors looked as fresh at the end as if it was their second or third match of the campaign . . . such was the conviction and camaraderie beating in the heart of this side.

The Scottish Cup offered the inevitability of Rangers again locking horns with Aberdeen, and ultimately prevailing, though they had to surmount various obstacles before the trophy was secured. Sceptics might glance at their cup-ties, which were all away from home, and suggest that they had it easy. Once they had disposed of Motherwell, they might have faced sterner adversaries than Ayr United and Arbroath, but in the semi-final versus Hearts, Rangers fell behind to an Allan Preston goal scored on the hour, and for a spell seemed to be struggling to regain the initiative against fired-up opponents. 'It was one of those afternoons where you just have to keep battling away and getting the basics right, because Hearts performed well and they had reached a number of semis and finals in the previous few years only to come a cropper, so they were really desperate to make this count,' recalls Scott Nisbet, one of the unsung stalwarts of Rangers' success. As the atmosphere intensified and the Edinburgh club strove to exorcise the spectre of past disappointments, they were stunned when Dave McPherson, who had been one of their own in the previous season, produced the equaliser as the prelude to McCoist dashing Hearts' aspirations with a late winner. It was a familiar scenario. Frequently Rangers would find themselves under the cosh or struggling to find their rhythm, then one of their number, be it McCoist, Durrant or Trevor Steven, would orchestrate a piece of magic while the defence harassed adversaries out of their stride, even if it meant dwelling on the margins of legality. The statistics could not be faulted – the team's goal difference of plus-62 required no addendum – and the trust which built up among the players cemented the notion that any situation was retrievable. 'The pride the boys took in the jersey was incredible,' Smith observed. David Murray also marvelled at the transformation which had been implemented since the departure of Graeme Souness. Now for sure Rangers were still combative, but without the malice aforethought that had characterised the Souness-managed team. 'Everybody played hard for each other, and that pulled us through,' Murray declared. That assessment succinctly epitomised the qualities which underpinned the team's other outstanding achievements.

By the time they made the short journey to Parkhead for the Scottish Cup final on 29 May 1993, the Rangers team could have been forgiven for having one eye on their holiday destinations. If they were not quite at their peak on the day, Smith's tactical nous ensured that youthful precocity had a starring role in the match: forced into switching his line-up because of the long-term injury to McCoist, he called up Neil Murray for the biggest experience of his life, and the youngster unleashed a ferocious long-range drive which opened the scoring in the 22nd minute. It was one of those episodes where a footballing hunch is regarded as inspired, and as the Rangers hordes celebrated in anticipation of a treble, Mark Hateley doubled the advantage. Aberdeen, who had slogged their guts out all season without tangible reward, were deflated by ending as runners-up in all three domestic competitions, and their so-called consolation goal through Lee Richardson was nothing of the sort. 'Credit to them, they had snapped at our heels in the league and clung on determinedly in the cups,' Smith said afterwards, as he gazed around Celtic Park wondering whether there would be this number of jubilant Rangers fans inside the stadium ever again. But it was a fitting finale to what had been a tremendous feat by his squad, the only bone of contention what might have been, or perhaps should have been, in the European Cup.

If this account had been written in strict chronological order, Rangers' foreign adventures would have slipped in and out of the narrative, and clarity would have been obscured. Hence the decision to concentrate at length on the Ibrox club's protracted and devilishly-near flirtation with the prize that had eluded Scotland's representatives since the 1960s. The first-round tie against Lyngby of Denmark saw the Scots ease through as 3-0 aggregate winners, with goals from Mark Hateley and Pieter Huistra in Glasgow and Ian Durrant at the Parkenstadion. Such an outcome was expected, but thereafter Smith enjoyed a string of superb results against some formidable teams, starting with the second-round tussle against Leeds United. As usual with these affairs the cliché 'Battle of Britain' was rolled out, but even by the standards of hyperbole surrounding previous clashes of teams from north and south of the Border, this encounter provoked a torrent of comment, analysis and patriotic hogwash. Leeds had advanced to this stage of the tournament after being reinstated by UEFA following a breach of the nationality regulations by Stuttgart, who had beaten them on goal difference before the outcome was reversed, and Leeds won a one-off third match by 2-1. Then there was the contrast in the managers' personalities. Smith, an introverted figure at press conferences, was tagged by the English press as living up to PG Wodehouse's maxim: 'It is never difficult to distinguish between a Scotsman with a grievance and a ray of sunshine.' By comparison, his Leeds' counterpart Howard Wilkinson was one of the bright young things of the English circuit, who was tipped to take charge of the national team in the future. It was also a compelling tie considering that Rangers' achievements since the late 1980s were derided in England as owing more to the deficiencies of opponents than to genuine qualities. The English media asserted that when United travelled to Glasgow for the first leg equipped with such international-class performers as Eric Cantona, Gary McAllister and Gordon Strachan, they would soon highlight the paucity of Scottish football talent by sweeping past their rivals.

That verdict seemed justified when McAllister dispatched a brilliant 20-yard strike past the despairing Goram. Gloomy home followers, though, should have known that their heroes were as resilient as they were committed, and despite an opening spell when the likes of Cantona swanned around the Ibrox turf, the hosts regrouped and mounted their own attacks, and gradually the tide turned in their favour. It helped that Goram was the personification of solidity and poise in his goals whereas Leeds' John Lukic looked uncomfortable in pursuing crosses, and a succession of Rangers corners finished with Lukic punching the ball into his own net. A mere quarter of the way through the match the visitors' swagger had been made to evaporate, and it was no shock when another treacherous Durrant corner was met by McPherson for Lukic to parry the ball to McCoist, who seized the opportunity with the glee. I spoke to several Rangers supporters in the days that followed, and they were convinced that Smith had been too negative in not pressing for a third goal. When I sought to counter this with the opinion that they needed only a draw at Elland Road, whereas the balance would have been different if Leeds had snatched a 2-2 draw, their scornful countenances reflected one of the less appealing aspects of the Rangers brethren. Namely, their refusal to accept that Smith, an individual with 15 years of coaching experience under his belt, might just know his job better than they did. Fans are entitled to grow agitated when their team slump regularly, but this was the Ibrox men on the hottest of streaks, and still grumbling could be discerned. No wonder that one player involved in that Rangers victory told me (on strict condition that he remained anonymous): 'Most of our support are terrific, but there are some wee guys out there with a bag of chips on both shoulders, who have never forgiven their father for being only five foot six. When you're sitting on the bench, you can hear them screaming stuff like: "That was f***ing shite, McCoist. You are a disgrace to Rangers." And you just feel like walking up to them and saying: "Do you know that we are actually winning 3-0, you wee prick!" But you can't argue with these folk. We could be beating Celtic 6-2, and they would still be moaning that our defence was a shambles. Sometimes it's hard to take, but you just have to remember that for every little tube like him, there are a hundred other decent people who respond fantastically every Saturday.'

Even the most hard-to-please Rangers spectators must have been enraptured in the early stages of the return leg when Hateley, showing marvellous agility and precision, volleyed spectacularly past Lukic from at least 25 yards. In an instant Leeds United were transformed into a panic-stricken rabble. They piled on waves of pressure that was not particularly inspiring, and a group of their supporters were heard screaming abuse, but Goram remained in imperious form, and Richard Gough slowed the pace as if to rile watching Tykes even more. Rangers established a stranglehold which was reinforced when Durrant and Hateley conjured up a glorious sweeping move, from which McCoist's header sealed victory. Nothing could have been sweeter for Smith and his players than to overcome the English on their own territory, though Cantona scored towards the end. It was noticeable that the majority of the losing fans accorded Rangers a standing ovation, in acknowledgement of the quality football that they had exhibited.

Smith refused to gloat over the defeat of Leeds, preferring to concentrate on the European Cup's revamped format in which the last eight were divided into two groups of four, the winners of each section progressing to the final. Nowadays it seems an antiquated structure, but at least the Champions League did not break the trade descriptions act in that period by granting entry to clubs who had finished second or third in their championships. Rangers were drawn in a group with Club Brugge, CSKA Moscow and Olympique Marseille, which would mean testing examinations for their mettle, but the prospect was not too daunting from the Ibrox perspective. On the contrary, Smith maintained his calm exterior when confronted with a series of problems, including injuries and suspension to key players such as McCoist and Ian Ferguson, and despite being restricted in his options by UEFA's non-national policy. He prepared for the opening match versus Marseille in Glasgow on 25 November 1992, by fielding the callow triumvirate of Neil Murray, Steven Pressley and Gary McSwegan, who were asked to make their European debuts against the might of the French title-holders, who had reached the European final two years earlier. Smith's plans were undermined when his captain Richard Gough departed after 45 minutes with a knock, but Rangers clung on during a putrid winter's evening, though the visitors had threatened to run riot. Alen Boksic and Rudi Voller had handed Marseille a comfortable two-goal cushion, or so it appeared, but substitute McSwegan suddenly reduced the deficit with a stunning header, which just happened to be his first touch of the game and his maiden competitive goal for Rangers. For the home crowd, who had been silenced gradually by the appalling weather combined with the patent superiority of the Frenchmen, it was the cue to erupt into a clamour for an old-fashioned, roll-your-sleeves-up climax, so beloved by Scottish football worthies. It helped to do the trick. In the 81st minute, Hateley headed the ball home from a Durrant cross, and the faint prospect arose of Rangers snatching the unlikeliest of victories, when even their most biased fans would surely have admitted that they had been overwhelmed for three-quarters of the affair. In the event they had to be content with a 2-2 result, but the reaction of Smith and Archie Knox was that of men who had grown up watching *The Great Escape*, and who were delighted to have been involved in a football version of the movie. They realised that Rangers had to improve by several notches in subsequent fixtures if they were not to suffer an ignominious exit from the competition.

In gauging the company that Rangers were keeping, the next tussle was against CSKA Moscow, who had qualified for the group stages with a superb triumph over cup-holders Barcelona, rallying from losing 2-0 at the Nou Camp to eliminating the Spanish team by 3-2. Because of the ferocious nature of the Russian winter, the Muscovites were forced to stage their home matches in Germany, and they constituted a formidable threat when Smith and his compatriots made for the imposing Ruhr-stadion on December 9 accompanied by more than 8,000 fans. The supporters had begun to imagine that if Rangers could keep using their get-out-of-jail card as astutely as had been manifest against Marseille, then almost anything was possible. A galvanised Rangers team grabbed the lead within 13 minutes via Ian Durrant, and were the epitome of professionalism for the remainder of the tie, limiting their opponents' chances and demonstrating the scale of the improvement made under Smith.

That marked a three-month break for the Champions League during which the Scots continued to reign majestically over domestic rivals. The March resumption of European action brought a double-header with Brugge, which on paper seemed to offer the best hopes of points. On their crusade to Belgium's Olympiastadion Rangers were near the height of their powers, consistently troubling their adversaries. Despite falling behind to a Tomasz Dziubinski goal on the stroke of the interval, they assumed control of the midfield and gained the ascendancy throughout the second half, Pieter Huistra equalising in the 73rd minute for a share of the spoils. Thus the re-match assumed an increasing degree of importance, and what a spectacle it was! I can recall a nagging feeling that Rangers would come a cropper when they were cast as favourites, and Smith gave warning that the Belgians would be dangerous: he had been impressed with their quality during the first meeting. It seemed that he need not have worried, for the prolific Durrant broke the deadlock in the 39th minute of another rain-lashed evening in Glasgow. Scottish teams, though, rarely participate in such must-win encounters without introducing crises, and Rangers' fortunes suffered when Hateley was sent off in controversial circumstances, then Lorenzo Staelens levelled the match early in the second period. Smith appreciated that a draw was no use, and urged his men further forward. It was a risky policy that might have cost him dear on another evening, but not this one. Scott Nisbet's clinching goal is etched in the memory: it was a startling score, a slo-mo in real time that baffled a Brugge defence who probably still suffer nightmares about it. From wide on the right, Nisbet struck a swerving shot-cum-cross which took a wicked bounce to fly at a devilish angle past the bemused Danny Verlinden and into the net. Many have dismissed it as a fluke, but Nisbet – whose career was cruelly cut short three days later after he sustained an injury at Celtic Park – told me otherwise:

'Let's face it, in these conditions with the rain pouring down and the wind howling, the most important thing was to keep troubling their goalkeeper, and when I ran forward I thought to myself: "Let's fire this in, and see what happens." To that extent I suppose it was a speculative effort, but it wasn't just a hit and hope, as some have alleged. I was aiming at the goal, and although I couldn't have imagined that the ball would move as it did, it was the kind of evening when something like that was always liable to happen, and I am just glad that it worked in our favour, not against us, and we ended up getting the victory which we needed.'

If luck seemed to be favouring the Scots, their optimism was soon checked. On the evening that Nisbet attained his priceless goal, Marseille trounced CSKA Moscow 6-0, and suspicions began to circulate that the French club's voluble owner Bernard Tapie was determined that the Champions League would be won by his team, and that he was not especially bothered how that was achieved. His side were probably the most talented in the tournament, but resentment increased as the group moved towards its climax, and for Rangers the next few weeks turned into a classic tale of what might have been. When they ventured to the Stade Velodrome, they had already been angered by their opponents' underhand approach to providing tickets for travelling fans – only 1,000 were made available, breaching an agreement that 4,000 would be on offer – but that merely acted as an impetus. Rangers were far more convincing than they had been in tackling Marseille at home, even if the absence of the suspended Hateley ultimately proved costly. With one of his main strikers out of contention, Smith plumped for the emerging McSwegan, but the reality was that the manager needed all his luminaries when facing a team of the calibre of Marseille in their cauldron-like amphitheatre. The visitors did recover from ceding a goal after David Robertson's carelessness had allowed Franck Sauzee to score in the first half; Durrant equalised in another testimony to his perseverance. The French team might have secured victory on several occasions, but there again McSwegan, a replacement for Huistra, saw a scything shot flash narrowly wide. It was fast and riveting, but 1-1 was but a moral victory for the Scots, who now had to trust that they could beat CSKA Moscow at Ibrox, and hope Brugge could do them a favour against Marseille. But fair play took a beating in the build-up to these fixtures in what had proved to be a captivating group. Rangers' historian Robert McElroy noted that sufficient bad blood existed between Brugge and their French rivals for the Scots to be optimistic that Tapie's club would face a stern examination when they travelled to Belgium:

'Both the club and their fans felt that they had been badly treated at the Stade Velodrome on match-day two. The visiting supporters had been the subject of shocking abuse from the Marseille crowd, whilst home coach Raymond Goethals had insulted the opposition with disparaging remarks about Brugge following his side's 3-0 win. The Belgians had sworn revenge, promising that they would defeat Marseille at their home ground, where they had remained unbeaten for so long, and had made that very promise to Rangers following the two matches between the clubs in March: "Keep the group alive until match-day six, and we will defeat the French for you." The group was indeed still alive, but something had changed in the last few days. The Belgians had sworn that they would avenge their honour, yet on the eve of battle they mysteriously changed their tune. Three key players were supposedly injured, the next weekend's league match was now considered more important, and Brugge meekly surrendered a home record of which they were extremely proud, going down to an early Boksic goal after just two minutes. Meanwhile at Ibrox intense home pressure [against CSKA] failed to achieve a breakthrough, perhaps a dozen good chances being squandered, with again the absent Hateley being sorely missed by Rangers.'

The dream was over, but Rangers' misgivings and regrets were wholly justified, for reports subsequently emerged of Tapie's involvement in bribery and corruption. The controversial official was sentenced to four years' imprisonment, his club were relegated and stripped of the championship that they had won that season, and it remains a mystery why UEFA did not step into the affair with their own investigation of Marseille's conduct in the Champions League. Among the damning evidence against Tapie was a list of matches which the president had bribed opponents to throw, and prominent on this roster was their game in Brugge, which had proved so damaging to Rangers' prospects of reaching the final (in which Marseille beat AC Milan 1-0 thanks to a Basile Boli goal). Smith and David Murray refused to indulge in public breast-beating, but the bottom line is that Marseille had acted illegally and lost their French title in the process, and the logical extension would have been for UEFA to strip them of their Champions League prize, and to charge them with bringing the game into disrepute.

It had proved to be a watershed season for Rangers nonetheless, in that they had gone 10 games unbeaten in Europe's premier competition. They managed that feat despite a fixture schedule which obliged players to participate in 64 matches for their club, and the majority of their leading lights were also involved in international duty. It was a gruelling regime for squad members and the management team, which possibly explains why Smith chose to speak out about the ridiculous workload heaped on his personnel rather than be dragged into a debate about the French judicial system. He stressed his apprehension about the future if the SFA and SFL did not recognise that it was not viable to engage in 44 league fixtures every season, and though the domestic structure was overhauled 18 months later, that did not help Rangers as they attempted to fly the flag for Scotland singlehandedly on the European beat. From Smith's perspective in 1992–3, the principal weakness of the Scottish structure was its sheer inflexibility and the fashion in which the intense routine sapped the stamina and creativity of even the most talented and enthusiastic youngsters:

'Club managers have been preaching this message for years – that the number of games should be reduced, and that players should have fewer matches in midweek. That allows time for all of us to work with the players, and also allows them necessary recovery time in between games. That's time to have injuries treated, time to rest if that is what is necessary, time to hone their skills and to work on any part of their game which needs developing. But in my spell in charge at Rangers there has been no time for any of that. All we have been able to do with the players is try to maintain their fitness level during the season, and try to allow them time to shake off the nagging injuries which come with the general wear and tear that these heavy domestic programmes bring in their wake. During the Champions League run we even had to resort to taking the players for a walk and finishing up in a transport café for coffee and bacon rolls, because to work them any harder would simply have been counter-productive. But is that really what we want to be doing in the long term? Of course not, but we can't change it. The authorities have to change it.'

Despite the strength of his argument, Smith's views attracted scant support, which was a measure of the rather depressing antipathy which was felt towards Rangers at the time. The trouble was that though they had attained some of the success they coveted in Europe, their performances owed more to team spirit and strength of character than to free-flowing, adventurous football. But then many Scottish fans seemed to assume that they could saunter on to the field against the likes of Leeds and Marseille and indulge in 100mph, hell-for-leather action. It perhaps summed up the gulf between fact and fiction that some Scottish newspapers, *Scotland on Sunday* included, attempted to draw comparisons between Jock Stein's 1967 Lisbon Lions and Smith's 1993 Champions League squad, when it should have been obvious that Stein's side sprang from a wholly different culture. In that era tanner-ba' exponents such as Jimmy Johnstone had licence to spark mayhem in opposition ranks, and most defenders could do only one thing, namely defend. The Celtic team who triumphed in the European Cup fully merit their prodigious renown, and Johnstone was a wondrous sprite with a magician's expertise, but that does not mean that followers of the game should be dismissive of a Rangers squad who served up thrills of their own, even if these diminished as the Champions League intensity mounted and the emphasis was less on exciting audiences than on playing the percentages. Smith himself acknowledged that his team had limitations. They were more reliant on Hateley than should have been a side with genuine European aspirations; McCoist glittered in the early European ties, but went off the boil the longer the competition rumbled on. He suffered a fractured leg shortly after Rangers' elimination, which added to the injuries, strains and assorted niggles which had accumulated as 10 matches became 20, then 40, then 50 and more. Some of the stars were dead on their feet, and others could barely stand.

The disappointing nature of the conclusion to Rangers' European campaign should not be permitted to disguise the scale of their exploits. Only two years previously, Graeme Souness had lamented that he would never achieve anything on the Continent when restricted to 11 Scots, but here we had a predominantly home-grown team packed with redoubtable figures such as McCoist, McCall, Goram, Brown, Ferguson, Durrant and Gough, who did club and country proud in a volatile environment. If there was a problem, it lay in the fact that Europe nagged away at Smith and Murray like the toothache. They appreciated that their supporters were desperate for as many domestic prizes as could be accumulated, but as the manager countered, what was the point of reigning supreme at home if that could not be translated into tangible rewards outwith the country? Unfortunately, as subsequent events emphasised, there were several reasons for the prognosis that this Rangers squad had gone as far as they could without major surgery, and that future signings would have to involve sophisticated and versatile performers who could grace the grand stadiums of Europe. Which made all the more mystifying the club's summer investment in 1993, which was more or less limited to the purchase of the gangly and scowling Duncan Ferguson from Dundee United for £3.75m, which was, and still is, an astonishing figure. But then managers are not permitted the benefit of hindsight in these transactions, and football history is littered with stories of men who were proclaimed as superstars in the making and initially applauded by the fans, but who turned out to be anything but super.

It would be remiss, however, to conclude an appreciation of the heroics of 1992–3 on a sour note. Instead, I recall watching Walter Smith on the periphery of the action as Rangers battered away at CSKA Moscow without being able to pierce their resistance. Afterwards a friend of mine named Ally Scott, who had no allegiance to the Ibrox club beyond wishing all Scottish teams success in Europe, faxed me from Germany, where he was based, with the message: 'Hi there, just watched the Gers go out of the Champions League, but not without giving 100 per cent effort and going so close that I actually feel a bit sad tonight. You look back on the tournament and think that Hateley shouldn't have been sent off against Brugge. And if he had been available in these last two matches [against Marseille and CSKA] I would have put money on him scoring at least two of the chances which were missed by other people. So near and so far. But they have gone through the competition without losing, and that is one hell of an achievement. Here's to 94!' Maybe hard-luck stories are too frequent in Scottish sport, but in the final analysis Smith's demeanour throughout that Champions League foray was symbolic of the man. On occasion he quietly bemoaned losing Hateley to suspension while launching into a reasoned debate on the best way forward for Scottish clubs, as the major European tournament developed into a schism between the haves and have-nots. But for the most part, he seemed thrilled to be pitting his brains and his blackboard against the best coaches from the rest of the Continent. The problem was that once you have won a treble and reached the equivalent of the semi-finals of the European Cup, where else is there to go? It was a question which would induce much head-scratching and soul-searching for Smith, Archie Knox and David Murray.

CHAPTER TEN

PAPERING OVER THE CRACKS

*'Smith had discovered yet again how fickle
the soccer public can be'*

Walter Smith is usually portrayed as a phlegmatic character, a stoical man in the face of adversity, and he required these qualities in abundance when the euphoria of the treble-winning season had passed, and he was forced to endure a string of travails as Rangers, without any great success, attempted to crank up the momentum generated by their exploits in the Champions League. Such achievements served the manager well, as it was easier to attract high-calibre players to Ibrox with the incentive of appearing in several European ties in each campaign. On the debit side, he discovered that the tremendous team spirit that he had established within the ranks was not easy to replicate after signing new personnel, especially when negative stories started seeping into the press. As a hard-nosed newspaper reader since his youth, Smith knew the score with the tabloids, so if one of his men was caught over-indulging in alcohol or in a melee at a taxi rank, he realised that the ensuing publicity would hardly be pleasant, but it would be no more than a two- or three-day wonder before life returned to normal. He could handle that, but when repeat offenders threatened to disrupt the harmony at the club, that was another matter. Hence the common perception that as Smith pursued domestic and European honours from 1994–7, scarcely a week passed without some lurid misadventure cropping up in the papers, to delight the club's detractors. Ally McCoist has responded to the allegation that Rangers' philosophy could be summed up as: 'The team that drinks together wins together' with the logical riposte: 'If we had drunk as much as some people had made out, we would all have needed to book into the Betty Ford Clinic.' Some scurrilous rumours were spread by mischief-making Celtic supporters, and these were of such a libellous nature that even at this stage they dare not be repeated. But all the same, Smith certainly didn't have his problems to seek from the moment that Duncan Ferguson walked into Ibrox.

It might be harsh to describe the big striker as a ticking time-bomb, but more than a few eyebrows were raised when Smith confirmed that he had recruited the 22-year-old Dundee United player for a whopping £3.75m, not least because he had an aerial expert in his squad in Mark Hateley. Yet Ferguson's arrival seemed apposite in what turned into a surreal season for Rangers, in which 11 first-team players required surgery at various times and in which Smith was occasionally left striving to convince opponents that he had not sent out a bunch of fans by mistake. On the disciplinary front the manager's views were fairly ortho-dox: he asked for respect and courtesy, and for well-paid profes-sionals to behave as if football was their vocation. If anyone swaggered around acting as if he was a law unto himself, felt inclined to criticise Smith's selections publicly, or worst of all appeared to be picking and choosing which matches in which to offer 100 per cent, he would step in with a final warning, and woe betide the transgressor. 'It's a tough job, and you can't afford to be sentimental,' was his attitude. 'At the end of the day the club matters more than any individual, so you can't let star players do things which others in the team are forbidden from doing. That creates disharmony, and I won't have that. As soon as the players have walked into the dressing room, they are all equals in my eyes.' Smith meant it. Andy Goram had been one of the most luminous personalities in securing the treble, but when he started amassing excess weight towards the end of the outstanding season, and initially did not seem to notice that an issue was building up, Smith stepped in and placed him on the transfer list. To some observers beyond Ibrox this was regarded as a piece of shock therapy, but the manager was adamant and held a lengthy discussion with the goalkeeper during which he delivered his opinion that a hefty Goram could not possibly perform to his familiar, lofty standards. Goram, rather shame-facedly, pointed out that part of his training routine had been curtailed by injury, but he recognised that was no excuse, and when he returned for pre-season he was more than a stone lighter, and he subsequently shed additional poundage in preparing for a gruelling schedule.

Smith's man-management skills had reaped dividends again, but when Rangers were drawn against Levski Sofia in the opening round of the European Champions Cup – another new title – we were offered the first signs that the incessant struggle to master such European forays might be gnawing away at his confidence. Smith's options were limited by injuries to Goram, Gough, John Brown and McCoist for the first leg at Ibrox on 15 September but general incredulity was the reaction when Duncan Ferguson was included in the same line-up as Hateley, and asked to play wide on the left wing. Nor did the presence of Ally Maxwell, Gary Stevens and David Robertson at the back inspire huge confidence, even if this was widely assumed to be a fixture in which the Scots would canter to victory. For much of the home tie that view appeared justified, with Dave McPherson and Hateley sending their team into a 2-0 lead within 55 minutes. Whether they considered that the job had been completed or simply underestimated their opponents, they slackened their grip and the Bulgarians roared back into contention. Their two goals were a consequence of cringe-inducing gaffes from Maxwell and Ferguson, which were seized upon by Daniel Borimirov and the gifted Nikolai Todorov in the last 15 minutes. Even with the addition of a second headed goal from Hateley, a 3-2 score provoked jitters: it was as if Rangers could continually discover new methods of applying the self-destruct button. When they ventured to the intimidating arena of the Stadion Vasilij Levski, they started well enough during a deluge and seemed to be taking the sting out of the hosts' threat, only for Gough to make a hash of a clearance attempt and to hit the ball directly to Sofia captain Nasko Sirakov, who opened the scoring in the 36th minute. So far so inauspicious for the Ibrox men, but when it appeared that they would enter the half-time break in arrears, Durrant ghosted in at the far post and latched on to a Gary Stevens cross for the equaliser. That should have been the cue for a more aggressive approach, but having ripped Levski apart once, Rangers retreated into their shells, and they drifted further and further back as the match progressed . . . almost as if they feared that ignominy might be lying in wait. Dave McPherson probably should have steadied his team's nerves when he was allowed a free header from a Trevor Steven free-kick, but his powerful effort was within range of the home goalkeeper Nikola Nikolov, who produced a stunning save. The Bulgarians could not have anticipated that their winner would arrive in such dramatic circumstances. The travelling band of followers had endured the gamut of emotions throughout the 90 minutes, and suddenly their heads were in their hands as Rangers lost possession, Levski launched a breakneck assault and Todorov's ferocious shot from all of 30 yards was too much for the flailing Maxwell as it crashed into the net.

It was a wonderful strike from a gifted individual, but the angry shakes of the head among Rangers fans told the story, and recriminations arose over Smith's tactics and team selection: such questions were raised virtually for the first time in his managerial reign. Why had he chosen Duncan Ferguson and fielded him out of position? Why wasn't Alexei Mikhailichenko, a footballer who would have been perfectly suited for stemming the Levski menace, included in either match? Why was he persisting with Ally Maxwell in goals? Worse still from Smith's perspective was the perception that this most methodical of men had not carried out his research on the Bulgarians properly, and had paid a heavy price in failure to reach the Champions League group stages, which was to become a recurring theme as the decade advanced. Smith responded by stating his faith in the men he had picked – he could scarcely have done otherwise – but expressed disappointment at the fact that his club, who had gone ten games unbeaten in the previous season's tournament, had actually lost ground in the UEFA seedings. This baffled and angered him, and these issues festered in his mind throughout his attempts to pilot Rangers to European success. What could not be denied in the defeat to Levski Sofia was the fact that the Scots had initiated their own downfall, for three of the four goals they conceded sprang from the sort of basic errors that professionals should not commit.

An equally difficult start was noted on the home front as the club pursued their sixth consecutive league title. Several Scottish rivals showing signs that they no longer feared being thrashed by Rangers, and despite a 2-1 triumph over Hearts on the opening day of the campaign, their form was dreadful in the main. A number of performances left Smith seething during a spell in which they attained a solitary win in eight matches as a combination of injury accentuated by the absence of the hugely-influential McCoist, inconsistency and dearth of inspiration conspired to provoke an angst-ridden August/September. Smith worked harder than ever to pilot his team beyond the turbulence, as Craig Brown confirms:.

'Walter is one of those guys who doesn't blame others when problems arise. He knows that it is impossible to enjoy success all the time, so when things go wrong it only stiffens his resolve. Even the best managers go through rough passages where there is some negative flak from the fans and the media, but if you react to that or allow the criticism to affect your judgment, it usually backfires on you. Basically you have to say to yourself: "My methods were successful last year and the year before that, so I have to stick to my principles." And, if you do that, as Walter did, the good times will return again.'

By the start of October indications were that the mini-crisis was abating. Rangers secured an important 3-1 victory at Tannadice, then boosted their morale substantially by beating Celtic in the semi-finals of the League Cup at Ibrox. The result itself, a tight 1-0 win with Hateley making the vital breakthrough, came as a terrific fillip for all connected with the club, but it was the manner of the success which provided most of the reasons to be cheerful. Rangers were rediscovering the spirit of solidarity and tireless commitment, and that allowed them to transcend the red-carding of Pieter Huistra and still dominate their Old Firm rivals. By that stage too the redoubtable McCoist had recovered from his leg fracture, and he had played two full games for the first team and another substituting as Rangers prepared to meet Hibernian at Celtic Park in the League Cup final on 24 October 1993. As if to stress the impact that Smith had brought to Ibrox, he had in his sights a sixth successive domestic cup, and he had a dual motivation for wanting to maintain his sequence since Hibs had been the last club to beat Rangers in these competitions, eliminating them from this tournament at the semi-final stage in 1991. Ian Durrant sent his team in front only to see his effort swiftly negated by an own-goal from Dave McPherson, and with the contest finely balanced Smith cast a gaze at his substitutes' bench, and espied the glint in McCoist's eyes. With 20 minutes remaining it was time to play his trump card. Smith did admit that he was unsure whether the striker would be able to make a serious contribution, considering how little football he had experienced in recent months, but he need not have worried. Suddenly McCoist surged towards a loose ball with proceedings still locked at 1-1 after more than 80 minutes, and he sent the Ibrox fans into hysterical cheers when he scored with a spectacular overhead kick. 'Only Ally could have done that – and I told him that after the game,' said Smith, emphasising the bond which the men shared. 'It was a gamble to have him involved at all, but he can sniff out goals better than anyone.' But then McCoist had been Europe's leading goal-scorer in two consecutive seasons, and had gained the cherished Golden Boot for his prodigious exploits. To those who reckon that he was nothing beyond a high-class poacher, studying a video of that cup final will confirm that a master was at work, and that conjured out of nothing, his pivotal effort was blessed with a magical quality. One only has to scan the incredulous expressions of the Hibs players nearest to McCoist to understand why Smith valued him so highly.

Despite the surge of relief which enveloped Rangers in the wake of that cup victory, season 1993–4 continued to suffer from glitches. On the field the team were bolstered by the arrival in November of the effervescent Gordon Durie, who was an astute £1.2m signing from Tottenham Hotspur, but it would be straining credibility to suggest that the team achieved anything beyond grinding out wins. Nor did the ceaseless stream of injured warriors help to bolster morale, and in facing the press on Fridays Smith seemed to spend more time in medical mode than talking about football. Gough joined the sick list, followed by Durrant, and as New Year approached the manager went into the Old Firm clash at Celtic Park with his club filling the unfamiliar role of underdogs. Rangers stormed into battle though, given Smith's ability to lift his troops for these contests, and barely had the match kicked off before Hateley had pounced for the opening goal, after 58 seconds. It triggered a tremendous tussle, and the visitors were as resilient in this game as they had been prosaic in much of their Premier League challenge. Celtic, whose very future was being debated in the press and in the hostelries of Glasgow and elsewhere, were eventually overcome by 4-2. Watching from the technical area, Smith quietly nodded his approval of that display, and as the season progressed and his men clung on to their crown with unquenchable desire, he refused to criticise them for failing to replicate the stylish performances evident during the season past. As has been stressed on many occasions, Smith was a devotee of the virtues of substance and hard graft. His players reacted to victory over Celtic by mounting an unbeaten sequence stretching to 17 matches between February and April, including seven successive victories, which all but clinched another championship. 'It wasn't pretty for much of the time, but it wasn't just about their footballing ability, but also the physical and emotional reserves they had left to draw on,' Smith reflected. 'There was no time for them to relax or sit back and say: "Haven't we done well?" Instead it was on to the next game, the next competition, the next challenge. Week in, week out. And I couldn't have asked them for any more.'

The boss, however, could have expected better from Duncan Ferguson, whose arrival at Ibrox had become shrouded in controversy. From the outset the youngster had looked ill-at-ease coping with the burden of expectations, and he repeatedly failed to convince the sceptics in serving up a series of indifferent displays which, coupled with his persistent injury problems and volatile temperament, marked him out as a liability. Worse still, having demonstrated an alarming penchant for turning any minor incident into a major stramash, the player found himself in the dock after head-butting Raith Rovers' John McStay. Given that this was not his first or even a second assault conviction, he had no grounds for complaint when he was sentenced to three months in Barlinnie jail, though his incarceration lasted only 44 days. Few among the Rangers' support regarded him as anything other than an expensive luxury, a 'ned with cash' as *Scotland on Sunday* described him succinctly. Smith though had some sympathy for his player, and he maintained contact with him during his imprisonment and even after Ferguson had departed Ibrox, as if to highlight his understanding of the pressures that surround those asked to dwell in the Old Firm goldfish bowl. Not that he was condoning the player's actions, but he recognised that when any young person is festooned with money and publicity, there is always the possibility of him going off the rails in a splurge of negative headlines. Especially if, like Ferguson, self-control did not come naturally.

Comprehending the dynamics of human frailty allowed Smith to contribute adroitly to establishing a sense of harmony in his dressing room. He knew it was impossible for 20 individuals to live comfortably in each other's pockets, and he accepted that rows, recriminations and even occasional violence would break out on the training pitch.

Some players required constant reassurance, others could communicate only by using the F-word, a few preferred their own company away from football, and others were desperate to become involved in as many late evenings as possible at Victoria's nightclub . . . without worrying whether the paparazzi ambushed them at the climax of proceedings. Smith appreciated these diverse attitudes without drawing the kind of ethical judgments which cropped up constantly in the tabloid papers. It was, and is, ironic that journalists, who are often less than moral exemplars, can heap opprobrium on young footballers for drinking to excess and enjoying other sins of the flesh. But while Smith's team selections or tactics might be the subject of criticism on occasion, most of his players revered him almost as a surrogate father. He could be grumpy and might scream at them, but he defended them to the hilt, and talked up their abilities whenever explaining was required in public. In return they invariably offered their utmost, and the consequence was a collection of trophies, a sixth successive league title, and a glut of media interest in everything relating to Rangers.

Perhaps it was appropriate, considering the troubled nature of much of the campaign, that the championship was sealed on an evening when the Ibrox side slipped to defeat, losing 1-0 to Hibernian at Easter Road. Though they finished the season much as they had commenced it, managing just two points from their final five fixtures, Rangers had done just enough to fend off their rivals. A weary, muscle-bound bunch of combatants journeyed home from Edinburgh that evening without enjoying a lap of honour after the final whistle, though the news that Motherwell had also lost in the twilight of 4 May ensured that six-in-a-row festivities could begin with a vengeance in Glasgow. According to one player, the gaffer proceeded up the aisle of the coach and thanked each of his men for the yeoman service put in during the season: 'Walter isn't a person for extravagant shows of emotion, but he was very grateful for what we had done, and I think that was probably one of the first occasions where it started to sink in that we were two-thirds of the way towards winning nine straight titles, and even though we were tired, there was this buzz about what might happen in the future. We had been warned not to raise the subject in any interviews, and Walter rightly thought we would be making a rod for our own backs if we made a big deal about chasing nine in a row, but let's not kid ourselves, it was high on our list of priorities. We had been ribbed about endlessly by Celtic fans from the days when we were growing up, so why shouldn't we talk about chasing their record, and if at all possible, beating it? And there was a feeling throughout the team that if we could win the league in '93–94 when nearly everything that could go wrong did go wrong, we could win it every season.'

Life was poised to change dramatically, at least for the other half of the Old Firm. In March, for a few hours at least, the unthinkable had almost happened when the Bank of Scotland threatened to send Celtic into receivership, before an outsider came to the rescue by acting as guarantor for the club's £7.5m debts. Some of us at the time believed that sum to be a drop in the ocean, but it was an indication of the sorry fashion in which the club had been managed while ruled over by the patriarchal Kelly and White families. It was Fergus McCann, a Canadian-based Scot, who marked the end of the fiefdom that had owned Celtic for the previous century, and set about remedying the malaise that had blighted the club since the mid-1980s. He had flown 'home' to Glasgow on 4 March and the following Monday he arrived as the new full-time chief executive and started to extricate Celtic from a financial mire, using expertise gained as an entrepreneur who had spotted an opening in the golf tourism market in Montreal, and transformed the business into a multi-million-pound operation. Some green-clad fans who were unfamiliar with stock-market procedures were initially unimpressed with McCann: to them he was a wee chap in a bunnet with a curious transatlantic accent. But there was no questioning his integrity, or his bank balance. 'I can now tell the fans that the club is safe,' he announced almost immediately. 'We have been able to resolve the critical short-term financing at Celtic, and shortly will be able to discuss long-term packaging.' If this sounded like the language of business rather than football, McCann was not fazed. He had a five-year plan for his new project, and claimed that he would not stay beyond that period. He wanted to inject the necessary funds to rid Celtic Park of the old Jungle and replace it with a gleaming, state-of-the-art stadium which would be the pride of Europe. And – music to the ears of the battle-fatigued supporters – he would release sufficient funds for the purchase of quality signings, who would terminate Rangers' hegemony.

David Murray viewed these developments from Ibrox with the studied indifference of one who would believe McCann's promises when they came to fruition, but not before. Walter Smith had never harboured the delusion that Celtic's slump would prove permanent, and in one respect welcomed the prospect of renewed hostilities, rather than being accused of profiting from the misery of another club. He recognised the fact that tribal loyalty requires a neighbour to beat, and that rivalry cannot exist in isolation. Obviously, given his position, there was no equivocation from Smith. He could neither afford to concern himself with his rivals' situation, nor would he concede that Scottish football was the better for a powerful Rangers and Celtic, a statement which he acknowledged was arrogant nonsense, the more so because the Scotland teams that qualified for five successive World Cups between 1974 and '90 contained only handfuls of Old Firm representatives. As Smith declared in the summer of 1994, he had enough issues of his own to address. He had to search for new blood for his squad and needed to ensure that there was no repeat of the Levski Sofia fiasco, so he scoured Europe in pursuit of players who would bring added oomph and sparkle to his line-up, and he enjoyed some success. He persuaded the gifted Danish internationalist Brian Laudrup to join Rangers from Fiorentina for only £2.25m – Duncan Ferguson had cost £3.75m – and recruited central defender Basile Boli from Marseille for £2m, which was a less gratifying piece of business. While Laudrup would eventually be acclaimed as one of the great foreign signings, there was no quick fix when Rangers launched their bid for a place in the lucrative Champions League against unknown quantities sporting the colours of AEK Athens. This was a pairing which again exposed Smith's inability to orchestrate a modified game-plan from the no-frills approach which worked in Scotland, but which too often appeared predictable and pedestrian against technically superior European adversaries, and this remains one of the more depressing of the club's continental encounters. Ewan Aitken, a lifelong Rangers follower and a bluff character who has visited many European countries, considers it to have been one of his most dismal footballing experiences, as he explained to me:

'We were basically treated like criminals by the Greek police, and there was no escape from them. The match was played early in August [the 10th] and the temperature was over 40 degrees, which might make you think would make anybody too lethargic to cause trouble. But it was just constant aggro from the cops, from the Greek supporters, from airport staff from the moment we landed in Athens, and we couldn't wait to get the match over with and get the hell out of there. When we got to the ground, we were manhandled outside the stadium, pelted with missiles inside, and as for the Rangers performance that night, they were just shite. Andy [Goram] was the only guy to do himself justice, and he actually saved us from a real tanking with a pile of excellent saves in the first half.

'But it was him against the world, and you can't keep them out forever when that happens. We were only 1-0 behind at the interval, but it could easily have been four or five, and when the striker [Dimitris Saravakos] scored his second goal with about 20 minutes to go, most of us thought to ourselves that we weren't going to pull this back at Ibrox. I have a lot of amount of respect for Walter Smith, but he screwed up big style that night. The defence [Richard Gough, Steven Pressley and Gary Stevens] was all over the place, and we read later that they had never played together in that formation before. Well, that is just daft, isn't it? And you can't blame anybody else for that but the manager.'

Smith accepted the responsibility: 'I tried the wrong defensive tactics for the game, and in the first half they didn't work.' He refused to shoulder any blame, though, for not preparing for the match as thoroughly as he should have done, pointing out that he and Archie Knox had watched AEK in advance, and had reached the conclusion that they were superior to Levski Sofia. Smith also mounted the valid argument that the tie had arrived before the start of the Scottish league season, and that it left such contests more reminiscent of a lottery than a Champions League. The defeat was swiftly followed by a reverse against Celtic, and suddenly a section of the fans who had been rejoicing in the spring reverted to appalling barracking of Smith and David Murray. I attended that Old Firm match, and reported in *Scotland on Sunday* that one or two supporters disgraced themselves by calling their chairman 'a f***ing cripple' within earshot of the press and a security guard. Some revisionists have alleged that this incident did not happen. It did. I was there. Smith had discovered yet again how fickle the soccer public can be, and the strain started to show. When AEK came to Glasgow bolstered by a home-made cushion, they again proved to be better than their opponents. Nearly 45,000 spectators howled for a sliver of inspiration or sophistication from their team, but Rangers kept punting aimless high balls towards Hateley and Duncan Ferguson, a double act that died on the big stage. Murmurs of unrest filtered through the stadium long before the end, and the nose-rubbing exercise was completed when Toni Savevski scored after 70 minutes, the prelude to a chorus of boos resonating around Ibrox. It had been a harsh lesson for Smith and his players, who crept off at the end, and the manager's latent frustrations exploded next morning when he was interviewed once again by BBC football reporter Chick Young. The unfortunate exchange went like this:

Chick Young, standing in the tunnel at Ibrox: *Would you agree that [Basile] Boli and [Brian] Laudrup didn't play well last night?*

Walter Smith: *I'm not answering that.*

Young: *What I'm trying to say is that you've gone out and spent at the highest level. But is the standard of play in Europe higher again? And are you going to have to match the likes of AC Milan to pay these types of fees?*

Smith: *I'm not following your line of questioning.*

Young: *Well, you spent £5m Walter, in the summer on good players, but these players are seemingly not good enough at the highest level in Europe.*

Smith, looking increasingly angry: *I don't think you can say that. How can you say that? I mean, they've just come here, and you've got to give everybody a chance to settle in. Are you saying that Boli and Laudrup cannae play in Europe?*

Young: *No.*

Smith: *Boli's won a European Cup-winner's medal, for f***'s sake, you cannae say he's no good enough to be in Europe. That's stupid, isn't it? You cannae say that Boli and Laudrup cannae f***ing play. Laudrup played seven out of ten games for AC Milan last season, and Boli played in the team that won the European Cup, and the only reason he didn't play last year was because his club [Marseille] were banned. You cannae say they cannae f***ing play in Europe. For f***'s sake!*

Young, getting more rattled: *At the end of the day . . .*

Smith: *Have you been up all night working that out?*

Young: *No, no, I'm . . .*

Smith: *Those were your f***ing words to me. That they could-nae play in Europe.*

Young tries and fails to interject.

Smith, shouting down the tunnel: *Archie [Knox], come and listen to this f***ing interview. He's coming out with worse shite than ever.*

Knox walks past with a furious glance at Young: *I'd have him out of here on his f***ing arse if it was up to me.*

Pause.

Smith: *Come on, you cannae be f***ing serious.*

Young: *All right, I'll do it again. The Rangers fans are demanding . . .*

Smith interrupts: *Your questions to the chairman [David Murray] last week were f***ing shite as well. If we had a bad night last night, then you are having a f***ing horrendous morning the now.*

Young, meekly: *You did have a bad night.*

Smith: *That's what I said to you.*

Young: *But would you agree that the two of them didn't play well?*

Smith: *Haud on, haud on, haud on, that doesnae mean they aren't good enough to play in Europe. Surely they have f***ing proved on many occasions before that they are good enough. It's just f***ing silly to be talking about this.*

Young: *Okay, I gather that you're not happy with that. Let's start again. What I'm trying to get at is . . .*

Smith: *That'll go down well at the Christmas f***ing party, won't it!*

Interview ends.

The edginess inherent in this salvo demonstrates that Smith occasionally has a short fuse when dealing with what he considers to be stupid questions, but there again it was not that clever of Young to suggest that a player such as Laudrup, a prodigiously talented individual, would not make the grade in Europe. However, if the fire which burned in Smith was doubted, his response to the AEK debacle was instructive. Within weeks of crashing out of the Champions League, the manager had revitalised his troops and had maintained his domination over Celtic, who were still in the process of adapting to Fergus McCann's arrival, with a 3-1 victory in the early stages of the 1994–5 league campaign. It proved the catalyst for another of the long stretches of supremacy which typified this Rangers' collective. The team went 14 games without defeat and gradually amassed an unassailable lead, but just as they were homing in on their seventh title, a deep sense of sadness enveloped Ibrox and the wider environs of Scottish football. Davie Cooper, one of the most talismanic characters to pull on the blue jersey, suffered a fatal brain haemorrhage on Thursday, 23 March while recording a coaching film for youngsters with Charlie Nicholas at Broadwood Stadium. He was 39, and Smith reacted as one who had regarded the player with unstinting affection and admiration throughout his outstanding career. At Hillhouse Parish Church in Hamilton on the following Monday, he spoke movingly and emotionally of Coop's talents, his eulogy a fitting testament to the man who was gone too early. 'God gave Davie Cooper a talent. He would not be disappointed with how it was used,' Smith declared to a funeral congregation including many leading figures of the national sport. His words were acknowledged because of a tacit admission by some in the throng that it had taken an untimely demise for them to appreciate his gifts fully, and to recognise the routine derring-do with which he had sustained Rangers when they were languishing in the doldrums. Smith did not make that mistake. He was enraptured by Cooper's skills, and subsequently made his feelings clear that this was a character with talent to burn, who had borne a heavy load during strife that had damaged Rangers in the first half of the 1980s. 'The pressure on him must have been enormous,' said Smith, 'but the arrival of players such as Souness and Butcher allowed Davie the freedom to play. It allowed him the setting he needed, and he responded wonderfully. You can discuss his many match-winning displays and go into the details, but all that really needs saying is that Davie was a magnificent footballer.'

The death cast a pall over the latter stages of Rangers' league season, but Smith told his men to go out and perform in the style that would have brought a smile to Cooper's countenance, and they obliged with a series of sublime showings, and Laudrup was at the forefront of everything positive. Aberdeen were edged out 3-2 in April, and eight days later the championship was settled when Rangers beat Hibernian 3-1 at Ibrox. Title No. 7 was achieved by a resounding 15 points from Motherwell, who had fought courageously to remain in touch, but had lacked the resources of their rivals. Celtic, even with the financial stability offered by McCann, were not in contention, and their supporters started to inquire about finance for serious investment . . . not merely in bricks and mortar, but in top-class players. They gained their wish eventually, but Smith and Murray were not about to relinquish their grip on the Premier League, confirming that intent during the summer of 1995 when Paul Gascoigne arrived at Ibrox from Lazio for £4.3m, and Oleg Salenko joined from Athletico Madrid, Stephen Wright from Aberdeen and Gordan Petric from Dundee United. Attracting the Geordie Gascoigne, despite the quirks and demons that lurked beneath his jolly exterior, proved that Rangers had not relinquished the capacity to draw big names. Though some suggested that he was a spent force and still leant on the reputation he earned at the 1990 World Cup, he confounded that perception within weeks of pledging his allegiance to 'Glasgow . . . er, Rangers', though not soon enough to prevent Smith from experiencing another painful series of lessons on his team's less-than-magical tour of Europe. At least there were no slip-ups in the preliminaries, the Scots defeating Anorthosis Famagusta of Cyprus with a patchy home display at Ibrox when Gordon Durie scored the only goal. A much-improved showing away from home confirmed a 1-0 aggregate victory, but Gascoigne looked sluggish in these ties, and conceded later that his confidence had been low and that he was not properly attuned to the intensity of these matches. But his vitality resurfaced as he forged bonds with McCoist, Hateley, Durrant and other team-mates, this to the detriment of the clubs vying to halt Rangers' lengthy winning streak in league fixtures.

In the Champions League the Scots were placed in a 'Group of Death' with Borussia Dortmund, Juventus and Steaua Bucharest. It would be pleasant to relate that they made a seamless transition from thrashing such as Kilmarnock and St Johnstone, but that was not the reality. The campaign commenced with a workman-like display in Bucharest, but as so often in close-run affairs, Rangers were sunk by a single strike, in this instance emanating from Daniel Prodan. His 20-yard volley with six minutes of the tie remaining screamed past Andy Goram, who otherwise had had relatively little to do in goals. The Scottish team served up a worthwhile showing when they entertained Dortmund, gaining a 2-2 draw courtesy of Richard Gough and Ian Ferguson. Yet it was a portent of their Champions League travails that Brian Laudrup limped off at the interval during the contest against the German side, and he remained crocked for the next dozen games. In his absence, Smith was forced to grapple with the knowledge that he needed at least one win from the double-header with mighty Juventus, who could field world-class talents in Gianlucci Vialli and Alessandro del Piero, and that all Rangers' leading players required to peak at the same time. With the exception of Goram, this failed to materialise, and as they trudged into the Stadio delle Alpi, the team seemed to be preparing for a siege. The sight of honest journeymen in the mould of Alex Cleland, David Robert-son and Stephen Wright preparing to do battle with maestros of their profession induced queasy feelings for those who had travelled to Italy. These did not abate, for in the first quarter of an hour Juventus weaved silky patterns through the visiting defence to such effect that they led 3-0, Fabrizio Ravanelli scoring twice with one from Antonio Conte. Men against boys, Armani v Barras, call it what you will: there was no disputing the evidence that for all the millions that had been spent by Smith in pursuit of a squad that could challenge the best opponents on the Continent, this was a humiliation. Neither did it offer consolation that they escaped from their ordeal with 'only' a 4-1 loss, because the suspicion arose that the hosts slackened their grip after netting a fourth through Del Piero: by then Cleland had been sent off for launching a swipe at the Italian icon. At least the Rangers man did not have to worry about meeting the same opponents a fortnight later. The manager, as was now usual, faced criticism for his tactics, though it was difficult to envisage any formation negating Juventus considering the depth of talent throughout their ranks. Rangers were forced to call up Gary Bollan for the re-match, and expectations were predictably low for the Ibrox clash. Despite a crowd in excess of 42,000, the atmosphere was dull and became even more so as the home team suffered a 4-0 defeat, despite mustering a performance that was considerably improved. All their commitment and industry counted for naught without a threat up front, and this was another evening on which, after Del Piero's early strike, Rangers pressed forward heroically and consistently without demonstrating the sharpness necessary to ruffle the visitors. If it was exasperating for the supporters, it was doubly galling for Smith as Ravanelli scored from an offside position and Moreno Torricelli and Giancarlo Marocchi completed the big haul in added-time.

Having amassed just one point from their four fixtures, it was surprising that Rangers still had an outside chance of progressing in the tournament, but this would entail beating Steaua at home and Dortmund away, and not even the most sanguine Ibrox supporters could envisage that scenario. To their credit, they produced some excellent football in both matches, including a magnificent solo effort from Gascoigne against Bucharest, which was worthy of a Champions League final. The Englishman's

50-yard incision past a swathe of Romanian defenders evoked memories of Diego Maradona's foray at the 1986 World Cup, but Adrian Ilie's goal ensured that his side left Glasgow with a share of the spoils. That trend continued in Dortmund where Rangers, basking in the Scottish trait of being carefree now that they had been eliminated, created myriad opportunities during a resplendent display which ended at 2-2: Brian Laudrup and Gordon Durie found the net, and German stars Andreas Moller and Karl-Heinz Riedle responded in kind. A downbeat group of players walked off at the end, not least because Gascoigne had been red-carded for two pretty innocuous offences, the second when he was furious not to be awarded a penalty in what seemed a credible claim. That incident perhaps summed up Rangers' European misadventures that season, namely that when they were not conceding soft goals or squandering opportunities up front, they were falling foul of officialdom, with Gascoigne alternating between classy and crass. Gazza's every action, gesture and indiscretion seemed to be captured by a photographer, presenting his manager with the dilemma of how best to save him from himself without extinguishing his innate enthusiasm. He embraced Gascoigne with human kindness and with verbal volleys when he felt these were required, as the former player recalls:

'I used to get it in the neck from him, and so did other players – but it was mainly me on the receiving end of his abuse. I seriously f***ed up one Friday night before a game, and he sent me away for three days. I was banned from Ibrox and told not to come near training. I was devastated by this, and never f***ed up again on a Friday. He also grabbed me by the neck on several occasions, and put the fear of death into me. I used to shit myself when he spoke to me – and that was when he was giving me praise.

'Yet I respected him immensely. I rate him right up there beside Terry Venables, and there are also touches of Sir Alex Ferguson in him. And the bottom line is that: I played for Walter Smith and Archie Knox. These guys were tremendous for me, they gave me my life back, and I will be forever grateful. With them, you had to be performing at 110 per cent, winning at half-time and full-time, and if you weren't, you were getting bollocked, because they were winners, pure and simple. There were times where I had scored one and set one up, and at half-time Walter would say: "You're just messing about, Gascoigne." And I shook my head, and he threw a boot at me.'

The other side to that dressing-room volatility was embodied in Smith inviting a lonely Gascoigne to Christmas dinner, after receiving a poignant phone call at his family home early in the morning. Within a few hours he and wife Ethel and their sons Neil and Stevie were sitting down to turkey with Gazza for company; I have a lingering notion that Mrs Smith might have been suprised, but reacted calmly, saying: 'Nuts, Paul?', 'Crackers, Paul?' until Gascoigne eventually asked his boss why he was being insulted. If one vignette epitomises why Smith forged a lasting relationship with one of the most troubled figures to perform for Rangers, his generous offer of hospitality was it. Ian Ridley wrote in *The Observer* newspaper: 'He had always been one of those people, like Sir Alex Ferguson who, when he first met the boy, saw something vulnerable in him that provoked a desire to take care of him. As Richard Burton's sister once said: "Rich had the kind of face that was too easy to forgive."'

A more pragmatic explanation for his benevolence was recognition that Gazza could act as an enormous asset to Rangers if his temperament and talent could be moulded to the task in hand. As 1996 unfolded the Rangers men were involved in a bare-knuckle scrap with a revitalised Celtic, who were as desperate as their supporters to prevent their Old Firm rivals from equalling or, heaven forbid, surpassing the fabled nine-in-a-row achievement. Fergus McCann was fulfilling his promise of bringing stability behind the scenes as well as delivering a magnificent revamp of Celtic Park, and just as Graeme Souness had done for Rangers under David Holmes, the club had recruited a series of high-profile signings. Dutch international striker Pierre van Hooijdonk had joined in 1995, to be followed by Jorge Cadete and Paolo Di Canio, a triumvirate who were swiftly branded the 'Three Amigos' by fans. As Celtic pursued their first title of the 1990s, where they had been porous, unconvincing and unable to mount a protracted challenge to Rangers, they were bursting with vim and vigour, and from Smith's perspective reflected a worrying sense of momentum. It was a measure of their transformation that they lost only one game in the league all season, at home to Rangers. The other Old Firm derbies were drawn, but pulsating spectacles in any case, the best being an engrossing clash at Ibrox which finished 3-3.

Smith required his elite players to carry the battle back to the opposition in such circumstances, and they responded. Hibernian were caught in the crossfire and demolished by 7-0, and Raith were briefly allowed to entertain thoughts of an improbable victory before a late McCoist double earned his side a 3-2 success. The pressure was on Gascoigne to help to spearhead a revival when Rangers, in one of their crunch matches, fell behind 1-0 to Aberdeen in Glasgow. Cometh the hour, cometh the footballer who would be the recipient of Scotland's Player of the Year award shortly afterwards and began to stamp his authority all over the visitors, bewitching and bewildering them to the delight of the home supporters. So what if there were occasions when it seemed that even he was not sure where his forays might take him? As McCoist remarked: 'If that was the case, what hope was there for the Aberdeen defenders who were trying to stop him?' Gascoigne scored two beautifully-worked goals which came with his trade-mark, and as the stadium was transformed into an inferno of tribal emotions, he coolly strode up to take a penalty and completed a hat-trick to cap what had been a personal triumph, a privilege to behold. That was instrumental in bringing Rangers their eighth title in succession, but the championship had proved to be a trek, not a sprint, and when it had been settled by a four-point margin, the club had to reflect on the fact they had lost two games more than Celtic, and would surely be confronted with even more fired-up adversaries in the season ahead. Smith remained objective: 'You can't get ahead of your-self in these situations. When you have won two or three championship titles, nine seems an awfully long way off in the distance. Then when you have six or seven, you feel that it might be coming within touching distance. But ultimately, getting this close just makes you appreciate what a great feat it was by Celtic in the first place.'

CHAPTER ELEVEN

NINE, NINE, NINE

❖

*'If you don't win the league this season,
the other eight don't mean a thing'*

As Rangers viewed the prospect of an achievement which would mean their supporters could counter mocking references to 'Nine in a Row' from Celtic fans, there was still no sign that the Ibrox club had cracked the code to guaranteeing better fortunes on the European trail. On the contrary, whenever football followers start to discuss whether Walter Smith or David Murray was more responsible for the successes of the 1990s, and whether Rangers would have fared better on continental business had they been playing in a more competitive domestic league, the answers tend to reflect the prejudices of those concerned, rather than answering why the light blues swept all before them at home, yet were constantly exposed on the bigger stage, give or take a few auspicious occasions. So far as the first question is concerned, it is undeniable that Murray's money was a massive factor in the metamorphosis from paltry crowds and an empty trophy cabinet in the early 1980s to the successful club that amassed silverware with ruthless efficiency a decade later. As numerous managers have proved when presented with wads of cash, and failed to transform it into tangible succes, there are few sure things in sport, and what counts in this debate are the opinions of the two men who led the Rangers' push towards nine consecutive championships. The mutual respect between them shines like a beacon. Walter Smith said in the mid-1990s:

> 'Basically in the modern game it is not managers who turn clubs into bigger clubs – chairmen do that. You need the right kind of driving force in the boardroom, and we have that in David Murray. He has never yet backed out of a deal. When we have needed players, then he has always found the money, and I just don't think that Rangers would be sitting in the position they are now without David. He is a hands-on chairman, and with the money which he has ploughed into the club, that's only right. But he won't stand still for an instant. He is an inspirational person, and it is a privilege to work with him towards a common goal.'

Murray reciprocated with a glowing tribute to the man that he promoted to the manager's role after the abrupt departure of Graeme Souness:

> 'Walter is the last of a breed, and I don't think that we will have another manager with his degree of integrity and loyalty. The Bosman influence on football is changing attitudes among managers as well as players, and no other manager will stay with one club for long periods. What we have to recognise is that Walter is one of the greatest managers Rangers have ever had.'

Thus the two men appreciated qualities in the other, which meant that though they had different areas of expertise, they were of similar opinion when it came to the weighty task of resuscitating Rangers and propelling them upwards. This is not to say that the club would not have thrived in Scotland had Souness remained in charge, though many have reservations on that score. What, for instance, would the fiery former Liverpool star have made of the chance to sign Paul Gascoigne? Would the obdurate Souness have relented in selecting McCoist, or allowed the striker to drift elsewhere, which would have been a horrrible example of man-mismanagement? How would he have coped with the chronic injury-list which bedevilled Rangers in 1994? One suspects that Souness would not have borne this burden as well as Smith, who implemented a superb patch-up job on his squad at regular intervals, and despite signing some players such as Basile Boli, Duncan Ferguson and Peter van Vossen, who at best flattered to deceive, could also point to successes such as Brian Laudrup, Gordon Durie and Paul Gascoigne, if one sticks to considering Gazza's contributions on the pitch. The puzzle over why Smith's Rangers struggled so badly in Europe is less easily resolved for those who recall how close his team came to beating Marseille towards the start of his tenure. By 1996 the majority of his players were well versed in the strictures of the Champions League; they acknowledged that it demanded a more patient and pragmatic approach from the helter-skelter of the Scottish professional game; and considering that Smith had enhanced his squad with Laudrup, Gascoigne and others, there genuinely was no excuse for the meek, tactically-naïve performances which were too often served up by Rangers.

Still, after being drawn against the Russian champions Alania Vladikavkaz in the qualifying round of the competition, it appeared that the Scots were poised to bring their A-game to the table when, having picked up a 3-1 advantage at home with goals from Derek McInnes, Gordan Petric and McCoist, they travelled to what seemed like the end of the earth – particularly for supporters who spent five days in transit from Glasgow to Vladikavkaz, via Copenhagen, Stockholm and Moscow – and produced an out-of-this-world display in annihilating much-vaunted opponents 7-2. It was one of those nights when McCoist buzzed in and out of the action like a cantankerous wasp, driving his rivals to distraction with a goal in just 33 seconds, and moving on to a hat-trick. Laudrup twice appeared on the score-sheet beside Van Vossen and Charlie Miller, and reverberations from the 10-3 aggregate were heard around the Continent. Could this be the season when everything fell neatly into place for Smith and

SILVERSMITH

his players? At first glance UEFA seemed to have handed Rangers a group, containing Auxerre, Grasshoppers of Zurich and Ajax, from which they had a definite opportunity to progress. However, any notions that securing the domestic title might be accompanied by a glorious march into the latter stages of the Champions League were dashed by a series of displays which varied from lacklustre to mediocre.

In preparing for the opening visit to Switzerland, which should have been targeted as a potential away win, Smith picked what on paper looked a formidable side, packed with flair and attacking threat from Gascoigne, Laudrup, Jorg Albertz, McCoist and Durie, but they produced what many Rangers' supporters believe was one of their club's worst performances on the European circuit in going down to a 3-0 defeat. Smith was furious by the climax, beseeching his men to remember the qualities that they had produced in eliminating Vladikavkaz; but there was no cohesion, a dearth of inventiveness and worst of all from the fans' perspective, a distinct lack of urgency within the visitors. They could, just about, tolerate their favourites being outclassed by AC Milan or Juventus, but certainly not by the unsophisticated efforts of the Swiss team. That reverse prompted derision at home from the non-Rangers' fraternity, and Grasshoppers' manager Christian Gross, soon to move to Tottenham Hotspur, dismissed his vanquished opponents with the words: 'They came here as holidaymakers.' Many Rangers' fans detected a semblance of truth in the comment, and Robert McElroy, faithful chronicler of all things Ibrox, was uncharacteristically apoplectic, summing up the evening with these comments:

'The Swiss could scarcely believe their luck. Rangers were lamentable, their appalling defensive errors typifying a pathetic opening to the campaign, and leaving many people to seriously question the tactical awareness of the coaching staff. Rangers, just possibly favourites to win the group given their results against the Russians, were rightly criticised, and scathingly so,

152

and from then on were always struggling to maintain any kind of impact.'

For the next match, a home date with Auxerre, Smith predictably made several changes, but the introduction of Derek McInnes and Van Vossen did not fill the compact and competent French side with trepidation. Despite a better showing, which was certainly not difficult, Rangers slipped to a 2-1 defeat, Thomas Deniaud twice beating Goram and rendering Gascoigne's goal academic. Several aspects were now growing wearily familiar. Rangers had amassed 10 goals in disposing of Vladikavkaz, but had scored once in 180 minutes against two distinctly average sides. That toothlessness was evident too often season after season, and McCoist's limitations had grown painfully obvious during European excursions, especially when he found himself pitted against defenders who could back-track quickly. In the midfield industrious toilers in the shape of Ian Ferguson and Derek McInnes, who could guarantee satisfactory shifts for Smith on Saturday assignments in the Premier League, were devoid of the vision and class to chart a path through their rivals, and for all that Goram and Gough were usuallly excellent, they frequently found themselves surrounded by colleagues who were out of their depth.

It was scant comfort for the manager. Off the pitch, the long-term failure of Rangers to invest in an academy structure, the norm across Europe, had often appeared to be a major mistake, and there was a limit to how much more investment Murray could pour into the Ibrox coffers. Hence the anti-climactic nature of the exit from the Champions League, with Rangers trounced 4-1 by Ajax in Amsterdam and edged out 1-0 in the return match, before finally mustering something for their fans to cheer about with a 2-1 success over Grasshoppers, sealed by a McCoist double. But the sorry saga concluded with a 2-1 defeat at the hands of Auxerre. Mitigating circumstances could be put forward in one or two of these matches: Rangers were missing a dozen players for their second tussle with Ajax, and their first joist with the Dutch club was disfigured by the adolescent behaviour of Gascoigne who, with no regard for his colleagues, aimed a petulant kick at Winston Bogarde, and was immediately dispatched from the field as an incredulous group of Rangers followers looked on.

At least for the beleaguered players and coaching staff, the quest for the Premier League title offered a smokescreen in the aftermath of what had developed into a thoroughly dispiriting continental venture, and the fans who had jeered with derision at the shambles in Zurich and Amsterdam were soon roaring approval as Rangers moved into the one setting which mattered more than any piffling European fixture: an Old Firm derby. Ibrox was packed to its 51,000 capacity when Smith's team entertained Celtic on Saturday, 28 September – three days earlier, when Auxerre had shown up at the stadium, the attendance was 37,344, the smallest of the season. 'Nothing could beat these occasions for the supporters, and especially with all the talk about us going for the ninth title,' said Richard Gough. 'One of the fans came up to me at the start of the season and told me: "You know, if you don't win the league this year, the other eight don't mean a thing." So, no pressure there then.' But as Gough and his team-mates recognised, this was a pivotal period for the traditionalists, men who had grown up routinely employing the F-word any time that they mentioned Celtic, and woe betide Smith's players if they did not keep to their part of the bargain. Smith observed mildly: 'It's not like in other countries where teams are allowed the occasional slip without having half the city screaming at them. Here Celtic and ourselves have to win every single week, or we don't hear the end of it. It means that we are constantly forced to attack and go forward, and when we come up against a side like Auxerre, who don't have the same pressures, they have the defensive edge over us.'

It was a valid observation, but as the manager well knew, words counted for little in the build-up. Hence the buzz around Ibrox as the hosts strove to shrug aside their Champions League disappointments, and attend to the sharp end of business.

Rangers were purposeful and penetrative from the outset, and despite the labours of an evolving Celtic team the afternoon belonged to the men in blue, their 2-0 win the consequence of goals from skipper Gough, described by Smith as his 'corner-stone', and Gascoigne, whose season flitted from joyous high to dismal low, and back again. It was indicative of the inconsistency of Rangers during that momentous season that their Celtic success was the precursor to a five-match sequence in which they managed only one victory. Then it was time for another Old Firm slug-fest, and an opportunity for Celtic to lay down a marker that they believed they could halt Rangers' title aspirations. Sadly for the Hoops, once again their strikers were posted AWOL in a scrappy, nerve-shredding affair at Parkhead, which appeared set for stalemate until Laudrup conjured up a mesmerising goal with a thundering effort from 25 yards. It was another reminder of the powers of this individual, as creative as he was carefree. Smith beamed at the media after the match, and confirmed: 'That is one of the things which makes Brian special. He can change the whole course of a match in a few seconds.' It was an apt summation to describe the Austrian-born Dane, whose exploits with his brother Michael had illuminated the 1992 European Championship, when they celebrated their country's unexpected triumph. Though sceptics might wonder why Laudrup, an individual of unquestionable European pedigree, did not hit the heights on a more regular basis in the Champions League, his talent was sufficient to induce approval from most objective Celtic stalwarts.

Rangers had established a 100 per cent record over their Old Firm opponents at the midway point of the campaign, and Smith's success against the principal rivals was, and is, a remarkable feature of Scottish football. I talked to a number of former players asking how he psyched up his teams for these high-octane occasions, and was half expecting to be told that the manager delivered a blood-curdling speech, full of copious references to 1690 and 1916 and 1972, but their response was surprising. One player said:

'Walter knew that we knew the history behind the Old Firm; he knew that we knew the songs and the religious baggage which goes with the territory; but what he didn't have control over was discovering how we would react to the massive pressure which comes with these games, and that was why he would sit us down and chat about it on the Fridays before the match. It wasn't all fire and brimstone, although Archie [Knox] would get us all fired up the closer we got to the kick-off. Walter's method was to tell us quietly, man to man, that Rangers was a club with proud traditions, and that he expected us to go out and perform as previous generations of players had done, for the club, for the supporters, for the honour of being able to play when there were thousands of supporters inside the ground who would have bitten off their right arm to have the same opportunity. And he told us that he wanted all of us to be able to look at ourselves in the mirror at the end, whatever the outcome, and know we had done our very best. Of course he was aware that even the most talented and toughest of individuals can crack in the Old Firm environment, so he tried to make us all feel part of a continuing story, and when I look back it was very, very effective strategy. Because anybody who might have been inclined to get tied up in knots in the countdown to the derby was constantly being reminded that they were part of a big family. And, as we always told each other, families look after each other, whatever is happening.'

That comradeship was one of the admirable facets of Rangers' charge, but controversy was never far away from several players, whether in Goram seeming to lend his endorsement to the UVF on several occasions, or Gascoigne's car-crash existence threatening to spiral out of control in an orgy of excess. There was also a growing campaign by Scotland's other clubs against what they perceived to be the pro-Ibrox bias of many officials operating within the Premier League structure, and that thorny issue reared its head for the third Old Firm meeting, in January 1997. Smith's team had accumulated a near-impregnable lead in the championship, and their rivals arrived at Ibrox knowing that only a victory would suffice, but they were rocked by a stunning Jorg Albertz free-kick. Despite clawing back into contention, they fell 2-1 behind in the 83rd minute when Erik Bo Andersen capitalised on a defensive lapse. Undaunted, the visitors roared back on to the attack, and suddenly Portuguese striker Jorge Cadete latched on to a header deep inside the Rangers' penalty area, and whipped the ball into the net for what would have been a deserved equaliser on the balance of play. But the celebrations were stalled when the stand-side linesman flagged for offside, and Rangers fans bellowed approval. Andersen added his second, and the hosts had one hand on the championship trophy once more. The controversy sprang from the fact that this did not constitute an everyday cock-up by an official. Television pictures proved emphatically that Cadete had been comfortably onside when he had collected the ball, and that he had not strayed offside when he had polished off his shot. Even to the naked eye it looked an awful call, and yet Scotland's two main tabloid newspapers hardly mentioned the incident the following morning. What they did eventually reveal was that the linesman at the centre of the dispute was a Rangers season-ticket holder, who drank in his local masonic club and was a self-confessed 'loyal' fan of the Ibrox organisation. None of which should have come as any great surprise, and yet it sparked a new surge of paranoia among Celtic supporters, some of whom hired a private detective to investigate the origins and backgrounds of those that they suspected of being too favourable to Smith's club.

I remember watching an interview with Walter Smith during that period. He was calmly discussing what it would mean for his players to collect the championship title, and standing next to me a normally quietly-spoken colleague of the Celtic persuasion became increasingly agitated until he could stand Smith's satisfied countenance no longer. 'Ach, awa and f*** yourself,' he shouted at the screen. 'Do you know why your team is so crap in Europe? It's because there are no masons over there to give all the decisions in your favour!' In three sentences this usually rational fellow encapsulated the hysteria that pervades the Old Firm milieu, explaining why the internet is a receptacle for barking-mad conspiracy theories. It's all in there lurking in blue and green cyberspace: rumours of SFA collusion in Celtic punishments, so-called coincidences, whereby a well-known referee will be spotted adjacent to an Old Firm player, rants against political correctness by those who see nothing amiss in wanting to be up to their knees in Fenian blood. And so on. Mercifully, the likes of Smith and Tommy Burns have been able to rise above the ordure which emanates from both sides in forging warm friendships, but anyone who still doubted that Scotland had a distance to travel before it could be regarded as a grown-up country should have been around the hostelries of Glasgow and Lanarkshire in March 1997, when Rangers completed a clean sweep of victories over Celtic with a scrappy, unmemorable 1-0 win, the deadlock broken by Ian Durrant, whose lob reached the net after a mix-up in the Celtic goalmouth. In anyone's language it was a rotten spectacle, but as the victors readied themselves for their celebrations, many Celtic supporters booked holidays specifically so that they could avoid being in their homeland when the ninth league championship in a row was secured.

Rangers' boss kept his counsel and attempted, vainly, to quell some of the triumphalism that had swept over the massed Ibrox ranks. On Wednesday, 7 May a date forever ingrained in the minds of thousands of Rangers acolytes, the team ventured to Tannadice, where a win would seal the championship. His side had been beaten 1-0 there earlier in the season by Dundee United, but in this instance nothing was about to ruin the festivities, and when Laudrup seized the clinching goal with a header, it was the prelude to a spree of gargantuan proportions. It was the early hours of the morning before the players arrived back at Ibrox, but the streets around the ground were jam-packed with thousands of celebrating fans, for whom the prospects of work next day, or the Friday even, would be as remote as the rings of Saturn. They howled for Smith and McCoist, Gough and Laudrup, and gradually the scale of what had been achieved sank in. Smith's principal emotion was to thank his lucky stars that it was all

Left. Starting out: the young Walter Smith soon recognised he was not a world-class footballer, but lacked for nothing in work ethic and determination (*D.C. Thomson*).

Below. Resisting the 'Tic: Smith offered yeoman service for Dundee United in his playing days and here, in the 1974 Scottish Cup final, stems the threat of two Celtic legends David Hay and Kenny Dalglish (*SNS Group*).

Above. The Tannadice Two: Walter Smith and the Dundee United manager, Jim McLean, plot further European success for their flourishing club (*D.C. Thomson*).

Below. A Pair of Greats: Walter Smith joined forces with Alex Ferguson to lead Scotland to the 1986 World Cup finals in Mexico, following the death of Jock Stein. The duo later worked together at Old Trafford (*SNS Group*).

Above. Fire and frost: Graeme Souness and Walter Smith were hugely contrasting personalities, but their partnership sparked a glorious resurgence at Rangers when they joined forces in 1986 (*Newsquest Media Group*).

Below. In the Ibrox tradition: Three of the stalwarts in the history of Rangers FC come together as Walter Smith banters with the club's former manager Jock Wallace and a youthful Ally McCoist joins in the repartee (*Newsquest Media Group*).

Left. No Mo' Blues: He was the most controversial signing in Rangers' history, but Mo Johnston, the former Celtic pin-up boy who crossed the great divide, soon became a hit with the fervent Ibrox support (*Scotsman Publications*).

Above. Pieces of Silver: Walter Smith and Archie Knox, two men with granite in their veins, soon began collecting silverware when they teamed up at Ibrox, winning the domestic treble in 1993 (*Scotsman Publications*).

Below. Smart men: Andy Goram, 'The Goalie', another Rangers hero, who was pivotal to the club's Nine-In-A-Row triumph. Here the men show off the Player of the Year and Manager of the Year awards for the 1992–3 season (*Scotsman Publications*).

Above. Gazza job: Paul Gascoigne was rarely out of the headlines during his time in Glasgow, but although not all the publicity was favourable, few people could deny that he had magic in his boots (*Newsquest Media Group*).

Below. Cheers!: Walter Smith and Archie Knox have often been perceived as being dour characters. But in the heat of the battle, both men relished the thrill of the chase, as witnessed in this dug-out delight (*Newsquest Media Group*).

Opposite. Hammer of the Hoops: A grateful manager embraces Jorg Albertz, an iconic player who often reserved his best for Old Firm derbies. This time he celebrates scoring against Celtic in the 1998 Scottish Cup semi-final (*Scotsman Publications*).

Above. Prize possessions: There were some who claimed that Walter Smith was lucky to enjoy so much success in his first spell at Rangers but his troubled spell at Everton had some high points as the Manager of the Month award attests (*Trinity Mirror plc*).

Below. Tough at the top: Life wasn't always rosy for Smith and Knox as they pursued their careers south of the border. Here, a pensive Smith and Archie Knox show the strains connected with the Liverpool derby (*Trinity Mirror plc*).

Above. Your country needs you!: Walter Smith inherited a mess from Berti Vogts when he became the Scotland manager in 2004. But soon enough, he started to turn things round and make Scottish supporters feel proud of their team again (*SNS Group*).

Below. A new mood: The Scots, under Vogts, had slipped to embarrassing depths in the FIFA rankings. But Smith re-ignited the country's passion and here shares a joke with one of his predecessors, Craig Brown, as Scotland dared to dream again (*SNS Group*).

Above. In Old Firm hands: As Scotland started recording some impressive results, most notably a 1-0 victory over the mighty France at Hampden, the good work done by Smith and his Old Firm confreres, Ally McCoist and Tommy Burns, became obvious (*Newsquest Media Group*).

Below. You CAN go back: Walter Smith was accused by some Scotland fans of betrayal when he quit Scotland to rejoin troubled Rangers. But Smith had always insisted that he desired a return to club management, so the allegations didn't stick (*Newsquest Media Group*).

Left. We've done it! Walter Smith was understandably jubilant after adding another league title – his 10th – to his illustrious cv in May 2011 (*Getty Images*).

Below. Fans for the memories. The Rangers supporters bid a fond farewell to the man who had rescued and revitalised their club (*SNSPix*).

THANK YOU GAFFER

SIR WALTER SMITH - SIMPLY THE BEST

Above. Showered with glory: Walter Smith and his players can finally celebrate after wrapping up their third consecutive SPL title against Kilmarnock (*SNSPix*).

Below. Passing on the torch: Smith enjoys his latest title triumph with Ally McCoist, who knows he has a hard act to follow (*Getty Images*).

over: 'The feeling at the end of the game was relief. Knowing how much it meant to Rangers' supporters, it is something that we will never forget.' Nearby Richard Gough was awash with joy and exhilaration:

> 'I was very emotional. Even my wife commented on it. She said: "I saw you on the TV, and you had tears in your eyes when you received the trophy. You never even cried when I had the kids." But we just had to keep going until we did it. I was injured with about six games to go, but we were playing Celtic, so I said to Walter: "I'll play, because if we beat them, then we'll have won the league." And we won. But then we lost the next three matches, and we had to win one out of our last two games, so we almost took it down to the wire. I can't speak highly enough about the guys and about Walter and Archie and the chairman, and this is one of the greatest moments of my life. And, you know, the boys are legends now.'

That they were, and if critics attempted to raise the European issue, Smith and his charges could afford to shrug off the jibes, not least because no British club in the Champions League in the early 1990s at least came as close to marching to the final as Rangers. My belief is that Smith moulded a side in his image: unprepossessing, wholehearted, occasionally dour and defensive-minded, but prone to flashes of inspiration and panache. Perhaps his Rangers teams would have thrived if they had been allowed to enter some form of British league at their zenith, for no other reason than Smith, akin to Sir Alex Ferguson, understood perfectly the dynamics of the game as it was contested in the UK, where physicality and pace held sway over any aesthetic sensibilities. If it was his and his team's misfortune that their style did not adapt well to Europe, Smith could counter with the retort that Rangers were at least masters on their own patch. For tens of thousands of Ibrox fans who toasted their ninth title, that was quite enough.

CHAPTER TWELVE

Exit Strategy

'Nerves jangled to the accompaniment of
obsessive media coverage'

By the summer of 1997, Walter Smith was exhausted. His methodical approach to management meant that when he was not preparing for important matches, he was studying videos, checking on opponents, fulfilling behind-the-scenes functions which are the lot of any football boss, and committing himself to the intensive media scrutiny which demands a constant approach to fire-fighting and news management. He had been at Ibrox for more than a decade, and as manager he had copped the flak for six years and more, and as he neared his 50th birthday even this most passionate of football adherents was in urgent need of a break from the game. The players noticed it as did David Murray, who was also aware that there was no question of preventing Smith from fronting the Rangers campaigns for another season, particularly the pursuit of an unprecedented 10th consecutive championship. As the season started early on 23 July when the club were involved in a Champions League qualifying tie against the Faroese minnows FC Gotu, a sense of unease hung around Ibrox, exacerbated by the dearth of time afforded the manager as he strove to assemble virtually half a new team in the space of a few weeks.

Possibly recognising that it was no longer sufficient to persist with a largely-Scottish side bolstered by a few guest artists, Smith had signed an Italian quartet made up of Lorenzo Amoruso from Fiorentina, Sergio Porrini from Juventus and Perugian pair Marco Negri and Rino Gattuso, in addition to recruiting Swedish midfielder Jonas Thern, whose previous career had been spent in the main at Napoli and Roma. On the face of it, several of these individuals boasted obvious qualities, and the acquisition of Gattuso, who was considered one of the brightest youngsters in his homeland, hinted at a long-term policy for adapting to the rigours of the Champions League. There is little purpose, though, in spending millions of pounds on new players – the above cost £14m in total – if they are not permitted time to integrate into the existing structure and to find their feet in a new country, whose football philosophy is radically different from the domain of Serie A. Sad to relate, if this was Smith's last throw of the dice, it yielded a pretty dismal return.

European missions had begun to morph into Smith's version of the film *Groundhog Day*. He could change the names on the jerseys and tinker with tactics, but he seemed unable to alter the outcomes. No-one was surprised when Rangers cracked a bundle of goals past ineffectual FC Gotu for an aggregate of 11-0, with McCoist and Durie contributing three goals apiece. While they were able to luxuriate in the role of dominating small fry, it was also no surprise that the team would encounter problems when pitted against Swedish club IFK Goteburg in the second qualifying round. The contrast between the performance of Rangers' strikers when they met second-rate adversaries as opposed to those who belonged in Europe's top tier was conspicuous. Events at the Stadion Ullevi followed the well-worn path for supporters who had kept faith only to behold another demoralising collapse by Rangers, after they had seemed to weather the storm in progressing to half-time without their goals looking especially under threat. Any delusions of adequacy were quashed upon the resumption when the Scandinavian side scored twice in two minutes through Stefan Pettersson and

Par Karlsson. It might have been supposed that Rangers would seek out a precious away goal, but they retreated into their shells apparently unsure whether to strive for containment or to risk being expansive. In the absence of clear guidance from the technical area, the visitors succeeded in conceding a third goal, finished by substitute Peter Eriksson. One could criticise Smith for the second-half slump, and a section of supporters did begin to raise misgivings over what they perceived to be the manager's inflexibility and persistent tactical blundering. This was justified in the circumstances, and the trickle of complaints quickly intensified when Rangers bowed out of the Champions League after drawing 1-1 in the second leg. The tide of frustration turned into a deluge after the club's short-lived sojourn in the UEFA Cup, in which French club Strasbourg, who were struggling in their domestic league, beat the Scottish representatives by 2-1 in both matches, the first of which was notable for Brian Laudrup visibly appealing to Smith to alter his approach. As the jeers increased from the brassed-off support and the media rounded on the management, it must have seemed a long, long time from May to September for those in charge, but if change was required, it would not be rushed.

Murray had resolved that he would not be railroaded by the tabloids or by any interests into implementing precipitate moves, yet the financial implications of his club's latest European fiasco could hardly be ignored. He recognised that Smith was unwell and suffering from the strain of such stalwart service, so the two discussed the situation at the beginning of October, and decided on a compromise. Smith would stay in the job until the end of the 1997–8 season, and his exit would be confirmed at Rangers' annual general meeting later that month. It was not an ideal arrangement, but it confirmed two things: that Murray, despite his reputation as a hard-nosed businessman, could be impelled by motives which, if not sentimental, had less to do with the stock market than ensuring that his long-term ally was not dispatched with indecent haste, and that Smith was not interested in hanging around unless he felt that he could continue to drive Rangers forward. He offered initially to stand down immediately, but that proposal was peremptorily rejected by the chairman. When the agreement was announced on 28 October Smith received a standing ovation from shareholders before he had had an opportunity to speak. He explained, as he struggled to hold back tears, why he considered it best to pave the way for a successor:

'There were pressures on the players which led to difficulties in the European scene. That to me has been a disappointment. However, I felt that a lot of the pressure came from me as the manager and that, after Strasbourg, I was beginning to become a problem with the players. There was a growing sense of anti-climax about the job. Rangers were not given any credit for beating Hearts in the Coca-Cola Cup last year. I went to the press room after the game, and it was like a morgue. There was no sense of achievement. It was: "Oh, they've won it again, now let's get on with it." There was a realisation on my part that things were changing for me. The next day's papers all focused on complaints that a foul had been committed on the halfway line in the build-up to our fourth goal. That had an effect on me. I didn't get any feeling of a great sense of achievement. But I decided to carry on because of Nine in a Row, and what it meant to everybody.

'The expectations of the club became greater with every championship we won, and obviously that led to more pressures. There have been times when I have been through periods of severe criticism in the press. A lot of demands are made on you. There are lots of pressures, but it's the same for the players. In Europe last year [v Auxerre, Grasshoppers and Ajax] I felt that we could have done far better than we did, and I felt there was a lot of pressure placed on the players because of the pressure on me. After the Strasbourg defeat, there was a cry for the manager to leave, and I felt that me being manager was going to create a problem for the playing staff. There is no divine right for any club to be successful, but I do feel that in the next few years we will have the opportunity to play and compete at the highest European level more than we have had so far.

'A new coach will need support. We need to be slightly more tolerant than we have been, and I hope everybody will look at the club in a new light. The fact is that a new coach could lose out early in Europe, and nobody will blame him, and quite rightly in my opinion. We need patience, but I have every confidence that we will succeed.'

The jumble of thoughts was not typical of Walter Smith, but it revealed the conflicting emotions beating in his breast. Denunciation from Rangers' fans had clearly riled him, though he could live with or without the media's views, but he recognised his complicity in the unacceptable string of European results. What may have irked him most was the tacit assumption that any manager could have enjoyed similar success in his position, which was manifestly untrue. When asked later about whether he was aggrieved that his achievements at Rangers had been unfairly overlooked, his reply was illuminating. 'I probably do when I look back on it, but my personality has a bit to do with that. I don't actively seek headlines, and I like to keep myself to myself. But, still . . . 13 trophies in seven years . . . nobody else in modern times has done it, and I am proud of that. Generally, things went pretty well.' Smith was entitled to a spot of self-congratulation, but true to type preferred to leave the tributes to others, and these personalities could speak for themselves. Tommy Burns, the former Celtic manager, struck the right chord in commenting:

'The old cliché will apply, but it will be true. Namely, Rangers won't know what they had in Walter until he's away. In fact the Scottish game won't realise what it had either until he has gone. I do not have the slightest doubt that Walter would be a success if he moved to England. I sincerely hope that he has not grown too disillusioned with the game, because he has what it takes. He has shown that repeatedly, and while figures like Alex Ferguson are exceptional, Walter Smith could come down here and do something similar.

'The truth is that I have never had anything other than total respect for Walter. I always held him in the highest esteem, because he knew what managing a club of Rangers' size was all about. He always conducted himself with dignity, especially when he was living with the added pressure of trying for nine in a row. And I always felt comfortable and safe whenever I was in his company. That for me was a true measure of the man. Even though he won nine titles in a row, Walter still found himself under pressure if he lost a few games. That's very tough to deal with, but he has handled himself marvellously throughout the years. So no-one should ever undervalue what he has done, and even though he was able to spend a lot of money, there was much more to it than that.'

As for chairman Murray, his words reflected the relationship that he had established with Smith over a decade, but also indicated that whatever the desires of the fans, he was not obsessed with amassing records for records' sake. His priority lay in making the correct appointment, and if that meant missing out on a tenth championship, he was sanguine about the prospect:

'I will work closely with Walter to find the right manager. We are looking at someone who will be northern European and certainly English speaking, and it would be beneficial if the new manager could settle in during the last couple of months of Walter's reign. We aim to be properly focused and move towards a future, which I am convinced will be bright. There will be changes because we have to move with the times, and these changes mean there will be no more bouts of indiscipline at the club. I couldn't believe the standing ovation Walter got at the AGM. I have never heard anything like it. It was very emotional, and I have to admit that I had a tear in my eye. Walter feels he needs a change in his life, and we respect that entirely. He is one of the greatest managers Rangers have ever had.'

The words about indiscipline point to Murray's exasperation at the fashion in which Rangers players were as likely to feature on the front pages of Scotland's newspapers as in the sports sections. There was a spat in a kebab shop involving Ian Durrant and Derek Ferguson, which also involved the constabulary; Andy Goram blundered into murky sectarian waters when he agreed to switch on the Christmas lights in Belfast's Shankill Road, and subsequently sparked fury by allegedly wearing a black armband in honour of the UVF terrorist Billy Wright; as for Paul Gascoigne, whose marriage to Sheryl had ended with sensational stories involving wife-beating and drunkenness, the disintegrating player was caught mimicking playing the flute, a ubiquitous instrument in Orange walks, in front of Celtic's supporters. There were few depths left to plummet. It might seem strange that all this, and more, transpired under Smith's stewardship, but there again the manager was a disciplined figure in a rock-solid marriage, who stuck to his own limits when it came to socialising, and refused to be a nursemaid for adult players. This did not mean that he ignored responsibilities, but acknowledges that Smith had a hundred chores to attend to on a day-to-day basis, and he could not be expected to issue curfews to his stars, particularly when so many of them were injured for sustained periods between 1995 and '97. The fact that most of his leading personalities, including Goram, McCoist, Hateley and Gascoigne, were sidelined for months at a time allowed them to be out of sight, if not of mind, and it is a dangerous situation when young men consumed with self-pity seek refuge in alcohol and decide to pour out their hearts to the nearest football groupie.

❖

In the aftermath of Smith's declaration at the annual meeting it appeared that he would be offered another post at Ibrox, and for a few days at least the club was a haven of sweetness and light. Having thanked his players for their efforts prior to delivering a paean to Murray, Smith paid homage to his back-room staff in terms which explain why, wherever he has ventured, Archie Knox has rarely been far behind: 'The boys in the coaching room have been fantastic, and it hurts me a bit when they are criticised for their efforts, as none of them could possibly have given any more. Archie could have been an outstanding manager in his own right and has loved being here, while the rest of the staff have been wonderful, and have contributed greatly to our success.' It was patently the end of an era, and Smith emphasised how much he was moved by the spontaneous applause that he had received at the AGM:

> 'Of all the things that have happened to me during my time here, that ovation before I spoke was probably the best of them all. It was totally unexpected. As a manager you often feel alone in the middle of it all, and it is easy for people to criticise what you are doing. But without a doubt that ovation was the best thing that has ever happened to me, and it was very difficult to start talking afterwards. I couldn't believe what the shareholders did, and I will always be grateful to them.'

The search for his replacement commenced with the media speculating on the appointment of, say, Kenny Dalglish, Bobby Robson, George Graham or Terry Venables, disregarding Murray's insistence that he was looking to Europe for Smith's successor. As the hype intensified, many so-called exclusives amounted to nothing more than a journalist phoning a name and asking if he was interested in the job; if the answer was anything but a blanket refusal, the story would be turned on its head and appear under a headline similar to 'Rangers Swoop for X'. Eventually tiring of some of the more ludicrous suggestions,

David Murray agreed to conduct an interview with BBC Scotland, telling viewers:

'Walter has had far too much to do. It was unrealistic, and the guy badly needs a break. What's more, the days of the football manager as we have come to know it, doing everything, are gone. We are looking for a coach as opposed to a manager. There is a football side to the job and a business side to the job, so we will do exactly that. The coach's job is a massive job in itself.

'I have read with interest several newspaper stories linking the likes of Dalglish, Graham and Robson with the Rangers job. Now that gets these names out of the way, and we can get on with things. Basically we need a top-class first-team coach, someone who has a proven track record in Europe, someone who has done it. But you can rest assured that we will have the new coach well in place by the end of the season to give him and Walter as long as possible together before the new coach takes over completely.

'Walter will be very much involved in the process of finding the new coach, and there is no doubt that we need continuity with the coaching. Walter was recently away for a couple of days looking for players, and that meant two days where he was away from his own players and the coaching. We can't have that. We want the coach to identify the players he wants, and then it will be up to a chief executive or myself to take the negotiations forward.'

Most of these discussions seemed to assume that Smith would carry on in some capacity at Ibrox, yet those who watched Smith and Knox for the remainder of the season had no doubts that they would not be outstaying their welcome. One such evening at the old and dilapidated Brockville Park was witnessed by a Falkirk supporter, Robbie Strang, and he related his memories of how the Smith regime sputtered towards its close. 'It wasn't a good night. The rain was pouring down, and the wind was howling, so you wouldn't have anticipated Smith and Knox being in the best of moods. But their shoulders were slumped, they both looked absolutely knackered, and the expression on their faces screamed the message: "We would rather be anywhere else than here!" It was pretty clear that some of their older players were either reaching the end of the road [Durrant, McCoist] or were on the verge of being moved on elsewhere [Goram, Gascoigne] and although their fans chanted "Nine in a Row" every so often, even the majority of them seemed to appreciate that it wasn't going to be ten titles, given the upheaval around Rangers at that stage. My own belief is that the team had shot its bolt, and perhaps the axe should have been wielded a bit sooner by David Murray, because once you have announced that somebody is leaving a job but is not actually exiting for the best part of seven months, he is dead in the water.' Such a verdict might be considered slightly harsh, considering the manner in which the Premier League race developed into a white-knuckle ride before the outcome was resolved at the start of May. As for the Old Firm derbies, Richard Gough's goal settled the first meeting and Marco Negri secured a draw for his team at Celtic Park. Something rather arthritic was noted about Rangers' display on 2 January and Laudrup was correct to observe that Celtic 'were just hungrier than us today' as his side slumped to a 2-0 reverse. And yet there was nothing between the clubs when they met again in the final league fixture of the season at Ibrox on 12 April.

The force was with Smith's line-up on the day. They had eliminated Celtic from the Scottish Cup the previous weekend, and they had recorded five consecutive victories as they prepared for battle, a pattern that was maintained in a furious struggle. The visitors enjoyed most of the territorial advantage in the opening quarter, but could not break through; then Jonas Thern produced a magnificent 30-yard strike which flashed past Jonathan Gould in the Celtic goals. Smith's men held a vital advantage which they did not relinquish. This was vintage Rangers, a throwback to the days when they had toyed with opponents, and Jorg Albertz, who was at the centre of the action, sealed the spoils with a goal in the

66th minute. This left the Old Firm rivals locked on 66 points each with four games to go, but Rangers boasted a superior goal difference and were clearly on a roll. No. 10? Surely! That assumption might have been justified if Smith had been presented with the option of tackling Celtic over the course of these matches, but a minefield of awkward games had to be negotiated instead. Nerves jangled to the accompaniment of obsessive media coverage reflecting views from both sides of the great divide as if the issue was as important as the Middle East conflict, and the scope for mishaps grew. Celtic were first into the fray on the weekend of 18/19 April and beat Motherwell emphatically by 4-1, which meant that Rangers had to travel to one of their bogey grounds, Pittodrie, to eke out a win. In a contest which demanded discipline and precision, the Glasgow club missed several fine chances and paid the price as Aberdeen edged home by the only goal, which handed the initiative back to Celtic. The following week Rangers weighed in by trouncing Hearts 3-0 at Tynecastle, which added fuel to the fire of conspiracy theorists who claimed that the Edinburgh side would lie down to Rangers when required; Celtic could only draw 0-0 against Hibernian. Pulsating stuff. On 2 May, as pressure on both teams reached absurd proportions, Rangers hosted Kilmarnock and their striking profligacy again let them down as the well-organised and efficient visitors silenced the stadium by orchestrating a 1-0 success, which even with news of Celtic's 1-1 draw with Dunfermline dealt a severe blow to hopes for Ten in a Row. The scenario was now straightforward: Rangers had to win their final match away to Dundee United, and hope that Celtic would come unstuck at home against St Johnstone. Smith was on the verge of departing Ibrox and knew that he would be remembered as a Rangers hero whatever occurred on 9 May, but nagging away was the question: is there room in the script for one more shock? Celtic soon made sure that their own script would go according to plan with a 2-0 triumph that rendered Rangers' 2-1 success irrelevant. So near, but blue-garbed fans reflected that matches which their team had strolled through in previous seasons had now become difficult exercises, and where once the likes of McCoist could taunt opponents, now it was as though he was running into a stiff breeze. Hence the need for a new Rangers coach.

One last date remained on Smith's calendar, 16 May, which brought the opportunity to mark his farewell from Ibrox by winning the Scottish Cup final against Heart of Midlothian. Two years previously, Brian Laudrup had been in devastating form as Smith's side thrashed the Edinburgh club, and it was predictable that Rangers were overflowing with sentiment along the lines of 'We'll do it for Wattie' as they headed to Celtic Park, though the departing manager would take nothing for granted. Hearts were awarded a contentious penalty by referee Willie Young, which was calmly converted by Colin Cameron . . . with fewer than 90 seconds on the clock. Thereafter came a series of vignettes rather than a full-scale performance from Rangers. McCoist at 35 was still capable of precipitating panic within opposition ranks, but the parts did not add up to a convincing whole, and the Ibrox men seemed down and out when Stephane Adam scored for Hearts early in the second half. Rangers launched a sustained offensive, as if recalling their lines from memory, and Gilles Rousset was forced into a couple of excellent saves before McCoist struck with seven minutes remaining. It was a cracking contest, but it finished as it had begun with thousands of Rangers fans screaming derision and disgust at Young after McCoist was denied what seemed a certain penalty, the official decreeing that he had been pulled down outside the penalty area. Laudrup's ensuing free-kick drifted wide, and despite a lengthy stretch of extra-time, Jim Jefferies' team hung on for a victory which was well merited over the piece.

Smith was dignified in the aftermath and congratulated Hearts on their success, praising the improvements that they had made in the previous two seasons. As he soaked up what he must have envisaged would be a last hurrah from the Ibrox support, he refused to hang around and gatecrash the winners' parade. It was not the result that he had desired, nor had the season unfolded as planned, but no individual in football who achieves 13 trophies in seven years can be adjudged to be a failure. Though weary of fighting the good fight, Smith had only recently turned 50, and other battles would ensue and other disappointments would need to be endured. For the moment, though, he could afford a wry smile of semi-satisfaction, for was that not the cry 'Walter, Walter' ringing out from the blue-and-white ranks encamped around the stadium? Not bad for a Rangers man who had stood amid the throng 40 years earlier.

CHAPTER THIRTEEN

BAD TIMES AT GOODISON

'The voices of doom were in full cry on the Mersey'

After he left Rangers, Walter Smith was able to relax on holiday and to spend time with his family and to catch up with Iron Maiden, Bon Jovi and other choice selections from his rock collection. But considering his exploits in Scottish football and the high esteem in which he was held by Alex Ferguson, Kenny Dalglish and other prestigious names in the English Premiership, it could only be a matter of time before he was persuaded to dip his toe into the water in England. Would he go to the right place, a setting in which he would be allowed appropriate amounts of money and time to forge the camaraderie which had been one of his priceless assets at Ibrox? Critics who believed that his success had been due to David Murray's financial clout would not be slow to pounce if he walked into a high-profile post south of the Border and fell flat on his face. Any job offer can look attractive, though, if it happens to include false promises. Everton was where he chose to pledge his future, despite the fact that the Goodison Park club had been routinely lacklustre for a long time. The Liverpool club were not the first prospective employers to contact him, for Sheffield Wednesday had made an initial approach; but Smith was tempted away from entertaining Hillsborough's offer by promises made to him by the Everton chairman, hamper tycoon Peter Johnson, which were never delivered. The problems stacked up almost from the outset, according to BBC football writer Phil McNulty:

'Johnson had said there would be massive transfer funds and unlimited ambition. Walter was given money to spend, and invested it wisely on the then unknown midfielder Olivier Dacourt, and the Scotland and Monaco star John Collins. But Smith was then stunned to discover that his brave new world was being financed by money which Everton didn't actually have. The banks were banging on the door, the club were facing a financial crisis, and Smith was shown the signpost towards future mediocrity when terrace idol Duncan Ferguson was sold to Newcastle United behind his back by a desperate Johnson, who needed to raise quick cash. Goodison folklore even has it that Smith's wife Ethel knew about the Ferguson deal before her husband did, because he was otherwise engaged preparing for a game. Smith was tempted to quit, but it was Johnson who left and opened the door for [theatre impresario] Bill Kenwright to fulfil his dream of owning Everton, and the new chairman immediately handed Smith an extended contract – but some people called it a longer sentence.'

It did not require much study by Smith to realise that he was in a precarious position almost from the off. What should not be forgotten is that he had arrived at a club who had only narrowly avoided relegation under Howard Kendall, because their goal difference was superior to that of Bolton Wanderers, and prompted by Johnson any manager might have been captivated at the prospect of launching a renaissance for the other Merseyside organisation. Yet so much of what Smith had to deal with involved cost-cutting, entrenchment, seeking bargain-basement buys and resorting to purchasing senior players who were well beyond their prime. He assessed the situation from a clinical perspective, in hindsight:

'My time in the Premiership helped me as an international manager, because it showed the necessity of stability. We had 86 transfers in three-and-a-half years at Goodison. I never had a team which was mine. I signed [Marco] Materazzi and [Olivier] Dacourt when they were young. I signed [Thomas] Gravesen. But when Peter Johnson put the club up for sale, the bank said we had to start selling players. So I began my second season with 38-year-old and 39-year-old centre-halves Dave Watson and Richard Gough. If anybody thinks that was through choice . . . and it wasn't their choice either. I have to be honest when I look back and say that I made a number of errors, but . . . signing David Ginola, Paul Gascoigne, that wasn't the way that I wanted it. I was fire-fighting. And I'm sorry that was the case, because it's a great club with a fantastic following.'

Despite the friendship which blossomed between Smith and Kenwright, money was in short supply, and the Premiership was not meant to support charity cases, especially as Manchester United, Arsenal and Liverpool were threatening to pull away from the rest of the opposition. Yet one feels that Smith, with the knowledge that he had accrued from his spell at Dundee United, should have been rather more adept in the transfer market, particularly given his renewed links with Archie Knox. I ventured down to the club to speak to the two men on a Thursday in the winter of 1999, and they were courteous, good humoured and clearly relishing the chance to avoid the suit-and-tie appearance which was demanded at Ibrox. What was missing, though, was any sense that they were in the job for the long haul or that they genuinely believed they could drag Everton out of the bottom half of the division. Smith, probably realistically, had set his sights on the lowish side: 'The same rules always apply: you have to strive your utmost, even though your level of ambitions may be different at a club such as Everton. There wasn't going to be a situation where you would be aiming to beat Manchester United every week. But there was no reason why we couldn't accept the challenge to be as good as we could be.' A practical approach perhaps, but it was hardly designed to win over the supporters, and this helped to explain the antipathy which gradually increased between the Scot and a section of Everton's fan base, who saw him as dour, uncommunicative and set in his ways. By contrast, those followers who met the manager spoke of his warmth, sense of humour and restlessness at being unable to provide the punters with a squad that could mount a sustained championship challenge.

Alan Nixon wrote in *The Independent* newspaper:

'His desire for stability at Everton was ultimately undermined by his own lack of achievement. The manager who came south of the Border with silverware-strewn credentials from his time at Rangers took his time to sort out the squad he inherited, made some poor signings, fell out with too many players and was betrayed by some of the club's biggest earners. Duncan Ferguson's return was a catastrophe, Paul Gascoigne's high-profile capture a sad sham and the deal for David Ginola a badly-judged investment. When Bill Kenwright backed Smith with cash recently, he signed three midfield players when the side cried out for a striker. Smith is a genuinely nice man, perceived as dour for his interview style, but sociable away from football and with a dry sense of humour. Once, after I had written that he was considering quitting, we met in an Italian restaurant and rather than rant, he was warm and amusing. When asked how close the trattoria was to his home, he replied with a grin: "I just rent up the road. Of course, I won't be staying." '

And he did not lay down residential roots on Merseyside, as if indicating that his tenancy was destined to be brief.

It was surprising in some respects that he lasted as long as he did. Everton were humiliated 3-0 in the fourth round of the FA Cup at the end of January 2001, and a group of fans immediately called for his removal. Rumours of dissent in the dressing room were circulating as were allegations that he could not motivate some of his star performers, and Smith went on the counter-attack:

'If the players were not trying hard enough and the lack of passion was a recurring theme, only one man is to blame, and that is the manager. If that's the case, he should be sacked. A lot of things have happened over the period where we have been dogged with an inconsistency, and that is something that has never been more prevalent than this season. We have had a huge turnover of staff and we have had constant chopping and changing in terms of team selection almost since I arrived here, so it has not been an easy situation for anybody. But listen, you have to remain optimistic in football, because if you can't be optimistic then you shouldn't be in the job. So while our battle to push the club into a good position is still ongoing, hopefully we can do that in the future.'

Smith kept tinkering with his formations and recruiting new personnel, the abiding impression being of a conveyor belt of itinerants passing through Goodison rather than a team being created gradually. By March of 2002 the voices of doom were in full cry on the Mersey, with justification, as their heroes had managed but one win in their past 13 league matches. The final straw came on 10 March when they were bundled out of the FA Cup 3-0 by Middlesbrough, almost without a whimper of defiance. Kenwright's face told the story – he recognised that the axe must fall, but he hated having to sharpen the blade. There was no alternative, and within 48 hours Smith had been sacked for the first time in his career, unemployed at the age of 54. 'I think after nearly four years working at Everton, there is bound to be a painful feeling on the morning after you learn you have to leave,' he reflected. 'I think every manager faces the possibility of being asked to leave, but you hope it doesn't happen to you. But it has happened, and I just have to face up to that." He pointedly refused to use the word sacked or dismissed, which hold dishonourable connotations for a person who had grown up in an industrial heartland. 'At this stage it is very difficult to say that I have enjoyed being here. There have been highs and lows, there have been lots of good things and a lot of things I have enjoyed during my time here. It hasn't been easy, but overall you feel a sense of frustration, coupled with a level of disappointment.' Kenwright's regret could hardly have been more evident: 'The difficulty here was the finality of ending a working relationship with someone who, on a level of integrity, stability and honesty, is as fine a human being as I have ever been associated with. We made the decision which we felt was right, and he took the news like the true man of honour that he is. In fact, Walter was absolutely extraordinary, because he ended up talking about trying to be helpful for the future of the club. It has been a privilege to work with him during the last three years.'

Smith's spell in the Premiership must be judged as a failure. He failed to pull Everton out of the bottom half of the division, and they were in danger of being relegated when he was replaced by the more youthful David Moyes, who responded with diligence and guided Everton to the safe haven of 15th place: the club grew stronger with each season thereafter. It sums up the essential decency of Smith that even his detractors could not accuse him of being anything other than honest and committed in his dealings with players, supporters and administrators. 'Perhaps I made a slight error in picking Everton, in that it was the right club, but not the right time,' he said. 'I wouldn't make that mistake again.' Where would he go next? His analytical skills made him a personable television pundit, but there was no great urgency to manage again if the circumstances were not right. At least until he heard the Tartan Army wailing in the style of the First World War recruitment slogan: 'Your Country Needs You'.

CHAPTER FOURTEEN

REVIVING THE THISTLE

'Everybody is happy to join up with the Scotland squad now'

As Walter Smith's life moved into 2004, it resembled that of a resting leading actor with ample finances earning interest in the bank. He had been released from the irksome task of having to deal with agents and reporters on a regular basis, could spend as much time as he desired with his family, and attend to business at his Glasgow hostelry The Rosevale. He could fit in rounds of golf whenever it suited him and his coterie of former players and managerial contacts, and even develop an interest in gardening. But an individual such as Smith was never likely to be content with bowing out quietly from football, and if he did not actively seek employment, he kept his finger on the pulse. He watched aghast the decline of his country's team under Berti Vogts, and maintained lines of communication with senior figures in the game. It was with a slight sense of incredulity, however, that Smith received a telephone call one morning early in March from the Manchester United manager Sir Alex Ferguson, asking whether he would be interested in travelling to Old Trafford and working as his assistant for the remainder of the Premiership season. He would be filling the shoes of Carlos Queiroz, who had departed previously for Real Madrid. Smith declared that this was not the sort of invitation that any person in soccer refused, and though the invitation 'felt like something out of a movie', he had barely informed his wife before he was heading down to join his Glaswegian friend: 'The chance to come to Manchester United was something that I couldn't turn down. There are few bigger challenges in football than helping a successful side sustain their achievements. I have huge admiration for what Sir Alex has achieved at United, and I am excited to be a part of it.' He knew in advance that his stint would be a short one, and he recognised that Ferguson's team had suffered an unexpectedly difficult season, but that was immaterial. As the tracksuit was pulled on again in readiness for dealing with players of the calibre of Ruud van Nistelrooy, Ryan Giggs and Paul Scholes, he felt refreshed and back on the beat where he belonged, even if the scale of the Premiership club's resources took him aback:

'It was incredible, even after everything which I had been party to in the game. It wasn't just the 67,000 people at every home match and the worldwide fan base, where you received constant reminders of being way in excess of what is attached to any other club, but I also wasn't prepared for the demands placed on the players. Everyone wanted a piece of them. All the time. I knew what I was brought there to do, and I would like to think that I justified the faith shown in me by Sir Alex. In my opinion, to judge United on this season is to take their achievements out of context. In the past 11 years they have had a third-placed finish, but in winning eight titles in that time they have never failed to claim the championship in back-to-back seasons, and that is a marvellous record by anybody's standards. In fact before I came here I always considered that Sir Alex was one of the best managers the British game has produced. But now after seeing him at close quarters in a club environment, seeing how he pulls together the vast number of strands of the job, I know he is the best.'

After his brief spell at Old Trafford Smith's return to the footballing mainstream with the Scottish national side thrilled not only the man himself, but the frazzled onlookers who followed the team's relentless slide down the FIFA world rankings to the high 80s, which was below Burkina Faso and Syria. A cottage industry of grim humour was up and running (*If the Scots couldn't do well against Iceland, they could arrange fixtures with Tesco and Asda*) as a demoralised group of individuals found confidence draining away with every fiasco against the Faroes or mess-up in Moldova. Though Smith became an obvious candidate to replace the ineffectual Vogts, he was far too diplomatic and mindful of his own experiences to be seen actively touting for the post. His response to inquiries: 'Taking charge of your country would appeal to the majority of managers, but I don't think that it helps the man currently in the position to talk of replacements. I had to deal with this when I was at Everton and to a degree at Rangers, and I feel for others who find themselves in the same circumstances.' The clamour only heightened in the months ahead, and though some criticism of Vogts may have been excessive, with whiffs of xenophobia surrounding several columns written in his denunciation, it was absurd to hear a few Scottish players complain that there was a language problem with the German manager, considering that one or two of them could hardly string a couple of coherent sentences together. Vogts' deficiencies were self-evident: he lost the media, lost the Tartan Army and lost to most of the minnows in Europe, or so it appeared, and the outcome was inevitable as 2004 neared its end. Alternatives to Smith were limited, not least because he was available at short notice and seemed ideally equipped for the job of Scotland manager. The expected dismissal of Vogts and appointment of Smith, confirmed on 2 December were greeted with a mixture of delight and relief. Craig Brown commented:

'This is terrific for Scotland, and it will be applauded by the media, all the supporters and the players, who will realise they have got a great manager. His main quality is his coaching ability backed up by excellent man-management. I don't know a single player who says anything other than that Walter is outstanding, and he will definitely change things for the better and gain a positive response from the players.'

The view of the ex-national manager was echoed by former Scotland internationalist Gordon McQueen, who touched on one of the key attributes which Smith would instil in his men – the belief that while miracles happen rarely in sport, they were always possible in the febrile sphere of football:

'We have the most optimistic supporters in the world, but at this moment in time even the Tartan Army has lost confidence in the side. I think he has got to win the fans back and do things that Berti wasn't doing, and I have every confidence in his abilities, because he has seen it all before. The great thing about this job as well is that he will have the whole nation behind him.'

During the first weeks in charge, Smith sought to reinforce that impression by asking the former Celtic manager Tommy Burns to work with him, and persuading his old Ibrox comrade Ally McCoist to bring his enthusiasm and ebullience to the Scotland hierarchy. These appointments earned him popular acclaim, as did the positive front that he immediately displayed towards press and broadcast representatives, many of whom had felt ostracised by Vogts. 'Media-wise you need experience,' he said. 'We have a population of only five million in Scotland, yet we have more newsprint than England, more national dailies than England. So part of handling any situation in Scotland is handling the media, and Martin O'Neill did that brilliantly when he was at Celtic. Now when I took over, the Scotland players had been threatening a boycott of the media because of the level of criticism they had been getting. That isn't the way to go. And as an experienced manager, I was able to come in and point that out to them.' He also sought to engender good relations with the clubs by trimming the excessive number of friendly fixtures which had been orga-nised by Vogts. Friendlies were the bane of a club manager's life, according to Smith, and his methodology was clear. There would be a cessation of internationals organised simply to bring money into the SFA or Sky TV's coffers, and he would concentrate on establishing a scenario where every match was invested with significance. When Smith had stepped into the role, Scotland's prospects of qualifying for the 2006 World Cup were slight, but he was focusing on the wider picture, which meant that no player was ruled out of contention, and these included exponents who had retired prematurely in despair over the chaos which had permeated the previous regime. He quickly assembled his first squad, and delivered an honest assessment of his priorities to the players in the affluent surroundings of Mottram Hall in rural Cheshire, where he had linked up with Burns and McCoist. As usual there was no soft soap or flannel, but a lucid exposition of where everybody stood in his plans:

'I felt it was more important to get these lads together to outline the future than to play a match at this stage, because it is a matter of urgency that we reduce the number of call-offs the Scotland squad has been suffering over the years. We had our first talk last night, and I told these players that I thought they were the ones who should represent their country. But I also emphasised that they would all have to show willingness to come along whenever they are selected. It's a question of achieving a club mentality with an international squad, and you can't do that if players keep failing to turn up.

'Some aspects of the previous regime had to be adjusted. There were some poor results in friendly matches. This led to a poor spirit amongst the players, and the heavy criticism they took over their performances and results proved to be demotivating. So we need to address how many games we tackle. As things stand we are insisting that players join us when selected, but we have to create an environment where they are keen to be involved. It's part of the first step of the process, which is to regain a little respectability in terms of everybody's view of the national team.

Hopefully that will lead on to improved results, because my goal is exactly the same as that of any other international manager – to help steer the team to qualification for European Championships and World Cups.

'I know that it will not happen overnight. But equally we don't have time for boys. Whoever comes into the team will have to stand up and be counted straight away. Younger players have no time, in the same way that the manager has no time. It might be hard on them, because international football is a difficult arena in which to gain the necessary level of experience, but that's the situation we are in at the moment.'

Smith's debut game as manager came in March against Italy, who were heading towards being crowned kings of the world. It was a tough proposition in the forbidding setting of the San Siro in Milan, and considering the limitations in resources at his disposal. It is instructive to examine the footballers that he selected to confront the Italians. There was no sign of a Baxter or a John-stone, a Law or Dalglish: this was a functional group of hard-working individuals who were being asked to shoulder a nation's expectations. The line-up that started comprised Rab Douglas, Jackie McNamara, Steven Pressley, David Weir, Gary Naysmith, Gary Caldwell, Paul Hartley, Barry Ferguson, Nigel Quashie, Lee McCulloch and Kenny Miller. On the bench sat Craig Gordon, Neil McCann, Andy Webster, Brian O'Neil, Stevie Crawford, Garry O'Connor and Russell Anderson. Smith declared in advance that the performance was more important than the result, and that he wanted his men to be disciplined and strong-minded and prepared to chase every single tackle for 90 minutes. It may not have sounded like an aesthetically-pleasing formula, but Smith had few options when pitted against opponents who were world class in most positions, and if the Scots had to resort to being honest artisans, so be it. The most-capped player in their ranks was David Weir, who was back after a 30-month absence, and at the other end of the spectrum the wide midfielders

McCulloch and Hartley had amassed four minutes of international experience between them. The visitors' aspirations may have extended no further than exorcising the spectre of recent drubbings – 5-0 versus France, 6-0 against the Netherlands – but the Scots at least performed with the gritty resilience which can be anticipated from teams under Smith's tutelage. They blocked their opponents and disrupted their attempts to ease into a silky passing game, their energy and industry beyond reproach. After AC Milan defender Andrea Pirlo had swept a resplendent free-kick past Douglas after 34 minutes, and the stricken goalkeeper had to leave the field, still Scotland scrapped and snapped at their rivals' heels. If the Tartan Army did not have many thrills served up in attack, the majority realised that this was a night for consolidation and composure, and they roared their approval on every occasion that McCulloch or Weir or another Scot stifled the threat of Totti, Gattuso or Pirlo.

Smith looked on with an appreciation of the qualities of the hosts – 'They will be up there with the best at the World Cup next year,' he noted presciently – and with obvious pride considering the robust display from Scotland, who showed tenacity in greater measure as the contest progressed without looking capable of redressing the balance in goals. There were occasional moments to savour with Quashie latching on to a Miller flick which forced the Italian goalkeeper Gianluigi Buffon to parry the ball narrowly past his post, and Miller being released by Barry Ferguson for a run through on Buffon, which should have asked more of the keeper: Miller was able only to muster a stabbed shot that was comfortably saved. These shafts of menace were encouraging, because Scotland's recent efforts at posing a striking threat in their Group 5 fixtures had been thoroughly unconvincing. As the game approached its climax, one or two hopeful Scottish supporters started to harbour hopes of a late goal and a memorable outcome, but it was the Italians who scored in the 84th minute when the peerless Pirlo profited from a rare Miller transgression with another masterly free-kick, which he drove past the diving

Craig Gordon. A 2-0 score probably better reflected the gulf between the combatants, but Smith's side had soaked up considerable pressure and handled the occasion well enough for the press to be fairly appreciative of their efforts. The verdict of *The Sunday Herald* was typical of the tone. 'Losing by just a couple of goals represented a precious return to some form of respectability,' wrote the estimable Michael Grant. 'Without getting too excited about what was no more than a stuffy, dogged performance, Scotland at least showed an ability to compete with clearly superior opponents, and this is a time to be grateful for small mercies.' Smith had never been under any illusions that this was a long-term project with a limited squad, and though talented youngsters were emerging from within the SPL, he would have to grow accustomed to perspiration rather than stardust.

A sprinkling of green shoots of recovery had been witnessed in Italy, and the consequence was a capacity crowd at Hampden Park for Smith's next match, a World Cup qualifier against Moldova at the beginning of June. This was a chance for the Scots to recompense fans for the dreadful display that they had served up when the sides had met towards the end of the previous year. Despite the reveries harboured by the Tartan Army that a renaissance was underway, Smith remained cautious and mindful of the dangers of meeting east European opponents and underestimating their abilities. Other managers might have reacted angrily to the words of the Moldovan coach Victor Pasulko, who ventured to suggest that the Scots were no better than his own side and had no outstanding talent, but Smith was canny enough to respond in measured tones:

'It is a realistic appraisal on his part. We drew over there, and in their home game with Norway they drew and we lost, so he has every right to say what he has said, but now we want to show him a different Scotland side, and prove him wrong. He's not out of order in his comments, but it is up to us to change his opinion. We have to take responsibility for giving the fans something to shout about, and I have said as much to the players. What I am looking for is consistently improving displays. If we get them, the results will follow, but we must achieve a good standard, especially when in possession of the ball. Moldova have set out their stall to be defensive even in home matches – that is the way they play; good luck to them – and the onus is on us to counter that tactic and impose ourselves on the game. But I am not expecting it to be easy.'

His suspicions were well-founded. Scotland were cheered on the turf as if they were conquering heroes, but were by no means convincing for much of the occasion, and their opponents belied their negative reputation with a series of fine attacking moves which, with the benefit of cooler heads, might have granted them the lead. There was even that unnerving sound of mass murmuring at Hampden, denoting the crowd's grumbling or fears, or both, over what they were watching. A blank score-sheet after 45 minutes was not what they had envisaged. Smith refused to flap, and the introduction of Christian Dailly and James McFadden eventually paid dividends as both scored goals. The visitors were eager opponents, constant thorns in the flesh and bones of the Scottish defence, so the 2-0 victory represented a minor success in the grand scheme of things, and Smith was quick to embrace Pasulko when play ceased, as if to tell him: 'You were right.' Given the horrors which had induced a deathly pallor among Scottish followers in 2003 and '04, any victory was to be savoured, and it helped to lift Scotland off the bottom rung of the group table. When they gained a no-scoring draw against Belarus in Minsk a few days later, the signs were definite of solidity returning to the ranks. A record of played 3, won 1, lost 1, drawn 1 was hardly the stuff of legends, but Smith was warming to his national task, and Burns and McCoist had slotted into their berths with the harmony which can prove so productive between Old Firm protagonists. Smith dealt out praise all round:

'The reaction from my players, every single one of them, has been fantastic, and while we have only got them for a short period of time before every match, we have worked hard to build up a good atmosphere, and there is definitely a buzz now. The back-room staff are a big part of that, and Tommy and Ally have been tremendous. I got Ally involved because I'd had him as a player, and I knew he was one of those lads with a personality that can lift any room and body of people, and he has done that.

'Everybody is happy to join up with the Scotland squad now, which was maybe not always the case in the last couple of years when there was a lot of despondency. Now we have a decent level of intensity on the training pitch, and more importantly we now have get-togethers where we talk, play golf and have a couple of drinks. It has worked very well, and we have moved forward. But clearly there is still a long way to go.'

The Scottish mood had changed dramatically. Where once it had appeared that their team's World Cup dream would have to wait until the next qualifying campaign, a rising tide of confidence envisaged Scotland fighting back into contention despite a hazard-laden fixture schedule in the autumn, with trips to Norway and Slovenia and the return meeting with Italy. The Tartan Army tend to be a volatile unit, and in detecting renewed reserves of discipline and desire in the side's efforts under Smith, it was only a short step to imagining that they could start making tentative travel plans for Germany 2006 the following summer. Come September the Scots prepared to entertain the Italians in a match from which tangible reward was required if Smith's men hoped to prolong their involvement in qualification. The fans knew what to expect from the bold Walter and his players, and his sensible approach to making the best of his raw material simply added to the unity between the players and their acolytes. Marcello Lippi, the cerebral Italian coach, recognised that it would not be sensible for his compatriots to indulge in an overly-sophisticated game plan and plumped for the towering front pairing of Christian Vieri and Vicenzo Iaquinta with the imposing if ageing presence of Francesco Totti set behind the duo. Smith and Scotland were undaunted, and as *The Glaswegian* paper commented: 'These are the kind of days you dream about.' For long stretches of the game the Tartan Army were able to wallow in what-could-be after Kenny Miller scored with a 12th-minute header, which vamped up the atmosphere into a frenzy of nationalistic fervour. What made Miller's contribution all the more critical was the fact that he was the only fit first-choice striker available to Smith, which cast the Wolverhampton Wanderers player in a lone role in front of a four-man midfield of Barry Ferguson, Darren Fletcher, Paul Hartley and Nigel Quashie. Living on their nerves and wits, the Scots survived a barrage of pressure from the Italians, for whom Vieri squandered a golden opportunity in ballooning a short-range effort over the bar. It was a reprieve which allowed those watching to wonder whether the *Azzurri* might fail to breach the home defence, but cold reality returned in 76 minutes when substitute Fabio Grosso scrambled an equaliser after a corner from Mauro Camoranesi. It was no more than Lippi's team merited, considering the fashion in which they had constantly striven to be enterprising and attacking, but it was a 'scunner' in the local parlance. The match finished 1-1, which still gave the Scots something to play for against Norway, but the mission was near-impossible.

Which made the performance in Oslo four days later a triumphant vindication of the sense of purpose and unity that had spread through the ranks of Scotland's finest. The mission to the Ullevaal Stadium would constitute a pivotal test of Smith's leadership, for this was the type of fixture which his countrymen had lost the habit of winning. From the outset Scotland bristled with intent and served up a dominant first-half display, which was too hot for the Scandinavians. After 21 minutes James McFadden headed on a Ferguson cross, and Miller sent the ball past the stranded Thomas Myhre; after 30 minutes the prolific striker capitalised on Andre Bergdolmo's error and again lashed a shot past Myrhe. A third goal would have killed off Norwegian hopes, and Miller had the opportunity to collect his hat-trick as half-time approached, but his effort struck a defender and bounced to safety. Despite a rally from Norway in the second period after they had made three changes, the Scots were tenacious when they had to be. Craig Gordon pulled off a string of fine saves, and Neil McCann almost sealed matters in the 75th minute with a fine shot which this time was parried expertly by Myrhe. It was a superb performance despite Ole Martin Aarst's late goal, and Smith leapt in the air at the conclusion of the game. On taking the job he had stated that one of his key objectives was to make Scottish people proud of their national side again, and this showing provided stark proof that his team were on the rise. The manager had no control over results elsewhere, and Norway could derive comfort from the knowledge that if they beat Moldova and Belarus in their remaining ties, they would progress whatever the Scots did in their corresponding fixtures. Perhaps Vogts should have been sacked earlier by the SFA, with Smith granted the whole of the World Cup qualifiers to weave his magic.

Such speculation was rendered irrelevant when Belarus travelled to Glasgow in the first week of October. It was widely perceived that they would pose minimal problems at Hampden, but they emerged with a 1-0 success, courtesy of an early goal from Vitaly Kutuzov, and Scotland could not retrieve the situation. That confirmed their elimination from the final list of World Cup participants, and it created a miserable climax to an impressive second half to their campaign. But then the Scots ventured to the Petrol Arena Stadium in Celje to meet the Slovenians in their final group fixture, and reverted to the stunning form which had been evident in Oslo, winning 3-0 after Darren Fletcher, James McFadden and Paul Hartley had found the net. If ever a four-day period exemplified the contrary nature of Scotland's footballers and helped to explain why so many managers have walked away from Hampden Park engulfed in profound bafflement about the national psyche, this was it. But Smith could not afford to linger on the Belarus setback. As he glanced back on his first year in office the manager could embrace conflicting emotions, and he picked his way past the thorns to accentuate the positive aspects of a spell in which Scotland had climbed almost 40 places in the FIFA rankings:

'I should have been prepared for the goodwill I have encountered through the year, because Craig Brown primed me for it even before I started. He told me I would be amazed by the amount of affection and support there is for the national team across the whole of the country. Craig was right about that, but it was still a terrific surprise to go out and discover the depth and the extent of it. It comes from everywhere, wherever you go, from supporters of all clubs, from the people at the clubs themselves and yes, even from the media. Of course there is a critical side to the press as well, but that is just part of the business. However, this year has definitely shown me that, if you are a bit settled and seem to have something going for you, they are very supportive. I have told our players that, and that they shouldn't allow media criticism to be an excuse for not producing good form. I have also told them that everybody does want us to do well, but it is not something we should be afraid of, something that should put us under pressure. On the contrary it should be embraced and seen as a positive thing, because it is. I knew even before I took the job that Scotland supporters themselves are rather a special group, and I have seen plenty of things to strengthen that opinion. We have been fortunate with them.

'When I look back, my attitude is that not getting to Germany was a disappointment, but it wasn't a massive one. From where we started [two points from the opening three matches] we were going to be dependent on an entire sequence of results involving rivals in matches which were beyond our control. You always hope that things will work in your favour, but from the beginning I had suspected that it wouldn't happen. As long as we were not mathematically out of it though, the hope remained, and that was what made the first half of the home match against Belarus the biggest disappointment of the whole year. We had beaten Norway in Oslo a month earlier, and that day at Hampden everybody was desperate for us to do well, and we didn't. In the first half particularly we just didn't get going, and they seized the goal which eventually won the match.

'All the same I think, unlike 12 months ago, we have now got ourselves into a decent starting position. I don't mean that in terms of the whole squad, of course, but in certain areas of the team. Every new manager's first objective is to sort things out defensively, to make his side difficult to beat, and I think we have made progress in that area, while I've thought from the outset that we were pretty strong in midfield. But it is doing the hardest bit that we still have a bit of work to do. That is taking the initiative and going on to win games. The Belarus experience was a reminder to us all that you don't just have to turn up in order to play well. You have to maintain the progress in the level of performance.

'Whether we can go on to the stage of being able to overcome teams with an attacking game will depend to a great extent on how our younger forwards mature over the coming months. Kenny [Miller] has reacted very well to the pressure of the international game, and James [McFadden] looks as though he has come through a sticky patch at his club [Everton]. Others have to mature and develop. We have given chances – and will continue to do so – to individuals such as Shaun Maloney, Craig Beattie, Derek Riordan, Garry O'Connor and one or two others. They are they key to whether or not we can achieve a more comprehensive game, one in which we can defend solidly, but also create and convert scoring opportunities on a regular basis. And I think that the forward play will be the crux of the matter in determining how well we fare in the forthcoming European Championship qualifying competition, no matter whom we are drawn against.

'But ultimately 2005 has been quite productive. If the goodwill I talked about has been the most pleasant surprise, the most pleasing aspect of the entire exercise so far has been the response we have had from all the players in the squad. During the period we have asked them a variety of questions, and they have tried 100 per cent to come up with the answers. I don't think it is ever possible to say that you are on track or ahead of the game, or that targets have been hit. More accurately it is an ever-evolving process with the primary objective of continuous progress. But from my perspective and that of the other coaches the players could not have offered more, and that is immensely satisfying.'

It was a characteristically sober analysis delivered by a professional who had witnessed almost every foible that football has to offer. If Smith had a complaint with the demands of the Scotland job, it lay in his conviction that these simply were not sufficiently demanding. It was satisfying being responsible for picking up where he had left off with a disparate collection of players only around six or seven times a year, but for the workaholic Glaswegian the national post was a tremendous privilege, and a source of some restlessness. 'Even at 58 I feel the frustration of not having enough to do, of not being involved with the players more, but that just comes with the territory,' he admitted.

If Smith was seeking a major challenge, he could not have asked for a more probing examination than that which emerged from the draw for the 2008 European Championship, which was conducted in Montreux, Switzerland, on 27 January. On that day I was covering a press conference at Heart of Midlothian during a surreal period when the Tynecastle operation seemed to have managers acting as translators and tea-boys running the commercial operation, or vice versa. Reporters had become accustomed to hearing mind-boggling declarations from and being harangued by the Edinburgh club's chairman Vladimir Romanov, but a genuine sense of shock gripped the team's training complex at Heriot-Watt University as the Scots were paired with Italy, France and Ukraine, not to mention Lithuania, Georgia and the Faroe Islands. It was a shark-infested pool, and Scotland would have to knock out one of the sides that had contested the most recent World Cup final to have any chance of reaching the finals of a major tournament for the first time since the 1998 World Cup. Some blanched at the news, but Walter Smith once more impressed European colleagues with a precise summation which confirmed his belief that this was exactly the sort of challenge that could galvanise the Scots to great deeds, considering the manner in which they had traditionally tended to reserve their best displays after they had been written off by the media. There was no self-delusion in this approach: 'Of course it will be hard. France are a wonderful side. So are the Italians. The Ukrainians have been formidable in recent years, and we know that this will be tough for us. But down the years we have relished meeting the best and testing ourselves, and nothing has changed in that respect. We have a few months before the campaign starts, but we have to be positive in our approach. And we will be.'

The obvious media response was to refer to a 'Group of Death' once more and to offer pessimistic forecasts, which rather missed the point that Smith's players were growing in stature. They demonstrated that in resounding fashion by venturing to Japan in May 2006 and winning the Kirin Cup, a tri-nations competition also involving the host country and Bulgaria. In the performance against the eastern Europeans it was possible to detect the blossoming of a new confidence and swagger, Smith having chosen a number of fresh-faced youngsters who responded superbly. Debutants Kris Boyd and Chris Burke produced touches of the sublime in marking up two goals apiece, McFadden joined them in the demolition job, and Scotland recorded a 5-1 victory which was better than any observer could have predicted. The Japanese proved a stiffer proposition and occasionally left Smith's men struggling in defence, but a goalless draw was sufficient for Scotland to lift the silverware, and though it hardly compensated for not being at the World Cup finals, the momentum was building.

That was evident from the clamour for tickets for the opening match of the European qualifiers against the Faroese, opponents from the far north who had sparked embarrassment for Scotland under Berti Vogts when they scored twice in the opening quarter-of-an-hour and were denied victory only thanks to a late rally from the likes of Barry Ferguson, the Scots scraping a 2-2 draw. Smith's squad were in no mood for a repeat, and sent out a ringing declaration of intent with a 6-0 win at Celtic Park, which was as convincing as the result suggests. Boyd led the charge with two goals and Miller, Fletcher, O'Connor and McFadden also contributed. Scotland flew to Kaunas to tackle Lithuania the following week, and again demonstrated their increasing confidence and freedom of movement in achieving a 2-1 success with goals from Miller and Christian Dailly. Scotland's 100 per cent record was maintained in a treacherous group, but next up were France, who had dismantled Scotland frequently in the past and who arrived as runners-up from the World Cup final in Germany. It was an occasion in which logic would have to be ignored for Smith's men to prevail, and yet a strange feeling was abroad in Glasgow on the morning of the game. Foot soldiers from the Tartan Army at Queen Street Station were not merely confident; they had placed wagers on a home win, which seemed somewhat rash. 'You see the French are a bunch of fancy dans. They want to walk the ba' into the net, and we will be in their faces from the kick-off, so I think we'll piss them off so much they'll lose the plot,' ventured Michael from Stonehaven. Alastair from Broughty Ferry maintained to me that Walter Smith would prove the key difference. 'Their manager [Raymond] Domenech is a bit of a flake, and he is also fu' of himself. He will tell his boys it is going to be a walk in the park, and if they go out with that approach, they will find themselves hitting a big brick wall.' Chris from Falkirk said simply: 'They couldnae score at the World Cup. They want it all on their own terms. If we mess with their heads, then we can beat them.'

Scotland's starting XI were Gordon (Hearts), Dailly (West

Ham), Caldwell (Celtic), Pressley (Hearts), Weir (Everton), Alexander (Preston), Hartley (Hearts), Fletcher (Manchester United), Ferguson (Rangers), McCulloch (Wigan) and McFadden (Everton). Domenech called upon some glittering personnel in Coupet (Lyon), Sagnol (Bayern Munich), Thuram (Barcelona), Boumsong (Juventus), Abidal (Lyon), Ribery (Marseille), Vieira (Internazionale), Makelele (Chelsea), Malouda (Lyon), Trezeguet (Juventus) and Henry (Arsenal). For all their recent improvement, Scotland still had to beat a team of significant pedigree under Smith, while France journeyed to the stadium with innate confidence springing from their record of losing just once in 49 previous qualifying games. The optimism expressed by that Tartan Army triumvirate was certainly contagious, and anticipation arose of a performance from the hosts which would shake the French, and the stage was set for one of the great afternoons in Scottish sport.

Smith expected his team to be under siege at the outset, and his concern was justified. The visitors pressed forward with the fluency and flourish expected from talents such as Thierry Henry and Claude Makelele, and they could easily have been a couple of goals in front within 20 minutes, but efforts by Patrick Vieira and David Trezeguet were denied because of offside. The Scots initially struggled to stem the flow, but Smith's unsung heroes gradually repelled their adversaries in stirring fashion . . . and began orchestrating little forays of their own. Hartley launched a series of darting runs which irked then worried the French, and Graham Alexander belied his first division status with a fine display. At the back Gary Caldwell was obdurate, Pressley covered most of the blades of grass on the pitch in harassing and hounding, and Craig Gordon was typically solid as the last line of defence.

The Scots did lose the opening half on points, but Domenech wore a slightly worried expression at the interval. Smith was in his element, praising his men for their discipline and professionalism, and reminding them that they could play a bit themselves. The watchwords were vigilance and precision, for the manager recognised only too well that if France conjured up one goal, they might finish with three or four, so there would be no cavalry charges upfield. On the other hand, if McFadden or McCulloch could carve out one chance, they had to do their damnedest to ensure that it was not squandered. Because, as the Tartan Army chap had suggested, France were one of those teams who could be breathtaking in full spate, but who often struggled to make supremacy tell when it really counted. That thought increasingly inspired Scotland, and suddenly they were on the march, the influential midfield pairing of Fletcher and Ferguson stamping their authority on an increasingly cantankerous Vieira, Makelele and Florent Malouda, as the more discerning supporters cranked up the tempo and the decibel level in recognition of the inspirational exploits which had started to trouble the French resistance. The question on everybody's lips was whether this would bring a breakthrough for Scotland, and in the 67th minute the prayers of a nation were answered when a corner from Hartley swung dangerously into the French 18-yard box, and Caldwell bustled past Eric Abidal to get his foot to the ball and power it into the net. For a few seconds it seemed as though the action had been frozen with supporters en masse checking out whether an offside flag was flapping in the air, but no. It was a priceless goal for Caldwell and his country, and across the land whoops of delight reflected the fact that nothing binds Scotland together more closely than victory against the odds. As I set out to meet friends that night, I recall that everyone seemed to be smiling and that a wee jink had been added to the step of the nation. Constant re-screenings of Caldwell's goal were allied to praise for Walter Smith, who had been close to tears as the fans applauded him. He summed up the action and the outcome:

'It's a tremendous result, and certainly the best I have ever had as a manager. We were under tremendous pressure in the first half and they had one or two chances, but we got stuck in, defended stoutly and benefited from a bit of luck. We want to remain competitive throughout the qualifying campaign, and this is a great start with nine points from three matches. We knew that France would have a lot of possession, and territorially they had us pinned back for a while. But in the second half we improved our passing, and they didn't create many clear chances after that. It is a fantastic win, and a great reward for all the hard work that every single player put into the game.'

Scottish football commanded front-page banner headlines for the right reasons, and though there came a hangover a few days later in Kiev when Ukraine comfortably defeated the team by 2-0, the French triumph embodied most of the prime qualities which the manager had displayed in the service of club or country for the best part of 25 years. Sports journalist Brian Viner wrote in *The Independent*: 'Waiting for Walter Smith in the lounge of the Holiday Inn at Glasgow International Airport, I reflect that if Scotland had won in Ukraine earlier this month, having just dispatched France at Hampden Park to top Euro 2008's killer qualifying Group B, then I might be waiting in the Walter Smith Lounge at the Holiday Inn, or maybe in the lounge at the Walter Smith Holiday Inn, or even in the lounge of the Holiday Inn at Walter Smith International Airport. "Aye, we do tend to go a bit over the top when we win," said Smith, with a smile.' Well, why not? Victories of this magnitude happen infrequently enough for the majority of Scottish people to be uncertain how best to respond. But then Scots with only a marginal interest in football were sufficiently roused by the unexpected defeat of France, and Smith received the accolade of Scot of the Year at the Glenfiddich Spirit of Scotland Awards in December. It was fitting recognition for his success in transforming a bunch of disillusioned young men into a potent fighting unit with the capacity to beat one of the best countries in the world. For a while, at least, he made Scots feel better about themselves and more optimistic about the future. Football may have problems, but it can be an inspirational pursuit, and Smith acknowledged as much when he accepted his prize to a standing ovation and bearing a rather sheepish grin. He promised that he would try to keep up the good work, but further drama was about to unfold.

CHAPTER FIFTEEN

BACK TO IBROX

'He will get the lads playing for the jersey again'

Walter Smith's first love in football was Rangers. Once that passion was ignited as a schoolboy, he cherished the club with his heart and his soul. When he departed Ibrox Stadium in 1998, it was with the sinking feeling that in sport as in life you can never go back. Yet even when he and the redoubtable Archie Knox were ensconced at Everton for three-and-a-half years, the first thing they listened out for every Saturday evening was how Rangers had fared. It should not have been regarded as a surprise then that when the Ibrox club stumbled into difficulties in 2006 and Smith was eventually offered a second chance to assume the manager's role, he weighed up the pros and cons, reflected on what his departure would mean for the Scottish Football Association, and reached his decision within a few minutes. To some, Smith's behaviour in returning to his roots at the beginning of 2007 was an act of betrayal, and the SFA confirmed their intention to take legal action against him, claiming breach of contract, and against Rangers for alleged inducement to breach the contract. David Taylor, the outgoing chief executive of the governing body, summed up the widespread mood beyond the vicinity of Ibrox: 'Walter's departure is a serious blow to the SFA. He has done an excellent job for us and the Scottish national team. We are very disappointed that he has chosen to leave us at this critical time in our Euro 2008 qualification campaign.' In a statement issued on 10 January the SFA added: 'At a meeting this morning with the CEO of the association, Walter Smith delivered a letter of resignation with immediate effect from his position as national coach of the Scotland team. No agreement has been reached with Mr Smith or Rangers Football Club on any compensation payment to be made for the early termination of his employment, which is in breach of contract with the SFA.'

The verbiage obscured the reality that Smith had already signed a three-year deal at Rangers, which would offer him security for the rest of his life. Paying heed to some comments in the Scottish press and on football phone-in programmes, one could have been forgiven for imagining that he was guilty of selling his birthright and his country down the river. The explanation was more prosaic, and embodied Smith's sense of priorities. He had taken the Scotland job while he was unemployed, he had succeeded in resuscitating the moribund patient, and now he was being presented with a fresh challenge by the organisation that he had always supported, and he would be rejoining David Murray, a man he admired enormously. Why all the fuss, hate mail and slanders? I believe that Smith had no reason to apologise for renewing his links with Rangers. He had watched from the sidelines as the sophisticated Frenchman Paul le Guen was wheeled out as Alex McLeish's successor to a fanfare of trumpets and a rapturous reception in the media. But almost as quickly as his star was in the ascendancy, Le Guen's stock plummeted in a flurry of poor transfer signings and miserable results allied to his failure to command the respect of key players and his deficiencies in adapting to the demands of the Scottish game. It was not as if Smith had wakened suddenly and thought: 'I'm scooting off to Rangers.' He had highlighted his frustration at not having access to his international players except on a sporadic basis, and his pronouncements during the previous autumn, when he spoke openly about his desire to get involved with club football again, could hardly have carried a clearer message that he was not prepared to commit himself indefinitely to the Scotland post. Smith at 58 knew the clock was ticking, that he could not afford to hang around in what he regarded as part-time employment, and that he would be obliged to stay with Scotland whether or not they qualified for the finals of the leading competitions. That held no appeal, hence his itchy feet.

As for those Celtic followers who have alleged that Smith took the Scotland job to get back into practice for Rangers, I would simply ask: are they seriously arguing that he deduced that Le Guen would prove to be a flop over a year before he was appointed? Is it not more probable that if the French coach had lived up to his star billing and steered the Ibrox team towards the Champions League, that Smith would have found another club in the English Premiership or the SPL? He had declared to *The Herald* in November 2006:

'To return to club football it would have to be the right job, and I would need to be able to do what I wanted to do. Everybody is competitive, and I suppose that I feel I would like to redress the situation [in England] and have another crack at it down there if the circumstances were right. When I left Everton, I considered myself a failure. I wanted to make them a stable, top-six side like they were in the 1980s, but I was there at the wrong time, and I never left anything for David Moyes except a young Wayne Rooney, and even then that had nothing to do with me, so David had done a better job at Goodison than I managed. But yes, returning to club management is something that has occurred to me, and I haven't ruled it out.'

These are not the words of a man who was waiting patiently to fill Le Guen's boots as soon as he had exited Ibrox under a cloud. Instead they serve to indicate that Smith was pleased to be able to assist his country in extricating themselves from the mire, but he did not consider it a long-term career option. This makes perfect sense for those acquainted with Smith's relish for training-ground banter, the daily exchange of news, gossip and jokes which are the lifeblood of any club, and which were denied him when he was meeting up with his Scotland squad five or six times a year.

No sooner had Smith arrived at Ibrox again than he was orchestrating another revival. The title race had long since been settled through a combination of Celtic's early-season supremacy and Le Guen's errors, but Murray assured his old friend that there would be money to spend in the summer, and the priority was for Smith to ensure that his team qualified for the Champions League. It was as if the rewind button had been set for a decade before. There was the manager marshalling his troops with the sturdy invective which had not changed throughout his career; and alongside was Ally McCoist, a coiled spring of energy, grins and remarks. The message from both was straightforward: Rangers had under-performed this season, their results had not been good enough for a club of their reputation, and some players needed to take a hard look at themselves in the mirror and ask whether they deserved to remain at Ibrox. No-nonsense stuff. Though Smith knew from his first inspection of the Rangers squad that serious treatment would be required come the summer, he had immediate business to hand. On Saturday, 13 January he returned to what seemed like his natural dwelling-place, the technical area at Ibrox. He reinstated as captain Barry Ferguson, a player he admired and trusted to bring the side together. The Scotland player responded with a brilliant display capped by a goal in 88 minutes, as Rangers transcended awful weather to power to the kind of overwhelming victory which had eluded them under Le Guen. The home side subjected Dundee United to a 5-0 flogging, goals from Charlie Adam and Chris Burke and two from Kris Boyd preceding the Ferguson strike. This Rangers player has his critics, on both sides of the Old Firm, but here he was wonderful in full flow, and he directed the action as if orchestrating the tempo of the match. Round about him the young Scots Adam, Burke, Boyd and Murray were hives of industry, and while there were still occasional signs of the defensive vulnerability which had blighted the Ibrox men throughout the season, their midfield was a sight to behold. Several of the men in blue recognised they were fighting for their futures, but on a bog-like pitch whose state had persuaded referee Craig Mackay to consider abandoning the match at the interval, there was no denying the efficacy or pace of the Rangers showing.

As *Scotland on Sunday* saw it: 'This was more like it. This was a world away from what we have seen from them this season. Throughout the Rangers ranks there was industry and urgency, there was a desire to play at a tempo several notches higher than before, and a ruthlessness in front of goal that brought them, by far and away, their most thumping victory of the season.' Smith expressed pleasure at his side's performance, but declined to take any of the credit. Even in these early days he had twigged that Le Guen had recruited several players, including Karl Svensson and Jeremy Clement, who were not equipped for the hurly-burly of the SPL, and that he would have to strengthen his defence when he could. But the screams of delight from the Rangers faithful, who had been fed a diet of dross for so long, was music to the ears, and in the directors' box David Murray must have allowed himself a significant sigh of relief. And as Rangers grew increasingly impressive, it became clear that Paul Gascoigne had been correct in his analysis that Smith would be capable of implementing a swift turnaround in the team's fortunes. The controversial former player had opined:

'Walter knows how to get the best out of all different types of people, and mark my words, he knows what is required to get in front of Celtic, and it will be his aim to finish second in the league this season and then win it next year. He will get the lads playing for the jersey again, and will sign players who deserve to be at Ibrox. In recent years not enough players have actually deserved the honour of pulling on the Rangers jersey, but I am sure that will all change from now on. Walter will also bring fear and a winning mentality to the dressing room. Before games he demanded a 3-0 lead at half-time, and during the break he would want to see us win 6-0 by the finish. And he was as hard on himself as he was on his players, if he thought that he had made a mistake. So I have no doubts whatsoever that his return is terrific news for Rangers.'

In domestic terms the recovery was well under way, but there remained the tricky problem of transplanting impressive form to European competition, and Smith must have felt a twinge of *déjà vu* when he attempted to negotiate his side past Spanish opponents Osasuna in the last 16 of the UEFA Cup in March. In recent SPL encounters at Ibrox the Scottish team had been indomitable and created numerous opportunities in most matches, yet they seemed to suffer from stage fright against Osasuna, and were lucky to record a 1-1 draw in the first leg. Smith described it as the worst display since his return to the club. That underwhelming showing left his squad with a difficult away match, and once again they toiled on their travels. Bernardo Romeo and Gomez Juanlo squandered excellent chances in the first half as Rangers were confronted with sustained pressure. Despite Charlie Adam and Gavin Rae coming close for the visitors, there was a sense of inevitability when Pierre Webo scored in the 71st minute to send Osasuna through to the quarter-finals of the event. It was frustrating enough that Smith's side had not done themselves justice, but worse that there was a disquieting recurrence of a traditional problem from their followers. 'We hoped to play a little better tonight than we did, especially in the first half, but it was not to be,' said the manager. 'At the end of the day we simply did not create enough opportunities. We played reasonably well in some aspects, but overall we weren't up to scratch, and I was particularly disappointed with how we performed in Glasgow.'

If these words sounded familiar, so did some sectarian chants which echoed from the stands as a small but vocal number of so-called fans disgraced themselves and heaped trouble on Rangers in the process. UEFA fined the club £8,000 after 'improper conduct' by their fans during the Osasuna tie, but the rather sickened expressions of Smith and Martin Bain, the Rangers chief executive, spoke volumes for their vexation at how this issue kept arising and threatened increasingly stiff punishments for the club, including the possibility of being banned from Europe in the future. Thus they had barely returned from Spain when they launched a new campaign, Follow with Pride, in a bid finally to nail the blight of bigotry. 'Everyone at Ibrox is committed to showing Rangers in the best possible light on and off the field, and that is why we are launching this initiative,' said Ally McCoist, who once expressed his mystification to me that so many supporters could roar on Rangers teams containing Catholic players such as Lorenzo Amoruso and Rino Gattuso, and yet still resort to shouting 'F*** the Pope' at opponents. 'Follow with Pride is all about promoting sporting behaviour among fans and the great work that the club does in bringing together all types of people in the community. The club is constantly under the spotlight, and our fans more than anybody else realise the importance of setting high standards of behaviour. So for the good of everybody, we have to get that message across and show what a fantastic club this is, not for some, but for all.'

The sentiments were admirable, but one suspects that this fundamental malaise will not be solved in the near future, particularly with the prospect that the Old Firm will again dominate the SPL in coming seasons. Smith has proved that he is a master in the art of beating his club's biggest rivals, and it was no surprise that he should continue his successful sequence, courtesy of Ugo Ehiogu's rather surreal winning goal which silenced the majority of the capacity crowd at Celtic Park on 11 March and subsequently when Rangers encountered Celtic at Ibrox on 5 May. In fairness to the visitors, they had gone off the boil with their emphatic championship win all but wrapped up, but that should not detract from the supremacy which the hosts displayed throughout their 2-0 triumph, a result that could have been significantly better but for missed chances and last-gasp defending. 'I thought we started well, and I felt that we fully deserved our victory,' said Smith, reflecting on the goals from Boyd and Adam which had earned the three points. 'The main objective was to clinch the Champions League qualifying spot, but a lot of the boys have found a good level of consistency, and that is very heartening. We kept good possession, we maintained our discipline, and my squad have shown a terrific attitude since I arrived back here. We haven't lost a league game since that time, but we know that both ourselves and Celtic will improve next season, so the work never stops. In fact, I reckon that it will be a very, very busy summer.'

Walter Smith more than anyone recognises the problems that lie ahead for him and for Rangers. Close friend David Murray has spent nearly 20 years on the bridge, and he made clear at the most recent annual general meeting that he was prepared to sell the club 'to the right person'. In future there be a greater reliance on loan deals, bringing youngsters through the youth system, and operating at a financial level significantly below the majority of England's Premiership clubs. Yet it would be difficult to find anybody better equipped to handle that challenge. His grasp of statistics and the details of transfer dealing is illuminating:

'It's not any different from the last time when I was at Rangers. People say that it is, but that's a bit of a fallacy. We couldn't outbid most clubs in the 1990s. During my first three years at Ibrox we operated at a profit in the transfer market, and that was because we were fortunate enough to get £6m for Trevor Steven. Paul Gascoigne cost us £3.4m, but at that time that was just the market value. A lot of really good players were going for that kind of money, and it is just how the market goes. If you go for a number of players and make offers, it will not happen that you will have them all accepted. You always get to the stage where you have a figure you would pay for the player, and sometimes it takes a while before the to-ing and fro-ing reaches that level. No club ever gets all the players on their list. It doesn't happen. You hear about clubs with more financial clout than us getting beaten by clubs with even more financial clout. Quite a lot of clubs don't even start until September. Then there are the awkward bits, and it can be a wee bit frustrating. You know the sensible view to take is that it might not all come together.'

Irrespective of these considerations, Smith's forays into the transfer market in the summer of 2007 appeared to be shrewd investments. There were some initial reservations over the fitness of Bosman signing Jean-Claude Darcheville, but the French striker repaid the faith shown in him with an athleticism and single-mindedness that yielded a rich crop of goals. The recruitment of Spain's Carlos Cuellar was similarly a master-stroke, and as the summer faded into autumn a quiet sense of confidence grew around Ibrox that Rangers would present Celtic with a much stiffer challenge in the new campaign than had proved the case in the calamitous Le Guen regime. Yet no-one could have predicted how dramatic that resurgence would be.

CHAPTER SIXTEEN

ADMIRABLE ARTISANS SET TO WORK

'I thought I was at the stage of my career where European finals were well past me'

Walter Smith met the press at Ibrox for the manager's regular Friday afternoon conference on 4 April 2008. The gathering looked forward to that weekend's matches, and inevitably focused on transfer speculation, injury matters and other paraphernalia involving the club. Given the circumstances in which Smith found himself – his team were chasing a remarkable quadruple of domestic and European prizes – one might have assumed that he would be radiating positive vibes, or if that is asking too much of an individual at the centre of relentless and often irrelevant tabloid tittle-tattle, that he would be mildly satisfied about the transformation that he had orchestrated. On the contrary, Smith was aggrieved, angry even, at what he perceived as the slighting of his players' achievements in advancing to within touching distance of Rangers' first European triumph for 36 years. Bad enough, he remarked, that he should be on the receiving end of criticism and cheap shots from opposition fans and managers in Scotland and further afield. But worse, that vitriol was emanating from those who called themselves Rangers supporters, who had signally failed to appreciate the scale of the upturn in fortunes under Smith. It was a significant statement; and when one recalled Smith's expression the previous evening as he heard booing from the stands after Rangers' 0-0 draw with Sporting Lisbon in the first leg of the UEFA Cup quarter-final tie, one could understand the man's frustrations. Unlike the 1990s, there was no Paul Gascoigne or Brian Laudrup, or even a Mark Hateley or Ally McCoist in the ranks, and Smith was being expected to effect minor miracles without any major investment, to the extent that the single substantial piece of business at Ibrox during the January transfer window was the sale of Alan Hutton to Tottenham Hotspur for £9m.

'At the end of the day, if there are a lot of dissatisfied supporters, then one thing happens – a manager normally walks away. And we seem to have a lot of dissatisfied supporters at the moment,' said Smith. 'It has been apparent at Rangers since the first game of the [European] season – we were booed off at half-time against FK Zeta in the Champions League qualifier. So if that is the way that people want to support the club, then fine, it's not our choice. It is a disappointing factor in the sense that, away from home, we get terrific backing, but come the home matches, right from the very start there seems to be a dissatisfaction. It is difficult. When you are doing really well in a game, then that is not really the time that you need the support. It is those times when you are not doing well that you need the backing and, at the moment, that isn't happening.

'From a managerial point of view, it just happens – whether you understand it or not is another matter. Invariably, if a manager brings this subject up, there is an outcry that you should be doing better or whatever. Supporters pay their money, so they are entitled to react in the manner that they do. But at times it is difficult to understand, and I don't think it helps the club overall. In fact, I believe that a lot of the players coming here must find it difficult to comprehend, especially when the club hasn't enjoyed any level of success, and now, when there is an opportunity to turn things around, they are still hearing boos. Don't get me wrong. I appreciate the demands of the job here. I keep saying to the players: "If you can't meet the demands, then don't stay here." And that's from the chairman [Sir David Murray] all the way down. But somewhere along the line, there has to be a level of understanding, and there doesn't seem to be that at the moment.'

❖

From Walter Smith's perspective, his fusillade merely reinforced what had been obvious to the majority of Rangers acolytes from their first sight of the class of 2007-08. Namely, that the squad were replete with graft and grit supplied by individuals who would shed every last drop of perspiration for the cause . . . but they lacked an excess of flair. Under the wretched Le Guen, the team had been packed with fluffy nothings, who had buckled under the weight of expectations which habitually surrounds the Old Firm. Smith felt that he had no option but to bolster his resources with artisans rather than aesthetes, which explained the recruitment of craggy characters such as David Weir, Christian Dailly, Jean-Claude Darcheville and Kirk Broadfoot. The last-named suffered some ridiculous abuse on his home patch and in England – with a *Guardian* columnist going so far as to ask whether he might be the worst-ever footballer to reach a European final – and while he was hardly poetry in motion, Broadfoot knuckled down to his job, flourished within limited parameters, and was as honest in his labours as he was modest in abilities. Mud sticks though, and once the cry had gone up that Rangers were 'anti-football' according to Barcelona's Lionel Messi, or 'boring' in the view of Zenit St Petersburg's ex-Ibrox tearaway Fernando Ricksen, Smith's personnel increasingly performed to type, grinding out a series of efficient but lifeless victories and draws on the European stage. Considering where they had been only 12 months previously, with Colin Stein telling me: 'Christ, we were going to places like Dunfermline thinking were going to get gubbed,' it might have been imagined that the Ibrox clientele would have been thankful for wins of any description over clubs such as Lyon, Werder Bremen, Sporting Lisbon and Fiorentina. But there again, some of Rangers' fans have such a staggering superiority complex, which is untroubled by reality, that their displeasure was predictable.

For those of a more rational persuasion, Smith's achievements merited applause, particularly when compared to some of Rangers' 1990s X-rated series of meetings with Europe's elite. From the outset, his strategy was obvious: avoid conceding goals, and almost anything is possible over two legs. Hence, even as the boos resonated around Ibrox, Rangers disposed of FK Zeta by the comfortable margin of 3-0, their goals coming from Weir and Nacho Novo, and oblivious to the sending-off of Hutton, prior to DaMarcus Beasley adding the third on foreign soil. That left Smith's men needing to beat Red Star Belgrade to progress to the Champions League, and again pragmatism reigned, with Rangers' less-patient souls registering their displeasure. The job was completed in the end, the pivotal incidents arriving when the prolific Novo fired home the only goal of the tie in the last minute at Ibrox, and when Allan McGregor pulled off a string of excellent saves to deny his opponents in Belgrade. It wasn't pretty, it wasn't even entertaining, but there was something grimly heroic about the indefatigable, they-shall-not-pass mentality of the Scottish soldiers, which was characterised by Weir, whose visage was perfect for featuring on a black-and-white cigarette card of the type avidly collected by young fans in previous eras. This footballer confirmed repeatedly that age had not wearied him.

Champions League qualification secured, the prize for Smith and his men was a berth in Group E with Barcelona, Lyon and Stuttgart, which offered the sort of threat in triplicate that had the manager admitting that the task of reaching the last 16 would be tough. But he had devised his tactics to counter the rapid pace of the better European clubs, and was intent on making Rangers hard to beat and on providing them with the requisite self-belief to ignore the reputations of those pitted against them. According to Colin Stein, who had no truck with the notion that Smith was overly defensive in his approach:

'Walter did a fantastic job in that regard. You watched the body language of the players when Le Guen was in charge, and if they went behind they started looking around at one another, and it was as if they didn't know what to do next. European football is changing, and nowadays a 0-0 draw at home isn't a bad result, and Walter grasped that you couldn't send your team out all guns blazing at 100mph, otherwise the other side will just pick you off. What he did was to give them shape and discipline and instil in them the confidence to play in specific positions, and most of his summer signings were excellent. Big Cuellar was immense, so was Davie Weir, as was McGregor, and when you have three guys of that calibre working wonders at the back, it is amazing what a pick-me-up it can be for the rest of the boys further up the park.'

Though Rangers were underdogs in their section, they soon served notice that they would be no pushovers, performing with resilience and opportunism throughout the first half of their campaign, and it appeared that they were in perfect position to qualify for the knock-out stages of the Champions League. At Ibrox, Stuttgart went in front through Mario Gomez, but Rangers were well served by a marvellous display from Hutton, who set up Charlie Adam for a splendid equaliser as a prelude to the scorer gaining a penalty which Darcheville converted. If that result prompted the raising of a few eyebrows, an outbreak of Groucho Marx impersonations must have greeted the end of the next 90 minutes. Rangers travelled to Lyon and inflicted a 3-0 defeat on the French champions with a thoroughly-accomplished performance. Summer signings Lee McCulloch, Daniel Cousin and Beasley were on target, and with six points from two matches Rangers knew that one more victory would probably be sufficient.

Whether that knowledge assisted them is another matter. With Barcelona next at Ibrox, Smith retreated into his shell, arguing that he had to do everything in his power to prevent the Spanish giants from unleashing their attacking threats. In this he was justified, but given that the two matches against Ronaldhino, Thierry Henry, Lionel Messi, Deco and their colleagues were essentially grand irrelevancies in the wider picture, one might have wished that he had shown greater boldness. However, scars inflicted by heavy European beatings from such as Juventus in the previous decade had not healed over, and the match on 23 October was one of the more tedious in the history of the competition. It was reasonable that Rangers should choose to scavenge and kick anything that moved in their direction, but they should have considered attempting some form of counter-offensive, rather than merely sitting back. Unsurprisingly, the event soon developed into the sporting equivalent of watching paint dry, and while the 0-0 score was partial vindication of Smith's plan, the ensuing publicity was as negative as his team's tactics.

'It's incredible. Rangers didn't want to play football,' opined Argentinian wunderkind Messi. 'Right from the start they went for anti-football, and I am left with a bitter taste in my mouth at not being able to win the match, because we had a decent amount of chances. It's a real pain playing against teams like them, and it's very hard too. But it will be a different story when we get back to the Camp Nou.'

Even if these sentiments suggested that Barcelona arrogantly expected opponents merely to look on admiringly as they demonstrated their silky skills, there was no doubting the gulf between the sides when they resumed hostilities a fortnight later, with Thierry Henry breaking the deadlock after just six minutes and Messi wrapping up the points shortly before half-time. But it remained galling that Rangers seemed in awe of their rivals and looked intent on damage limitation rather than throwing caution to the wind, particularly given the fact that Barca were nowhere near the force that they had been in past years, as their subsequent league and cup form proved.

The next few weeks, tellingly, were storm-tossed for Smith. Rightly or wrongly, the 'anti-football' gibe struck a chord with commentators and supporters. 'We pay our money, and we are entitled to express our views,' one season-ticket holder told me in his denunciation of strategy on the pitch. 'In the old days it would have been unthinkable that we would have set our stall out for a draw at home, but by playing a lone striker up front and ignoring somebody like [Kris] Boyd, Smith is shooting himself in the foot, and he has to recognise that we are not interested in the idea of respectability.' Controversy arose off the pitch after Rangers were beaten 3-2 by Stuttgart in their fifth match, which meant they needed a point from the home Lyon encounter to be sure of progressing to the last 16. The game in Germany was a tale of could-have-beens. Charlie Adam opened the scoring in the 27th minute, Jeronimo Cacau levelled, then Pavel Pardo pushed the hosts in front. The influential Barry Ferguson restored parity with a fine goal in the 70th minute, and Rangers seemed capable of orchestrating a victory, but they squandered several openings, and Stuttgart grabbed the winner through Ciprian Marica with five minutes left. A Scottish team had again decided that straying down a cul-de-sac of vulnerability was preferable to walking on easy street.

It was here that Rangers made a strategic mistake which cost them dear in the longer term. Recognising the importance of the Lyon clash, Smith was obviously keen to prevent any personnel sustaining injury during the SPL match against Gretna in the midst of the build-up to the Champions League tie. But it was one thing for the manager to express the wish that he might be allowed to pick his best side, and quite another for his club to ask for the postponement of the Gretna fixture, which was the action that they chose. At a stroke they surrendered any semblance of good-will that might have been building up among the rest of the SPL contenders, and the speed with which the league acceded to their request looked suspect when Aberdeen subsequently sought a similar postponement, which was peremptorily refused. As the fixture schedule piled up for Rangers, they could have few complaints about the congestion, having started the process against opponents who were struggling for their very existence. Having been granted the luxury of time to prepare properly for the meeting with the French champions, it was perhaps predictable that Rangers should proceed to crash out of the Champions League. Fecklessly at that. Smith spoke in advance of how far his men had travelled, and of his pride in some of their perfor-mances. When it really mattered, though, they came up short. Nervy and unconvincing in the early stages, they fell behind when

Sydney Govou scored after 16 minutes, and despite the crowd whipping up a crescendo of noise and a chance to level matters that was spurned as a result of Darcheville's profligacy, the die was cast when rising star Karim Benzema added a terrific brace of goals in the 85th and 88th minutes. With supporters streaming towards the exits, Darcheville rounded off a miserable evening by being sent off for stamping in injury-time, and the promise that had burned brightly a couple of months earlier evaporated in stale anti-climax.

The manager did not attempt to sweeten the pill in the aftermath. On the contrary, Walter Smith displayed the candour which has always been one of his most admirable qualities: 'It was a disappointing result, and a disappointing performance overall. Just as we were making a change near the end, we conceded a bad second goal, which really killed the game. Now we have to sit down and reflect on what has happened. We have enjoyed some good experiences, and some bad ones as well, but I'm sure that the campaign will help the players in the rest of their careers. It [the UEFA Cup] is not a great consolation, but maybe in the next few days we will appreciate it a bit more.' He added: 'If you look at the situation realistically, when I came back to Rangers I never set out to think about progressing far in Europe. I felt it would take us the first year to build a steady foundation, and what I was looking to achieve was mounting a better challenge to Celtic. I looked upon the European side of things as purely financial from the club's point of view.'

If the man was hurting, his response was exemplary. Despite failing to land any expensive transfer signings during the January window, he snapped up youngster Steven Davis and veteran Christian Dailly, and both proved invaluable as Rangers did warm to the thrill of the chase in the UEFA Cup. As in the Champions League, it was a triumph for the muscular over the mercurial in the main, and again the team appeared galvanised whenever they left Glasgow. Few could quibble with the efficacy of their displays as one big European club after another were sent tumbling out of the competition, usually accompanied by the whining of their coaches and players. Panathinaikos were the first to depart Ibrox with self-satisfied smiles in the wake of a doughty goal-less draw in the opening leg, only to discover that their opponents posed potent threats allied to tireless resilience in the return. Lesser sides might have wilted when Ioannis Goumas established a 12th-minute lead for the Greeks, and Rangers were dependent on some tremendous goalkeeping from the rock-like McGregor, but the longer the match raged on and the more nervous the home fans grew, the better the visitors rose to the occasion. The pocket-sized Novo seized the priceless away goal in the 81st minute, and Smith's team had qualified for a last-16 tussle with the formidable Werder Bremen.

If criticism of Rangers' tactics continued to proliferate outwith Scotland, it was undeniable that the squad possessed an irrepressible spirit and a fierce determination to succeed. Perhaps Smith was harsh on Kris Boyd, who languished on the bench for much of the European odyssey, but individuals such as Darcheville, Cousin and Novo had shown a willingness to harry and chase for every ball wherever they were on the field, and the instinctively-selfish Boyd, by contrast, seemed an expensive luxury in an ensemble propelled by the power of collectivism. Bremen looked superior in most aspects on paper, but then football is conducted on grass, and Ibrox reflected the old-fashioned, sleeves-rolled-up rambustiousness which used to typify these euphoric European nights, and at least one of the Germans could not handle the pressure. The fact that the affected player was their highly-rated goalkeeper, Tim Wiese, only added to Rangers' delight: the No.1 committed a couple of costly errors, almost ushering Cousin's speculative shot into his own net, then weakly parrying a shot straight back to Steven Davis, who doubled his side's advantage. McCulloch was granted a wonderful chance to bolster Rangers' cushion, but dithered with the ball and wasted the opening, prompting many fans to wonder whether his gaffe might return to haunt the team in the second leg. In other circumstances that might have been the case, but where Wiese had been unconvincing, McGregor was the hero of the hour-and-a-half in Germany, producing a string of fine saves as the hosts laid siege to the Scots' territory and goalmouth.

It made for fraught viewing for visiting supporters, and when Brazilian Diego reduced the deficit in the 58th minute, signs grew that Rangers were creaking, but their custodian remained serene and pulled off an incredible late block to deny Boubacar Sanogo, sealing a berth for his club in the last eight.

It was understandable that Walter Smith was wreathed in smiles at the end, and he immediately paid homage to the stalwart McGregor: 'We knew that Werder would test our mettle, and they have come really hard at us tonight, but Allan was fantastic, and his form has been instrumental to us getting this far in the tournament. We rode our luck on occasions, but it always helps defenders when they know they have somebody of Allan's quality behind them, and he was simply immense when he needed to be. He has been extremely consistent, and I think he is now living up to the potential he has always had, even before I came back here as manager. Now we have Sporting Lisbon, and although they are a good team, we have proved that we are a good team too.' The last comment was pertinent. Some might have condemned Smith's tactics and alleged negativity, but no team can beat opponents of the quality of Lyon, Stuttgart and Werder Bremen without possessing virtues, and Carlos Cuellar and David Weir offered immense contributions in snuffing out Lisbon's menace at Ibrox. Though Rangers recorded another 0-0 draw in Glasgow, their ramparts were tested infrequently by the Portuguese, who had reached the 2005 UEFA Cup final, and a justifiable air of optimism could be detected within the Rangers camp, not least from Smith, whose energy and effervescence in his 61st year were inspirational. With the pressure and expectations rising in equal proportions, the manager reflected a cool disposition in the midst of the cauldron of Lisbon, and his players responded in kind. It was an opportunity for the Scots to bask in the spotlight – no other British clubs remained in the competition – and Rangers boasted solidity, precision and a degree of skill as the hosts' mounting frustration was ruthlessly pounced upon. Darcheville, exuding the resolve of a long-distance runner in his quest to burst through pain barriers, ended the stalemate with a dazzling goal on the counter-attack in the 60th minute, and as visiting supporters indulged in raucous celebration, Steven Whittaker proved adept at spinning a silky path through the home defence prior to scoring sublimely.

This offered a vindication of Smith's selections and strategy, but characteristically he refused to indulge in hyperbole. 'I'm surprised that we have managed to get ourselves into this position,' he revealed, 'but sometimes you get a season in football where a lot of things go for you, and you gain the wee bit of luck that is required at times. In general, the attitude and approach to the games has been terrific, and I can't fault any of the lads in that respect. Yes we have ridden our luck at times, but I don't think anybody who has watched us over the whole campaign in Europe so far would argue that we lack the right level of commitment and winning mentality. We don't have a lot of flair in our squad and can't afford to bring it in, so we have to try and enhance other aspects of football, and we have done that successfully this year. Yes I know we have had quite a bit of criticism for being defensive, so it was interesting to read [Barcelona coach] Frank Rijkaard's assessment of the English teams the other day, when he said they are far too defensive in the way they play. He felt that they should be playing more attractive and skilful football, so if clubs [such as Manchester United] are spending hundreds of millions of pounds and still being accused of being too defensive, then I think that says a lot about modern football. It's the pressure that is on you to win. That criticism didn't really affect us, because I just felt it was the way that Rangers had to go this season. We could be doing with more flair in the wider areas of the pitch, but there is only one legitimate winger in Scottish football at the moment, [Celtic's] Aiden McGeady, and we could be doing with somebody like that, but unfortunately it costs a lot of money, so experience tells you to look in another direction.'

As a semi-final meeting with Fiorentina beckoned, injuries, suspensions and the fixture pile-up were beginning to take their toll on Rangers' squad. Nonetheless, the Ibrox contingent persevered with their mantra that if your opponents can't score, you have won half the battle. Deprived of the services through injury of the talismanic McGregor, Smith replaced him with Neil Alexander, who immediately settled into the goalkeeping role, and that flexibility and *esprit des corps* were pivotal in Rangers being able to withstand and wear down a Fiorentina side, who offered attacking threat and youthful brio. But heaven knows what neutrals made of the convoluted affair – the Italian club's manager, Cesare Prandelli, subsequently rushed into print castigating the 'deliberately negative tactics of Rangers' – but it was somewhat absurd to hear the one-time masters of *'Catenaccio'* bleat about their rivals' safety-first philosophy, which had been dubbed *'Watenaccio'* by tabloids in honour of Mr Smith. Fiorentina did enjoy home advantage, and were blessed with numerical superiority when Daniel Cousin was foolishly sent off in extra-time; they enjoyed ample possession and territory to force the pace, but they still could not make the breakthrough in 120 minutes at the Stadio Artemio Franchi. They gained a foothold in the ensuing penalty shoot-out when Ferguson missed Rangers' first kick, but against all the odds and with Alexander sensationally filling McGregor's boots, the Scots held their composure. Fiorentina were let down by Fabio Liverani, whose penalty was saved, and by the vastly-experienced Christian Vieri, whose effort sailed embarrassingly over the bar . . . and Novo delivered the *coup de grace*. Smith and his assistants, Ally McCoist and Kenny McDowall, went into paroxysms of joy on reaching a European final. They had done it on their own terms and minus a battalion of leading players, or even one out-and-out world-class talent. It was a triumph for traditional, blood-and-guts football, and if that sat badly with some of UEFA's suits, more fool them.

Smith, architect of Rangers' nine-in-a-row and the Scotland manager who had masterminded victory at Hampden over France, had no doubts about the significance of his team's exploits: 'It is probably my most satisfying achievement in football. To put a team together, as we have done in such a short space of time, and for them to show the spirit and determination which they have done throughout the season has been tremendous. I thought I was at the stage of my career where European finals were well past me, so I am delighted from my own point of view. But I am more delighted for the club, for the chairman, and chief executive [Martin Bain], and everybody who has supported us through this period. When you see the level of commitment we put in to keep the game at 0-0 tonight, it was just fantastic. I was worried when it went to penalties, because David Moyes told me Fiorentina were excellent at them when they beat Everton in an earlier round. Then, when their keeper saved our first kick from Barry, I feared the worst. It takes courage for any player to step forward and take a penalty in these circumstances, so all credit to all our players for that. I was fairly confident that Nacho would score his, because he practises them all the time in training.'

Smith could be granted a few moments to contemplate his side's success.

Sadly, considering the cack-handed fashion in which the SFA and SPL colluded to exacerbate Rangers' fixture fiasco, leaving them with eight matches to fulfil within 20 days at the end of what had already proved to be an exhausting season, the odds were always likely to favour Zenit St Petersburg in the UEFA Cup final at the City of Manchester Stadium on May 14 2008. Much was made of the friendly relationship between Smith and his Zenit counterpart, Dick Advocaat, the former coach to Rangers who had done such a sterling job of relieving David Murray of vast sums of money to fund football during his tenure at Ibrox. So it was valuable to hear an honest appraisal of the two men from former Rangers striker Colin Stein: 'Walter is a real players' manager. He backs his guys 100%, and if he has any problems with them, it will be sorted out behind closed doors, and there will be no bad blood allowed to fester thereafter. One of the great things about Rangers this season [regardless of what would happen in Manchester] is that the boys are all desperate to play in every match, there is genuine competition for places, and they all look proud to be where they are and wearing the Rangers jersey. It's like night and day compared with where the club was 12 to 18 months ago, and that's why I can't believe that people are criticising Walter Smith and talking about Mr Advocaat as if he was some kind of miracle worker. Put it like this: one of the main reasons Walter has had to pull his squad together from Bosman signings and loan deals is that Mr Advocaat spent so much of the club's and Mr Murray's cash back in the late 1990s.'

Stein could not say when interviewed who would win the UEFA Cup final, but he considered that Zenit would start favourites after beating Bayern Munich 4-0 in the semi-finals, and he thought that going in as underdogs could play right into Rangers' hands. Much wishful thinking in this vein was apparent, but with the Ibrox personnel striving to maintain their SPL challenge in addition to contesting a Scottish Cup final with Queen of the South at Hampden Park – this less than 48 hours after tackling Aberdeen at Pittodrie in the finale of the league season – the rigours of Rangers' closing schedule were quite ludicrous. This was emphasised by the stance adopted by the Russian Football Federation, who granted Zenit a week to get ready for their final showdown. In these circumstances, it was not surprising that Sir David Murray entered the fray, asserting that Scotland would be a 'laughing stock' throughout the rest of world football, and even if it is sometimes difficult to sympathise with young men who are being paid thousands of pounds a week to kick a ball around a pitch, Rangers were clearly disadvantaged en route to Manchester.

None of which should be taken as a slight against the Russians, who possessed several individuals of international class, and who were worthy of their place at the denouement, given the exhilarating fashion in which the likes of Andrei Arshavin, Igor Denisov, Viktor Fayzulin and Konstantin Zyrianov had demolished high-class opponents in reaching the final. There was no disgrace in struggling against adversaries of this lustre, and for a lengthy period it seemed that Smith's tactics were once again destined to thwart a superior force, as he assembled his familiar cast of disparate talents. Kirk Broadfoot was very much to the fore despite the relentless sniping about the player's modest gifts from the English press, and Smith showed faith in the men who had beaten Fiorentina. Even so, one might have hoped that in this one-off encounter, and with tens of thousands of Ibrox supporters packed into the ground, he would have gambled a little by offering help to Darcheville, the lone Ranger who was left to plough a weary furrow up front while the Russians swept forward with panache. A recall for Lee McCulloch might have disrupted Zenit's impeccable tempo, while the sight of Kris Boyd slumped moodily on the bench spoke of his dismay at being consigned to the role of peripheral figure. Barry Ferguson looked dead on his feet, Brahim Hemdani suffered a bout of stage fright, and it was left to such livewires as Kevin Thomson and Steven Davis to provide much-needed spark. Granted, with over an hour gone and the match deadlocked, Smith's team were still very much in contention, but the suspicion lingered that the slick inter-passing of the Russians would create an opening. Thus it transpired in the 72nd minute, Denisov latching on to Arshavin's superb service to sweep the ball past Alexander. There was nothing left but for Rangers to throw caution to the wind, but Smith was strangely dilatory in sending on the cavalry in the form of Novo, McCulloch and Boyd, the last two arriving in the 80th and 86th minutes. By that stage the momentum was inexorably with Zenit, who sealed their victory deep in stoppage time when Zyrianov benefited from the flapping of a spent defence to cement a 2-0 success, which was no less than they deserved for their greater enterprise.

Despite failing the ultimate test, over the course of an adventure which had comprised 19 matches and taken Rangers to many corners of Europe, Smith could derive a significant amount of satisfaction from the exertions of his squad, with Cuellar, Weir, McGregor and Darcheville the pick of the bunch. In short, this was no time for being overly critical or seeking refuge in excuses, and he summed up what had been achieved:

'This is the end of the beginning if you consider that this is the squad's first season together. I think when you look at the player who has just been named man of the match [Arshavin], we have missed that something different. We have a team which works extremely hard, and that quality has taken them a long way. But in some games we have definitely lacked somebody with that bit of creativity. The over-riding emotion is disappointment, but what we have achieved is fantastic and it will stand these lads in good stead for the future, and in terms of us still trying to build a team, it has been pleasing to see their reaction to the challenges they have faced. I'm sure they will continue to grow, and I can't speak highly enough about them. Ultimately, I don't think anybody would have predicted that this season would lead to a European final, and that is a testament to how well they have handled themselves. Of course it is disappointing to lose, but at least we know now we belong in this company.'

Walter Smith maintained his dignity throughout this notable occasion. There was no shame in a group of honest artisans coming second to a side packed with Russian internationalists. The real shame, sadly, was being perpetrated on the streets of Manchester, where a limited, but substantial, number of Rangers' so-called supporters were besmirching the name of Scottish football with a series of violent attacks on police officers, cowardly destruction of property and terrorising of at least two women. They found themselves under siege in their cars from groups of knuckle-draggers pretending to represent Rangers even as they shouted 'UVF, UVF', inducing a shudder among the majority of Ibrox fans who were deflated, but not down in the gutter with savages who were intent on destabilising the efforts of those such as Sir David Murray and Martin Bain, who had sought to drive away the most insidious of the sectarian offenders. The grainy pictures of PC Mick Regan being set upon by these neanderthals were instantly beamed across the world, and provoked knee-jerk generalisations from some in the media. *Sunday Times* columnist Rod Liddle used the violence as a means of attacking the Tartan Army, despite the fact that they have ventured to many parts of globe without feeling the need to embark on drink-fuelled terrorism of honest citizens. In *Scotland on Sunday*, meanwhile, an

English-born journalist penned a doom-laden piece about how 'we' would all be affected by the negative images . . . a view which could only make one think of Basil Fawlty taking a twig to chastise a faulty car in the classic comedy TV series that the character stalked.

Perspective took a vacation in the aftermath, but it was soon restored, albeit in tragic circumstances. Early the next morning, Walter Smith received a phone call at his hotel in Manchester informing him that his friend and colleague and erstwhile Celtic rival, Tommy Burns, had died of cancer at the age of 51. The return journey to Glasgow was a saturnine affair, and many tears were shed across the city in the next few days, but in death there came myriad illustrations of how the bonds linking the Old Firm need not involve bigotry or festering prejudice, but can be life-enhancing. Smith demonstrated as much in his behaviour during the next few days, when he might have been preoccupied with football business. He acted as a pall-bearer at Burns' funeral, and paid a warm tribute to his Scotland colleague:

> 'There are few people who epitomise a football club more than Tommy Burns did Celtic. He was a Celtic man: a supporter as a kid, all the way through to having a terrific career for them. For me, Tommy showed everything that was good about Celtic. I think there is a respect among Rangers supporters for someone whom they know to be a true Celtic man. He was there as man and boy, and I think Rangers supporters respect that. Tommy had a respect for Rangers too – a dignified one in the sense that he never criticised Rangers about anything, and he held the club in a great deal of respect.'

For a few days at least, Glasgow's tribal divisions ceased to matter. Rangers had lost a cup final, but they would have other opportunities in future. Burns, on the other hand, was gone forever, snatched away before his time. Smith recognised where his priorities lay, and Celtic supporters applauded him for that.

CHAPTER SEVENTEEN

REWARDS AND REGRETS

❖

'Rangers ventured into Hampden preparing to undertake their
fifth match in 11 days'

By the close of play on 24 May 2008, Rangers had finally and wearily completed their itinerary for the season. They had just finished their 68th match. For Walter Smith, the CIS Cup was secure in the trophy cabinet, sealed after a fraught contest with Dundee United, while the last rites saw his team collect the Scottish Cup with a tempestuous 3-2 win over Queen of the South, which owed much to the contribution of Kris Boyd, whose two goals raised further questions about why he had been such a peripheral figure in the previous month. But it was obvious from the expressions of the manager and his squad that their achievements in regaining Rangers' dignity and reputation were overshadowed by thoughts of what might have been. That was understandable, but with the benefit of hindsight, the more pragmatic assessment was that Rangers over-achieved to a significant extent during a dramatic, pulsating and occasionally crazy period for the club. If there were people who complained about their collapse in the latter stages – which one critic described as echoing the proportions of a Shakespearean tragedy – the greater majority realised that it was little short of miraculous that an organisation which had been in freefall at the end of 2006 should be in any position to challenge for a quartet of prizes less than 18 months later.

Smith's personnel had an opportunity to prise the SPL title from under Gordon Strachan's nose right up to the climactic fixtures of Thursday 22 May, when Rangers ventured to Pittodrie, and

Celtic, ahead in the table on goal difference as the Old Firm rivals stood level on 86 points, travelled to Tannadice. There should have been little surprise about the fashion in which the Ibrox men, who had played St Mirren on 19 May, Motherwell on 17 May and Zenit St Petersburg in the UEFA Cup final on 14 May, succumbed to leaden legs and heavier pressure. Quite simply, Rangers were dead on their feet, and their mounting fatigue had been evident in the eight points they had dropped in three league matches in April – drawing 3-3 with Dundee United and losing twice to Celtic, 3-2 and 2-1, in both instances at Parkhead – as their traditional rivals fought back into contention, unburdened by having to focus on alternative competitions.

Naturally, that heaving fixture list was a bone of contention, and epitomised the procrastination and ineptitude of league officials, whose antics scarcely merited such a thrilling culmination to their competition. Quite apart from allowing Gretna to advance to the SPL and sanctioning a ridiculous ground-sharing arrangement with Motherwell, which predictably turned into a fiasco for all concerned – the promoted club going out of business and Fir Park being transformed into a quagmire, forcing the postponement of a slew of matches – the league management were consistent only in their inconsistency. They dithered following the death of Motherwell's Phil O'Donnell, who succumbed to heart failure during a tussle with Dundee United, and instead of calling for cancellation of all matches or pursuing the adage: 'The show must go on', the SPL nailed their colours to the fence, and created a situation in which the New Year Old Firm meeting was postponed, while Dundee United, whose players had suffered the trauma of watching O'Donnell collapse in front of them, were forced to proceed with business as usual.

That was bad enough, but there was no sign of flexibility or appreciation of the difficulties which were stacking up for Rangers as the SPL belatedly reacted to the club's heroics in Europe by unveiling a season extension – on 22 April – which no-one wanted, provoking consternation from Ibrox chief executive Martin Bain and his Celtic counterpart, Peter Lawwell. 'We are really bitterly disappointed in the SPL, on all fronts. It is hardly the best preparation in the lead-up to the UEFA Cup final – if we get there – to be required to play on the Sunday, Wednesday and Saturday in advance of that,' said Bain. 'I don't see what the SPL have done for Rangers in terms of aiding them in European competition. They have simply accommodated a fixture. It is all very well for them to go on about Rangers' co-efficient and how it is great for Scottish football, but they are doing nothing to assist us. As for the situation of not being in the UEFA Cup final, we have been asked to play four games in eight days. The SPL cite the preservation of sporting integrity in their decision, yet Rangers are the only club being asked to play four games in eight days, so there is no sporting integrity.' It was a horrible fudge, and Lawwell hardly emerged with credit by harping on about 'integrity', when he would have been more worldly to argue that he wanted no advantage offered to Rangers. But the spat was an indication of how tensions had risen between the clubs as the battle had grown ever tighter, and Smith, until then silent, made his feelings clear on the eve of an Old Firm match with a withering denunciation of the Celtic executive's double-speak:

'Peter Lawwell appears to be the person who is the chairman of the sporting integrity committee for the SPL. Peter would be better coming out and saying that he wants Rangers to play four games in a week, because it helps his team, and aids their quest to retain the championship. If it was the other way about, I would he hoping Celtic had to play four games in a week, so he should be honest about it, instead of trying to hide behind what he is calling sporting integrity.

'He is doing what he feels is right for his club by stating that the season shouldn't be extended, but he is doing it for his own reasons, and the thing that bothers me the most is that the SPL have this season acceded to every request which Celtic have made. I don't mind playing four games in a week. Celtic are using that situation to their advantage, but that's what it's all about. We have got to overcome them if we are to win the title.

'The most galling aspect is that they have given Celtic everything which they have asked for, and yet Peter is still complaining. I don't take part in conspiracies, and I thought it was a reasonably simple request to extend the season, but perhaps I was being naïve. If Rangers are helping raise the profile of Scottish football, helping raise the co-efficient, and giving us extra European places, then surely we should be getting a little bit of help from the authorities. If the SPL think that is the way to treat their teams, then that's fine for them. But over the piece, I think my own club has been treated unfairly.'

Coming from Walter Smith, this was unusually trenchant criticism, but it epitomised the grievances harboured by the manager, and reflected his opinion that there are many individuals in Scotland – from revenue collectors and traffic wardens to tabloid muck-rakers and New Labour politicians – whose jobs elicit minimum sympathy from the public, but that few have as thankless a task as the man picking the team at Ibrox.

By the night of 22 May, Smith's wrath had diminished. During the course of the epic league campaign, his side and Celtic had spurned myriad opportunities to steal a march on their opponents, with Gordon Strachan's team dropping nine points in December by drawing 1-1 respectively with Hearts, Hibs and Motherwell and losing 3-2 to Inverness Caledonian Thistle. That slump explains why many people believe that the postponement of the Old Firm match at New Year – for which Celtic's leading asset, Aiden McGeady, would have been unavailable through suspension – offered Strachan a chance to regroup and regain momentum. But whatever the more blinkered observers might retort, Celtic man for man and pound for pound were superior to their Rangers counterparts. The surprise was that they took so long to press home that reality in the only place that mattered. Eventually, the slow puncture that deflated their adversaries made things easier than they might have been. For over an hour, as the action raged in the north-east of Scotland, supporters on both sides listened nervously to their radios, and endured the exquisite torture which pervades such occasions. With Rangers required to attain a better result than Celtic, they could barely have chosen a less auspicious venue than Pittodrie, and matters came close to resolution in the 63rd minute when Lee Miller steered Barry Nicholson's finely-flighted free-kick past the despairing Neil Alexander. Ten minutes later at Tannadice, the predatory Jan Vennegoor of Hesselink executed a thunderous header from Paul Hartley's corner cross, and it was evident that the championship trophy was staying at Celtic Park . . . even before Smith endured the indignities of Darren Mackie's second goal and the dismissal of the often impetuous Nacho Novo for a wild challenge.

As the moments ticked away, Smith bore the countenance of a man whose worst fears had been realised, and looked every one of his 60 years. But those vaguely-moronic so-called supporters who responded to the defeat with calls for his sacking – they hit the airwaves almost before the cessation of hostilities in Aberdeen – were mercifully in a minuscule minority. Twelve months earlier, thanks to the combination of a late surge and a complacent end-of-term series of displays from Celtic, with the championship title wrapped up by Christmas, the Ibrox club had accrued 72 points. Now, despite the rigours of fighting on several fronts, Rangers had progressed to 86 points, without significant spending on new players. It represented measurable progress, but that did not prevent Smith from feeling deflated: 'We had an opportunity to win the championship, but we let it slip. Overall, it was our failure to handle a set of unusual circumstances. That is where we have fallen down. Rangers, like any other club would have done, tried as hard as they could to get the fixtures more spread, but when it doesn't happen, you have got to get on with it and play the games. The biggest thing to our detriment has been the amount of matches we have had to play – especially big league games at Celtic Park and the European fixtures – and I think that has taken its toll mentally. There is no doubt in my mind we have handled it physically, though mentally we have struggled a wee bit with a lack of sharpness. The one thing that bothered me about the build-up of games was how injuries and suspension would affect us. [DaMarcus] Beasley was out for most of the season, but when you have Lee McCulloch, Charlie Adam, Chris Burke and Steven Naismith all injured, then we lost all our wide players at the same time during the campaign. Ultimately, there have been a lot of highs this year for us, but on a personal basis I am more inclined to remember my disappointments, and I think that attitude helps spur you on all the time. This is the first occasion I can recall that we have been involved in the latter stages of all of the four tournaments we were chasing, and that's a measure of what we have done over the course of the season, but we just haven't been able to handle the vital part of it, which is the end part. Hopefully, we will learn lessons from that which we can carry with us into the future, because while we are obviously disappointed at the league outcome, we can derive a lot of positives from what we have achieved.'

One of the most significant of these was the camaraderie developed by Smith and his back-room staff, assistant coach Ally McCoist, first-team coach Kenny McDowall and sports scientist Adam Owen: the latter pair had previously been Celtic employees. While Rangers looked increasingly under pressure as the season marched on, there was no doubting their resilience nor their strength of character, and much of that was down to the methodology of those working behind the scenes. Gone was the prevalent drinking culture which had existed at Rangers in the 1990s, and in its place was a milieu in which players were encouraged to discuss health matters, organise their own diets and thrive on pasta, energy drinks and mineral water. Smith no longer took such a hands-on role in directing operations, and though he was swift to repudiate tabloid rumours alleging that he might be moving upstairs at the end of the season, he seemed comfortable with compartmentalising the roles of those within the Ibrox hierarchy. 'Not only have we had a lot of new players coming in during the last year, the entire back-room staff has changed as well. Ally and Kenny have worked extremely hard to create a good atmosphere on the training ground, and that has helped us a great deal in what has been a hectic season, because they have created an environment where people want to come in and work. Ally, Kenny and Adam take the vast majority of training, which is a different situation to when I was the manager here before, but it is all about being flexible and being receptive to new ideas. For example, I was always used to doing longer spells of running in pre-season training, but what we do now is much shorter and sharper. The whole staff has had to work hard to keep everybody going this season, but the players have battled on, and that is testament to the work they have put in.'

❖

Rangers may have crashed into a wall in April and May of 2008, but their fortitude and physical fitness had been conspicuous as they advanced to the final of the CIS Cup in March, to within touching distance of their first trophy in three years. En route to Hampden, they brushed aside East Fife 4-0, struggled past Motherwell 2-1, and were indebted to a controversial Barry Ferguson goal – the ball clearly striking his arm before he despatched his shot – in beating Hearts 2-0 in the semi-final, but they knew they would face a gruelling tussle with Craig Levein's Dundee United, not least because the Tannadice side were determined to secure a prize for their terminally-ill chairman, Eddie Thompson.

In the event, it was tougher than anyone could have anticipated, the result in the balance from beginning to end. Rangers twice had to come from behind prior to winning a penalty shoot-out, and the enigmatic Boyd was the hero for his team, emerging as a substitute after an hour and scoring a brace of goals before striking the decisive kick past Lukasz Zaluska. That turn of events had seemed remote during a whirlwind first half, which was dominated by Levein's men, Noel Hunt giving them a deserved lead in the 33rd minute, and Smith was sufficiently concerned to introduce Jean-Claude Darcheville for the ineffectual Brahim Hemdani at the start of the second period. United's claims for a penalty in the 53rd minute, when Carlos Cuellar appeared to pull back Christian Kalvenes in the box, were ignored by referee Kenny Clark, and Darcheville and Boyd became ever more influential as the conclusion beckoned, with Rangers equalising through Boyd with six minutes remaining. Even here, there was stroke of good fortune about the goal, with Mark Kerr inexplicably attempting a pass-back to his keeper, which was comfortably intercepted by the Ibrox striker. But if onlookers imagined that Smith's ensemble would find life more comfortable in extra-time, they were soon disabused of that notion when Mark de Vries restored United's advantage in the 96th minute by drilling the ball past Allan McGregor from the right side of the box. It was tense stuff, a classic clash of contrasting styles, and once again the clock posed as much of a threat to Rangers as their opponents when Boyd, drifting in and out of the action, suddenly proved their saviour as the Tayside team failed to clear their lines, and he headed the ball home at the back post in the 113rd minute.

The shoot-out was equally fraught for fans, managers and players. David Robertson, Craig Conway and Lee Wilkie missed their spot kicks, but Darcheville and McCulloch were similarly culpable, and the tension within Hampden was tangible. However, Boyd was an oasis of calm in the circumstances – nothing seems to worry this fellow, though that may be as much a weakness as a strength – and his penalty was converted with the sort of clinical assurance that some of the previous efforts had so manifestly lacked.

He was indisputably the pivotal protagonist of the drama, and Smith, who emerged relieved, exultant and exhausted in equal measure, had no choice but to applaud Boyd's contribution. Yet it summed up the febrile relationship between the two individuals that when it would have been easy for Smith to lapse into comments of the *Colemanballs* type and to rhapsodise about his player, he still felt it necessary to inject a sliver of criticism: 'I know that sometimes in his overall play he is a little bit of a frustrating character, but if you get the ball into the box a lot of the time, he will always get you goals. He also knows that, and it is a little frustrating for him sitting on the bench all the time, and for me. But I know that if I put him on he is not affected by it.' Smith's response was fuelled by the knowledge that in the Rangers heartlands widespread bafflement had greeted his decision to persist with the likes of the often anonymous Daniel Cousin when Boyd was such a prolific scorer, especially in the SPL, where subtlety matters less than goals on the ledger sheet. The manager added: 'It was a hard match, but we expected nothing else from United, who were excellent in the first 45 minutes. I felt that we had to impose ourselves and get the ball into their box in the second half, and we did that and got the goals. Then, when it came down to a final penalty, there is nobody better. He is a terrific penalty-taker, and I was as confident as I possibly could be that he would convert that one.'

This may seem like faint praise, but it embodies Smith's footballing philosophy and his indomitable work ethic. He was proud of his squad for emerging victorious in the CIS-sponsored competition a mere three days after eliminating Werder Bremen from the UEFA Cup, but there was nary a trace of complacency in his make-up. Smith had reached his 60th birthday, but he remained as restless for success as ever, and confessed that his passion for management had been rekindled during his three-month spell with the masterly Sir Alex Ferguson at Manchester United in 2004. 'I felt revitalised, and I got the bug back when I went to Old Trafford,' he revealed. 'I had been enjoying doing for the first time what I wanted to do – watching games, playing a bit of golf and having a break when it suited me. I was in a lucky position, a lot luckier than a lot of people who were unemployed. But going to United definitely gave me a lift, particularly when we won the FA Cup final against Millwall.' Smith explained that he had changed in some respects from the relentlessly-driven individual who had succeeded Graeme Souness at Ibrox in the early 1990s:

'Norman Mailer said that there are not that many good things about getting old, but one of them is that you don't really give a f*** any more. I think it's true. I don't feel quite as tense as I did, and I don't get as angry so quickly. Before I came back to Rangers, I spoke to Sir Alex and he told me it's a matter of how young you feel, and that if you can communicate, then age doesn't really matter. He was probably right, but it was something I had to think about when I was coming back. In other types of management, you are often apart from the workforce, but here, in the football world, you are involved directly with them all the time. But I enjoy that, and if I didn't, I would not be here. You have to love your job to do it well. I loved my period at Rangers first time round, and I am loving it now.'

That passion was witnessed often enough throughout Rangers' Scottish Cup run which, akin to everything else which surrounded the club in this protracted season, gradually developed into a marathon. Smith and his charges started with a comfortable 6-0 rout of lowly Third Division East Stirlingshire, a non-contest which allowed Kris Boyd and Lee McCulloch to add cheap goals to their account. Boyd, capitalising on the slipshod defending of the underdogs, claimed a hat-trick by scoring in the 30th, 45th and 62nd minutes, while McCulloch was on target after 25 and 50 minutes, but the more significant statistic was that Alan Hutton's goal in 28 minutes was his last tangible contribution to Smith's side before he was snapped up by Tottenham Hotspur for £9m. It was a piece of business which made financial sense, but was not the catalyst for Smith to splash out as the January transfer window opened and closed without serious activity, beyond the acquisition of the dependable Christian Dailly and Steven Davis. That Davis proved an auspicious purchase should have reminded fans that their manager was no slouch in the scouting field, but it was a world removed from the days when entrepreneur David Murray showered Smith with cash in search of the SPL title.

As one competition intertwined with another, Rangers knuckled down to the grind, as if determined to demonstrate that they could withstand any problems by the sheer force of their combined personality. Drawn away to Hibernian, they survived an arduous battle with the Edinburgh side, earning a goal-less draw despite losing McGregor, who was harshly dismissed in the closing stages for making minimal contact with Dean Shiels outside the penalty area. Come the replay, a first-half goal from Chris Burke eventually proved decisive for the hosts, but not before the fractious Novo was red-carded for a reckless lunge on Thierry Gathuessi in the 79th minute and pandemonium erupted with Smith and his Hibs counterpart, Mixu Paatelainen, exchanging cantankerous words, as the prelude to the more senior manager being sent to the stand with steam coming out of his ears – reinforcing the impression that football was as important to him as it had ever been.

Fixtures were clogging up the schedules, and the last thing that Rangers needed was more sweat created by their failure to win inside 90 minutes. Pitted against Partick Thistle at home in the quarter-final, they served up a desperately-disappointing performance that was devoid of flair or imagination, and it was just as well that their First Division opponents were of limited quality, or Rangers' progress in the tournament would have been abruptly curtailed. Thistle seized the lead in the 67th minute with a fine effort from Damon Gray, but the visitors were unable to settle on that lead before Boyd levelled the score to ensure a replay. When the Ibrox stands reverberated to the refrain: 'He gets the ball, he scores a goal', the contrast between the supporters' loyalty to the striker and Smith's scepticism about the player's worth was never more apparent. Whatever the feelings about Boyd's work-rate, or lack of it, he kept providing vital goals. The return encounter at Firhill was less stressful than Rangers might have feared. First-half strikes from Novo and Burke were sufficient for the cup favourites – confirmed as such after Celtic's elimination by Aberdeen – to ease into the semi-finals for what seemed a straightforward task versus St Johnstone.

By this juncture, however, nothing was straightforward, and Smith was forced to confront a daunting match schedule in the knowledge that his options were limited. Having lost to Celtic in the league on 16 April – a hammer-blow which ensured that Rangers were subsequently always playing catch-up in the title race – the manager made nine changes for the Hampden encounter with the Perth side four days later, retaining only his talismanic Cuellar and ever-reliable Dailly from the team that had succumbed at Parkhead. The reshuffled side proved to be mediocre, but they were hampered from the outset by the dreadful state of the pitch at the national stadium, in addition to suffering the loss of Burke and Steven Naismith within the first 20 minutes, both players sustaining serious injuries in challenges with Kevin Rutkiewicz and Martin Hardie. In these circumstances, the Ibrox men were entitled to look disjointed, but they still orchestrated good chances for Thomas Buffel and Novo without reward, as the precursor to the familiar sound of boos echoing from sections of the support who were oblivious to the severe depletion of their team's resources.

Perhaps stung by the jeering, they commenced the second period with greater urgency and Novo was presented with another golden opportunity, which he squandered in shooting weakly straight at goalkeeper Alan Main, before St Johnstone's Steven Milne almost broke the deadlock with a deft flick which required smart attention from Neil Alexander. As the hour came and went, Derek McInnes' men clearly scented an upset, and though Liam Craig had to be alert to deny Rangers a late winner when he cleared Davis' net-bound header, the First Division side never ceased battling, nor snapping at the heels of their opponents as extra-time beckoned. Daniel McBreen sent St Johnstone in front three minutes into the added period, nodding Paul Sheerin's cross beyond the helpless Alexander. It was a precarious position for a second-string team who were perilously close to running on empty, but whatever the skill level, their bravery and commitment could not be faulted, and they deservedly gained a penalty after Rutkiewicz fouled Daniel Cousin in the 103rd minute, with Novo making no mistake in crashing the ball low past Main. That sparked a frantic climax, Milne firing over from close range and Novo hitting the post, but the match had looked as if it would go the full distance, and once more Rangers entered a penalty shootout clinging to quadruple hopes by the skin of the teeth, and by the skill of Alexander. Predictably, neither camp attracted an urgent queue of volunteers for penalty duties: Milne and Hemdani missed for their respective clubs, but the crucial error was perpetrated by St Johnstone's Jody Morris, whose miss left the way open for

Cousin to secure victory. The job was done, but far from convincingly. Business as usual, then!

If some perspective was required on the scale of what Rangers were pursuing, it surely came from the torrent of events, controversies, disputes and front-page headlines which materialised between their beating St Johnstone on 20 April and meeting Queen of the South on 24 May. In just over a month Rangers celebrated a nail-biting success over Fiorentina, which guided them to the UEFA Cup final; they provoked a furious response from Dundee United's manager Craig Levein, who claimed that referee Mike McCurry had 'bottled' two major decisions, which might have earned the Tannadice club a penalty and a red card for David Weir during his side's acrimonious 3-1 defeat at Ibrox; and they experienced the heady prelude and sickening aftermath of a European showpiece in which they were undone on the field by Zenit St Petersburg and embarrassed off it by a cabal of alleged supporters with a craving for drink, violence and sectarian chants. All that transpired even before the hectic, bathetic conclusion to the story, with Rangers pipped for the SPL title by Celtic, but with the death of Tommy Burns casting a long shadow over mere sporting affairs. It was scarcely any wonder that by the time Walter Smith was asked how he would motivate his team for their Scottish Cup assignment, this most sedulous of individuals was almost at a loss for words. Almost: 'From memory, I don't think anyone could share this experience with us, because I don't think anyone has had to play in a cup final after playing 48 hours before. It's a new experience for us all, so we will just need to go along our normal route of trying to get everybody lifted again,' he reflected with the faintest of smiles. 'It gives us the opportunity to finish on a high after a couple of real disappointments in the last eight or nine days, but there's nothing you can say to cover the disappointment. As a manager I couldn't have asked any more of my players over the course of the season, and now we have to go out there again. I will consider the season a season from where we started out, yet it is a season which will always be tinged with disappointment, and we cannot get away from that. But winning the Scottish Cup would be a great thing and give us a couple of domestic trophies for the season, which would be great. I hope for the boys' sake that they do that. No disrespect to Queen of the South, who have worked very hard to get to this stage, but I just hope that we can get ourselves up for the game.'

Rangers ventured into Hampden preparing to undertake their fifth match in 11 days, and less than 42 hours after being beaten by Aberdeen in the SPL. If the SFA are wondering why their premier tournament does not have a sponsor, they may wish to consider setting up a working party containing members of all the SPL clubs, to ensure that such a scenario never happens again. Quite apart from the dearth of focus with which Rangers approached the competition's finale because of their mass of fixtures, cup final day was strangely subdued. This may have been down to sheer fatigue on Rangers' part, while Queens had endured a month's lay-off before their day in the sun, which meant that Gordon Chisholm's men were nearly as under-cooked as Smith's were burnt to a frazzle.

It was refreshing, then, that what could easily have developed into a forgettable occasion – such as the dire meeting between Celtic and Dunfermline in 2007 – was lifted by illustrations of courage, passion and no little flair from both sets of players, as they waltzed to a merry tune amid the sunshine on Mount Florida. The hero, as he had been invariably when presented with the opportunity, was Kris Boyd. Complete with comedy moustache and a deadly-serious intent to move elsewhere rather than spend as much time on the bench in future campaigns, he broke the deadlock in the 33rd minute, collecting Ferguson's free-kick and unleashing a ferocious shot past Jamie MacDonald. When Beasley was allowed a glimmer of goal following a collision between Queens' Jim Thomson and Ryan McCann, the American coolly made it 2-0 in the 43rd minute, which seemed to have guaranteed that Walter Smith would be picking up his fourth Scottish Cup without any shocks. However, it would not have been like Rangers to have accomplished their mission comfortably. Nor, to the credit of Chisholm's side, were they allowed to settle into anything resembling cruise control. On the contrary, a massive upset appeared possible when Queen of the South levelled the game within eight minutes of the second period opening, with goals from Steve Tosh, who diverted a Sean O'Connor cross into the net delicately off his groin, and Thomson, who leapt in balletic style while the Rangers defence slumbered. None of this should have been totally unexpected, given the stunning fashion in which the Dumfries team had risen to the challenge of beating Aberdeen 4-3 in their semi-final, but if ever Smith was inclined to raise a toast to Boyd, this was it. Without his bullocking menace, Rangers might have sunk without trace, but as the contest advanced towards the spectre of extra-time, Boyd regained the lead by heading in Beasley's delivery from a corner as if it was easiest thing in the world, and the jubilation, relief and slight aggravation etched on Smith's face at the arrival of the decisive strike was a picture to behold. Simon Buckland deftly described the subsequent scenes in *The Sunday Times*:

'As each player took their time to lift up the trophy, the cheer for Boyd was only surpassed by the ovation given to his manager. Smith took the cup in his right hand and raised it to the sky with as much delight as he could muster. He hasn't got everything he wanted out of the season. Neither has Boyd. Perhaps Smith should consider that the two are linked. Goals win matches. Boyd wins matches. If Rangers aren't careful, he could soon be winning them for somebody else'

It was an astute summation of the relationship between boss and employee, and in the wake of victory, Boyd, who accumulated 25 goals in as many starts despite the hours of frittering around on the periphery, emphasised that matters would have to change dramatically, or the exit door beckoned. 'I hope I showed the manager what I can do today. I would have been delighted to play more this season, but that's life,' said the Hampden hero, whose moustache might have served as a farewell to the fans. 'You go on, but I'll have a long, hard think about it over the summer. Obviously not playing gets to people, so I will go away and think about what has happened this season, and decide what's best.' For his part, Smith was content simply to avoid the humiliation of a third successive reverse in less than a fortnight, and commented: 'The amount of football we have played has taken its toll, so I am delighted for the players because of their efforts throughout the season. I worried about fatigue, but it was slackness that cost us the goals, and I wondered if we had enough left to come back again. We have had a lot to overcome, and I'm glad we managed to do it. It would have been a shame if we had lost out, and although it doesn't take away the disappointment of the last few days, it is a tangible reward.' Smith was not inclined to dampen the celebrations unduly with a fresh onslaught against the SPL and SFA, but he had already stated his case, logically, the previous day at the club's Murray Park complex. Non-Rangers observers will probably dismiss his sentiments as sour grapes, but his argument was tightly constructed and inherently sensible:

'I'm not one for statistics, but I read that we went on a 27-game run without losing, and that set us up to have a better opportunity to win the title than I imagined would be the case in the first season. After that, we have been confronted by the situation. We have kept at a reasonable level to qualify for the UEFA Cup final, but it has affected our form and our results elsewhere. Look at our block of games after that run – our form has been up and down. [He was referring to how Rangers dropped 15 of the last 27 points on offer, after relinquishing just 13 of the previous 87].

'We have dropped points after the last lot of European matches, and these are circumstances which we have not handled well. But there again, we had three spells of playing four games in 10 days, and it is difficult for anyone to handle that. The second part of the season has been difficult, and the last two months have been a hard test. It has been easy to sit and watch. The hard part is the footballers to keep physically and mentally prepared. The goals we were losing were not those we had been losing earlier in the season.

'At the start of the UEFA Cup, as soon as the Champions League campaign was over, if you were looking at it domestically, it would have been better if we had cleared the way. But I don't know. How do you look back on a season? What do you do? You can't plan to lose. You lose often enough without trying. During the run that we had, around about the time of the UEFA Cup quarter-final, we saw that we were going to be faced with a list of fixtures, and I thought then that it would be extremely difficult for us to keep going. So, to get to the last day of the title race [still in contention] has been a big thing.'

Ultimately, and whatever one's allegiance, the excitement and contrasting emotions conjured up by season 2007-08 at Ibrox marked a distinct stride forward for the club and demonstrated that, even after turning 60, Smith had no thoughts of quitting. Instead, he was intent on hunting down further prizes and surmounting challenges, no matter whether they came from opponents – or from within his own organisation.

CHAPTER EIGHTEEN

BEATING THE ODDS

'I can't remember a season when we have had so many difficulties
to overcome'

Life is never dull in the world of the Old Firm. At other clubs,
there may occasionally be opportunities to seal deals and map out
futures behind closed doors, but that luxury wasn't afforded to
Walter Smith and his Celtic counterpart, Gordon Strachan, as
they prepared to resume hostilities in the summer of 2008. There
were days when football seemed to be a secondary consideration
at Ibrox, whether with the club finding themselves under scrutiny
from UEFA because of sectarian chanting from a section of their
supporters, or with the fall-out from the mayhem from Manchester continuing to cast a blight over any attempts to drag Rangers
into the 21st century. As an engrossing SPL campaign progressed
from August onwards, Smith had, at various times, to deal with
questions about the 'Famine Song' and respond to the aftermath
of the notorious 'Boozegate' saga, involving Barry Ferguson and
Allan McGregor; he had to worry about the parlous financial
state of the business behind the scenes, even if the full extent of
that malaise wouldn't become clear for another 12 months; and
he even had to confirm, on one occasion, that his defender, Kirk
Broadfoot, had suffered burns after an egg exploded in his face.
(The player had been inspecting two eggs he had poached in his
microwave when one of them blew up and squirted scalding-hot
water over his coupon.)

If these had been story lines from a series of *Footballers' Wives*, they might have been rejected as being too implausible, but Smith had long since realised that his job was less a sporting post than a one-man fire-fighting shift. More predictably, perhaps, given the paucity of international class within his squad, was the fact that Rangers started the new season with little of the effervescence which had typified their previous campaign and, although, with hindsight, it may beggar belief, there were even question marks over Smith's suitability for steering his side forward. The doubts surfaced during a 4-0 trouncing by Liverpool at Ibrox, they intensified when the hosts could only manage a 0-0 draw in the first leg of their Champions League qualifying tie with Lithuanian minnows, Kaunas, and a minor agitation transmogrified into a full-blown crisis when Rangers lost the return leg 2-1, after Linas Pilibaitis swooped to head home a Rafael Ledesma corner in the 87th minute of the game, which the Scots had initially dominated, prior to succumbing to the nerves which arise when tens of millions of pounds are at stake.

The year before, Rangers had advanced through with a mixture of *esprit des corps*, sheer cussedness and a dogged refusal to accept defeat. They had also been fortunate on one or two occasions, and there was always the prospect that the luck might balance out. But the most frustrating aspect for Smith and his assistants, Ally McCoist and Kenny McDowall, was that their charges had begun brightly, with Kenny Miller spurning a wonderful opportunity to open the scoring, prior to Kevin Thomson breaking the deadlock by latching on to Nacho Novo's pass and slotting the ball past Marian Kello.

So far, so promising. Yet, when the situation demanded a battening down of the hatches, the visitors quickly conceded an equaliser, when Nerijus Radzius' 35m free-kick flew past McGregor and Rangers' initial poise was replaced by a decent impersonation of rabbits and headlights conjoining. 'A lot of the players believed their own publicity from last season and they didn't work as hard as they did back then,' said Lee McCulloch, once the post-mortems commenced. 'They need to take a good look at themselves.'

It was a fair assessment of an evening where the Ibrox men diminished under the glare of pressure which they had created through their own lackadaisical approach. Miller squandered another fine chance, then Andrius Velicka and Christian Dailly displayed similar profligacy, to the extent that when Pilibaitis struck late on in the proceedings, it wasn't any great surprise, least of all to the sprinkling of travelling fans who had spent substantial sums to be inside the Dariaus Ir Gireno Stadium. Basically, this wasn't a Rangers collective so blessed with sufficient talent that they could afford to choose their moments. On the contrary, they required to be at the peak of their performance for 90 minutes of every match and when they failed in that respect, they were very vulnerable.

Smith recognised as much. If truth be told, his resources had required bolstering during the summer, without any signs of significant transfer activity, but the bottom line was that Rangers should have been capable of negotiating their path past opponents as limited as Kaunas. 'We have gone from the sublime to the ridiculous in going from reaching a European final to losing in the qualifying stage, but it has happened and we have to deal with the consequences,' said Smith, exhibiting the pithy pragmatism of a man who knew only too well that this result carried serious ramifications for himself and his club. 'It is thoroughly disappointing, but if we had gone through, we could have counted ourselves fortunate, because our level of performance was nowhere near what it reached last year. Now, we have to pick ourselves up and concentrate on doing better in the SPL.'

There was a depressingly familiar pattern in the days following the defeat. Many so-called Rangers aficionados, the same people who had watched Smith guide a squad of honest artisans to the brink of winning four trophies less than three months earlier, suddenly popped up on Internet message boards and radio phone-in programmes, proclaiming that the manager should be replaced by McCoist, or a Graeme Souness, or a Terry Butcher . . . indeed, anybody from the glory days of the mid-1990s. This reaction reflected the myopic tendencies of the doom-mongers who cling to the coat-tails of both halves of the Old Firm, but it was desperately unfair on Smith, who was being forced to make the best of a bad job and was doing so with characteristic vim and commitment. Nor did the people who spouted these views carry on complaining when Rangers, under fire and out of sorts in the build up, roared out of the blocks to win the first Old Firm derby by a convincing and thoroughly merited margin of 4-2 at Parkhead on August 31.

In the prelude to the contest, Smith had lost one of his prime assets, Carlos Cuellar, who had moved on to Aston Villa in a £7.8m deal while Pedro Mendes had arrived at Ibrox from Portsmouth for £3m. This was a reversal of the spending policies which had surrounded Rangers during their march to nine consecutive league titles, but it demonstrated that those people who protested that Smith would have achieved nothing without a massive cheque book were almost as accurate as the pundit who told Sir Alex Ferguson he would never win anything with 'kids'. Straight from the outset, Mendes looked blessed with a touch of class and steel, which were necessities for anybody being thrust into an Old Firm clash and if Rangers fans were sceptical about their new man, and openly hostile about the return of Kenny Miller to their club, they had ample cause to be grateful to both performers as Celtic crumbled against the duo.

Smith, too, merited plaudits for the fashion in which he paired Miller with the Gabon internationalist, Daniel Cousin, up front. The latter opened the scoring and, even if he was subsequently dismissed for a second yellow card, after jumping into Stephen McManus, becoming one of two players to see red – the other being Celtic's Jan Vennegoor of Hesselink – the trial combination worked wonders in revitalising Rangers and ensuring that they dominated the contest, with Shunsuke Nakamura' 90th-minute goal proving to be nothing more than scant consolation for Strachan's hapless personnel.

Indeed, although they responded to Cousin breaking the deadlock immediately with a counter from Giorgios Samaras, Celtic were left on their uppers when Miller met Kevin Thomson's cross with a sweetly-struck volley, as the precursor to Mendes, a tower of enterprise and creativity in midfield, thundering in a wondrous shot from 30 yards, which surged beyond Artur Boruc and reduced the majority of the audience to surly silence or renewed criticism of Strachan. Their annoyance heightened when Boruc spilled an apparently routine cross from Broadfoot right into Miller's path and the latter wrapped up victory with all the practiced ease of somebody who has been scoring all his life.

Later in the evening, the aftermath of the match brought a new batch of lurid headlines when it emerged that Celtic's Neil Lennon had been assaulted in Glasgow city centre by the sort of so-called supporters who should be ostracised by any decent football people. But Smith had no authority over this disgraceful behaviour. What he could control was his team's performances in the Old Firm cauldron and he was quick to lavish compliments on Miller for marking his return to Rangers in such a spectacular fashion. 'If that doesn't win the fans over, then I don't know what Kenny needs to do,' said the manager. 'We were just pleased to get the goals, no matter who scored them, but it is funny how things like that happen in football. It was a good showing from the boys.'

The trouble was that, even while Smith addressed the media in the aftermath of the victory, the Scottish game was going through one of its periodic bouts of soul searching. There was no question that the pedigree of the Old Firm personnel had deteriorated since the end of the 1990s or when the likes of Henrik Larsson, Chris Sutton and Stilian Petrov were instrumental in steering Martin O'Neill's vintage to a European final. But these things tend to be cyclical and the reality was that the Scottish Premier League was nowhere near as attractive a proposition to would-be sponsors and broadcasters as it had once been. With the national team also getting out of the habit of qualifying for the finals of major competitions, while England's Premiership increased in stature, it was hardly surprising that the Scottish clubs were becoming increasingly irrelevant in the wider picture of Continental football. That much was pretty evident when Celtic were briskly swept aside 3-0 by a Manchester United ensemble, who were missing several of their key players, at Old Trafford in the Champions League. Yet, as one of the throng who watched the proceedings, Smith bridled at the remarks of Paul Ince, who described Celtic as an 'embarrassment' and claimed that the match had been 'men against boys'.

'You have to bear in mind there is a big gulf between Manchester United and a lot of teams in the [English] Premiership. If you look at United, Arsenal, Liverpool and Chelsea, they have made themselves fixtures at the top of that league. But the game in Scotland is as good as it can be, taking into account that football is a financially-based game and has been for the last 10 or 15 years since the introduction of huge sums of television money in England. Scottish teams do the best they can – Celtic acquitted themselves well in the Champions League last year and I felt that we also acquitted ourselves well. The fact is the English clubs have a level of finance that is greater than their Scottish counterparts, but football throughout Europe is like that as well. You don't see many teams from small countries getting into the latter stages of the Champions League and that is just the way it is these days. We managed to get to the UEFA Cup final, so Scottish sides have definitely proved that they can stand up and play and have a level of success. Of course, it is very difficult for us to do so every year, but it doesn't stop us from competing and I think that we do very well. Put it like this, I don't believe Scottish football is suddenly in a desperately poor situation just because Celtic got beaten 3-0 by a team who could probably beat any team in Europe 3-0. But I do worry that it will become too predictable – that is the biggest danger. The fact is that Manchester United can afford to leave out players who would make up a very good team. That has been the case for 10 years and, on a basic level, you need the other teams to have a very poor day and us to have a very good day if we are to achieve anything in Europe.'

These words met with little resistance from pragmatic surveyors of SPL fare. A more serious problem for Rangers, and Smith, lay in their inability to generate any sustained momentum on the domestic beat, following their early triumph against Celtic. Instead, with Kris Boyd continuing to provoke heated exchanges between those who thought him a messiah and a mess, and with the likes of Kyle Lafferty, an expensive summer purchase from Burnley, looking as comfortable in the Rangers ranks at Jeremy Clarkson at a Green Party conference, the Ibrox men regularly flattered to deceive, whereas Celtic established a lengthy winning streak, which pushed them seven points in front of their Old Firm opponents at the end of November. By this juncture, and especially in the aftermath of a significant 2-1 defeat to Hearts, where Rangers were gifted an own goal by Christos Karapidis, prior to the Tynecastle side being reduced to 10 men with the dismissal of Lee Wallace, it was evident that Smith's personnel needed to grasp two central messages. Firstly, they weren't good enough to thrive without offering 100% and, secondly, they had to stop conceding territory and goals to the likes of Marius Zaliukas, Laryea Kingston and Christophe Berra, all of whom shone for Hearts amidst their success. At the end, with the jeers of the Govan faithful ringing in his ears, Smith refused to offer excuses or pretend that the performance had been in any way acceptable. 'It certainly means that in the three Old Firm games that are left, the pressure is heaped firmly on ourselves,' was the gist of his post-match assessment. 'As I've said all along, we have a big enough group of players and that group have to handle the situation we are in.'

This was for public consumption. Privately, Smith appreciated that, despite the hype and hoopla which habitually surrounded the Old Firm's tussles, they were only worth the same number of points as away trips to Kilmarnock, St Mirren, or the rest of the places where Rangers' early-season displays were less the red-blooded variety of yore than positively anaemic. Yet, if he had problems with Boyd, who walked out on Scotland – under the then manager George Burley – in a fit of pique at being left on the bench, during a World Cup qualifying match against Norway at Hampden Park, Gordon Strachan was beset by a similar battle of wills, amidst reports of dressing-room unrest with Aiden McGeady. Sometimes it was as if football was a secondary consideration in the 2008-09 campaign, not least when the Old Firm locked horns. Style and subtlety, flair and finesse: if you wanted these, you had to switch your gaze elsewhere, to La Liga or the Premiership in England. But, all the same, the clash of temperaments between Rangers and Celtic still possessed an earthy fascination, particularly as the New Year beckoned and the Ibrox men strove to recover from producing a lethargic and wholly unsatisfactory display in slipping to a 1-0 loss at Ibrox on December 27.

In some quarters, this was portrayed as if it had been a title decider. *The Observer* reported: 'On a day when Celtic had the look of champions, victory that would open up a potentially-decisive seven-point lead over their would-be challengers seemed not to be enough. There was a whiff of humiliation for Rangers, beaten with almost contemptuous ease by opponents, whose personnel problems gave them a makeshift look, but who, in racing parlance, won "on the bridle". Scott McDonald's second-half goal may have been the decider, but it was obvious, from a long way out, that Walter Smith's team lacked the inventiveness, the incisiveness and even the will to deliver the victory for which their supporters ached . . . Rangers were in such disarray, during the last 30 minutes of the game that the champions were able to coast towards the finishing line. By the time that they got there, their opponents had become victims of a deep despair.'

It was true that the hosts had been ineffectual throughout the proceedings, but it was a tad premature to start dishing out SPL winners' medals. If anything, the result merely confirmed what Smith already knew: that his team were workmanlike performers without the cutting edge to spark havoc in rival defences, and were reliant on perspiration and a spirit of collectivism to help them compensate for individual deficiencies. On the other hand, though, Celtic had only secured the spoils with a spectacular effort from McDonald – the one genuine piece of class on a chilly Yuletide afternoon – and Smith possessed sufficient guile to recognise that there would be plenty of twists and turns in the pursuit of the championship. What can't have bolstered his mood was the knowledge that there was no money in the Ibrox kitty to strengthen his squad – a state of affairs with which he had to grow used to in the next 18 months – but he sat down with his players over the New Year, reminded them of their responsibilities to the supporters, and essentially spread the gospel that there could be no further slip-ups in the race with Celtic.

'There is not much between the two teams right now. The pride and determination they have at being champions has seen them through a period where they're maybe not playing their best football, but they're winning their games, and credit to them for that. We have not shown that edge; losing in this month alone to Hearts and Celtic has been disappointing for us and that's something that we have to try and develop. We have a situation where we know we have to go on that type of run [winning all their remaining matches] if we hope to get ourselves back into the championship race.'

In these circumstances, it might have been understandable if Smith had resorted to straw-clutching exercises, even as he learned about the sickly financial state of the club, but he was assisted by a brace of factors in his objective. Firstly, Celtic, who were in a far healthier fiscal position, elected not to bring in meaningful reinforcements during the January transfer window, amidst speculation that Strachan and his board did not see eye-to-eye on the best way forward for their club. Secondly, Smith had a heart-to-heart with Boyd – who, at this point, was being routinely vilified by the Tartan Army and even many Rangers fans – and convinced the striker that the best way to silence his detractors was to notch up as many goals as possible. It was the sort of motivational exercise at which he excelled – a former colleague described Smith as 'part-shop steward, part-agony aunt' – and Boyd went away feeling as if life was bearable again. Fragile egos or not, this mattered a lot in the psychological stakes, which became abundantly clear when the former Kilmarnock star upped his game as Rangers hunted down their prey.

Slowly but surely, the gap was reduced as Celtic stumbled on their travels and only two points separated the behemoths when they squared up for the third time in the season at Parkhead on the St Valentine's Day weekend. Predictably, there was little love in the air, either on the pitch or among the crowd. Perhaps, equally unsurprisingly, given the palpable tension which had crept into the performances of both sides, it wasn't an afternoon for pretty passes or aesthetic delights, but while Rangers were once again condemned by their critics for being overly negative, Smith secured the share of the spoils which had been his minimum requirement. If the hosts had won, and moved four points clear, it might have proved a bridge too far for the Ibrox side. But, as it was, the match not only saw John Fleck become the youngest debutant in the Glasgow derby since Derek Ferguson, but confirmed that Celtic's nerves were growing frazzled at the prospect of surrendering their title for the first time since 2005. Scott McDonald wasted one glorious chance to break the deadlock as early as the 15th minute, but sent his effort wide and thereafter, despite the usual spate of meaty challenges and handbags at ten inches, Rangers held firm. In fact, they might have seized victory when Madjid Bougherra eluded the attention of Jan Vennegoor of

Hesselink and Shunsuke Nakamura and surged forward, creating an opportunity which ended with Barry Ferguson driving wide of the target from outside the box. Neutrals – a rare species in the west of Scotland – bemoaned the dearth of class or va va voom on parade. Celtic aficionados wheeled out Lionel Messi's old reference to their adversaries serving up 'anti-football'. But Smith wasn't concerned by the opprobrium. He realised that the momentum had tilted back towards his charges and that Strachan, growing more and more cantankerous with every passing week, was facing increasing flak from his own supporters. Some of this was unmerited, but the ball was in Rangers' court and the fashion in which they reacted to the challenge testified to their boss's knack for making carthorses believe they are thoroughbreds.

Yet it would be stupid to pretend that there was any straightforward route to their destination. March, for instance, threw up disappointment on the pitch when Smith's side were beaten 2-0 by Celtic in the League Cup final (in extra time), and controversy off it when Barry Ferguson and Allan McGregor indulged in a marathon bevvy session at Cameron House, in the aftermath of defeat against Holland in a World Cup qualifying match on Saturday, March 27. If their Bacchanalian excess had been their only misdemeanour, the episode might have been swiftly written off as being another in the protracted list of Scottish football's unsavoury brushes with the hard stuff. Sadly, the Rangers duo weren't simply stupid, they were arrogant as well, infamously being photographed making V-signs in the media's direction, during Scotland's subsequent victory over Iceland on the following Wednesday – which just happened to be April Fool's Day – and Smith and his Rangers backroom staff were as incandescent at the ensuing furore as anybody else. Ultimately, both men were old and experienced enough to know better, and could have no complaints when they were summoned to Ibrox and suspended by the club, without pay, following an internal inquiry into their behaviour while on international duty. But this was another unwanted distraction at a time when all Rangers' focus should

SilverSmith

have been on their push for the SPL crown. In which light, it was hardly surprising that Smith, a man who recognised the pride the Tartan Army took in their team and how many of them would have given their right arm to have been offered the chance to pull on a Scotland jersey even once, was furious about the whole sorry saga. At a distance, one could argue that the affair was blown out of all proportion, but Smith made it clear that Ferguson would be looking for another employer come the summer and, although there were some who claimed he softened his stance as the dust settled, Ferguson was duly sold to Birmingham City, where, to the surprise of many observers, he seemed to discover a new lease of life in the English Premiership.

However, if March was a month to forget, April showered Smith and his troops with reasons to believe that they could orchestrate heroics. Bolstered by their ability to conjure up goals all over the field, they negotiated several tough hurdles, none thornier than their fraught 3-2 victory over Hibs at Easter Road, a result which brought them to within a solitary point of Celtic. Steven Whittaker lit the touch paper in the space of two minutes, claiming a precious goal with a superb volley from 25 yards, but as the hosts searched for an equaliser, the contest turned into a genuine thriller. Steven Fletcher levelled matters by heading a fine Lewis Stevenson cross past Neil Alexander and Smith urgently cajoled his men to push forward and close down their opponents quicker. It was nip and tuck for a spell, but Andrius Velicka, who was on the verge of being substituted, suddenly unleashed a magnificent volley to restore his side's advantage, prior to Maurice Edu adding a third in the 73rd minute. Even then, there was still time for John Rankin to seize another wonderful goal in a match showered with brilliance, and the visitors had to survive a few marauding forays from their rivals before the points were safely in the bag. By the climax, Smith was as much relieved as overjoyed – 'It turned out that we needed the early goal, because Hibs played very well' – but the click of his jaw and steeliness of purpose in his eyes in uttering these words proved that he could scent the apprehension building up among his Celtic opponents as the SPL denouement beckoned.

It was little wonder Gordon Strachan and his personnel were concerned. Between their defeat of Rangers on December 27 and their failure to beat Hibs at the start of May, they dropped points in eight out of 16 league fixtures, commencing with their inability to hang on to a two-goal lead against Dundee United on January 3. It was another statistic which epitomised why they had been wrong to keep the biscuit tin shut in January – Willo Flood was the only new man in through the door at Parkhead and he was hardly a Roy or Robbie Keane figure – but Celtic's capitulation owed as much to Smith's tactical acumen as the board's lack of investment. It was as if Dermot Desmond, Peter Lawwell and John Reid had looked at the Rangers squad and decided that they could coast to another title, impervious to the threat posed by Kirk Broadfoot, Steven Whittaker, Kevin Thomson and their compatriots. They should have remembered that Rangers had only fallen short in the previous campaign because of an absurdly congested fixture list in the last three weeks of the season. Even then, Smith was within touching distance of a unique quadruple. And if they believed he couldn't repeat those exploits, they hadn't done their homework.

Which brings us to a saturnine afternoon at Ibrox in early May, 2009. In the one corner, Smith had primed his comrades to exhibit the killer instinct they required and placed his trust in his stalwart defensive pairing of Madjid Bougherra and David Weir. In the other, Strachan appeared to have aged several years in as many months, had omitted Aiden McGeady from his starting line-up, and there were rumours circulating in Glasgow that, win or lose the SPL, he was committed to walking away from the job. As usual, when these combatants meet, there were lashings of perspiration and a slew of fierce challenges in the opening period, as the rivals vied for supremacy. It was close, it was tense, and the atmosphere was suffocating, but, amidst the hubbub and incessant rain in Glasgow, Weir basked in his domain as if he was coming on 29, not 39, and the threat of Vennegoor of Hesselink and Scott McDonald was virtually extinguished. This wasn't, in itself, a calamity as long as Celtic could stem the attacking menace of their opponents, but their frailties were exposed by Steven Davis in the first half and his goal was sufficient to evoke rapturous applause from the vast swathes of supporters inside the stadium. Indeed, their celebrations might have been more pronounced if Kris Boyd had added a second from close range, only to be denied by Artur Boruc, but Celtic, for all their huffing and puffing, could not pierce the fortifications of Weir, Bougherra and their team mates, and, although the result left Rangers with work to do, they had grabbed the initiative and were worthy winners on the day. Suddenly, with three games remaining, they stood two points clear and Smith's face was a picture. There was a hint of elation and a soupcon of relief, allied to a pinch of pragmatism, while conducting the obligatory post-match interviews. He had seen too many trophies vanish at the eleventh hour to be remotely complacent, but equally, he realised that his beloved club were in the box seat. It was theirs to lose and few pundits would have laid odds on that scenario at the turn of the year.

None the less, perspective was difficult to cling on to, as the pursuit took another twist, worthy of M Night Shyamalan, when Rangers ventured to Leith for a midweek assignation with Hibs. This always appeared a tricky proposition, a belief borne out when Derek Riordan sent the hosts in front and although Nacho Novo levelled things in the 80th minute, Smith and his colleagues were aghast that an earlier effort by the Spaniard – when he bundled the ball into the net from close range – was deemed not to have crossed the line. If that wasn't contentious enough, Celtic had rebounded from their Old Firm defeat with a hard-fought 2-1 win over Dundee United, whose manager, Craig Levein, was sufficiently incensed at a challenge made on Lee Wilkie to enter into a furious argument with referee, Stuart Dougal, and later claimed he had lost all respect for the official. It added up to another turn-around in the title sprint: Celtic were now ahead on goal difference and the only certainty was that the race was going to the wire.

By now, nothing was easy or being taken for granted. The more pessimistic Ibrox adherents wondered whether their side was destined for another demoralising finale, and Smith was one of the few people who retained a semblance of calm in the eye of the storm. Yet he wasn't immune to the fever sweeping Glasgow and the following weekend's home tussle with Aberdeen awakened memories of how recently the latter had rained on Rangers' parade. It wasn't a day for ostentatious triumphalism or even for flashy theatricals at Ibrox, but even so, meetings between these sides tend to be inflammatory affairs and this was no exception. Some of the blame for the rancour could be laid at the door of Stuart Dougal, who sent off two players, Charlie Mulgrew and Bougherra, while Kyle Lafferty's part in the former's dismissal – where he dived to the ground as if the victim of a head butt when there was no contact whatsoever – rightly earned the Irishman a torrent of dog's abuse. Eventually, in the midst of the niggle and snarling, a football match broke out, and Rangers established a 2-0 lead through a Richard Foster own goal and a Miller header from Nacho Novo's corner. Job done! Granted, it had hardly been a thing of beauty, and Michael Paton's late strike, induced fleeting trepidation in the home ranks, but the 2-1 success heaped the pressure back on Celtic and Strachan's side couldn't respond, failing to score on their visit to Easter Road the following afternoon. The equation was now crystal-clear – if Rangers defeated Dundee United at Tannadice on the final day of the season, they would win the SPL title, regardless of what happened between Celtic and Hearts at Tynecastle.

These were the occasions Smith had dreamed about as a youngster and even if a few of his fellow Rangers adherents were anxious in the build-up to 'Helicopter Sunday', the veteran plotted a canter on Tayside and watched as his plans came to fruition. Any early nerves were swiftly settled when the much-maligned Lafferty scored in the sixth minute and the euphoria heightened when Pedro Mendes doubled Rangers' advantage, slotting the ball beyond Lukasz Zaluska after United failed to clear a Sasa Papac free kick. That strike, on the stroke of half-time, broke the tension, and even though Smith warned his men against complacency at the interval, these players had listened well enough for long enough to appreciate they needed to keep pressing for a third. Within seven minutes of the restart, they had gained it, through Kris Boyd, and the party started in earnest, while a huge sense of deflation permeated the Celtic ranks as they laboured to an uninspiring goalless draw in Edinburgh. It was redemption time for Smith and when the 61-year-old walked off the Tannadice pitch alone and with trophy in hand, his raised fist testifying to how much this meant to him, the supporters, en masse, and even those who had moaned about Rangers' alleged negativity, cheered him to the rafters. Given the mess he had inherited upon his return to Ibrox, and considering the raft of personnel issues and scarcity of money which had hung over him and his assistants, winning the SPL was a sweet feeling, the more so because Celtic had been so dominant at the midway point of the campaign. In which light, and even before Gordon Strachan had announced, to almost nobody's surprise that he was quitting Parkhead, Smith spoke of his joy at the manner in which events had unfolded, and also revealed how the threat of redundancies at Ibrox had been a very real prospect from the beginning of the year onwards.

'I can't remember a season when we have had so many difficulties to overcome. We have a financial situation at the club, so it was important to win the championship. I was worried about the threat of compulsory redundancies for the staff at Ibrox and that has been one of the hardest things. Despite what has been said, there were no real redundancies after January. Some people left who would have left anyway as a natural progression, but that situation could have been compulsory if we hadn't won the championship. It was a factor which weighed very heavily on me when I was looking at the consequences of not winning the league; as the manager, I take responsibility for that. So, it was a tough thing to face, but my players are not daft. They knew what was going on around the club, and there was an awareness from those who read the papers that these things [job losses in a recession] were happening in all walks of life; this was something the players could do something about and they responded magnificently.'

There only remained for Rangers to maintain their focus for another week, in search of the Scottish Cup, when they tackled Falkirk at Hampden Park. In the build-up, Smith asserted that his men would have no trouble raising themselves for the match, but, as it transpired, there were a few in their ranks who looked as if they required a beach towel more than another high-profile fixture. Their opponents, in contrast, had narrowly escaped relegation and were determined to secure the Cup in memory of Craig Gowans, the youngster who had died in tragic circumstances at Falkirk's training ground. They were motivated, well-briefed by their manager, John Hughes, and basically played Rangers off the pitch for the opening 45 minutes without capitalising on their dominance. But that had been the story of their season and the same shortcoming deprived them of the chance to pull off one of the biggest shocks in the history of the competition. The Ibrox men, by comparison, were made to sweat on a glorious afternoon and were second best in most departments except, crucially, the one which mattered, courtesy of Nacho Novo, who scored a magnificent goal only seconds after arriving on the pitch as a half-time substitute for Kris Boyd. It was the one sublime piece of skill – a stunning shot from 35 yards out – in the Rangers repertoire throughout the course of the contest, but it was enough and the double was achieved, albeit not without a few scares at the end.

At the climax, Smith was candid in his assessment of Falkirk's menace. 'They had us worried. They were excellent and deserve credit for making this a very difficult afternoon for us.' But, in the final analysis, Rangers had weathered another storm and Smith had secured his fourth major prize since returning to Ibrox. He was entitled to bask in the triumph as the summer beckoned. Life was only going to get tougher for him.

CHAPTER NINETEEN

THRIVING IN ADVERSITY

'It is always mentally tiring, but that goes with the territory'

When Walter Smith started out on his managerial reign at Rangers, the arrival of summer was as joyous a time for him as it was for barbecue salesmen, ice-cream vendors and midges in various parts of Scotland. Whatever the results in the previous season, there would be significant amounts of money for Smith to bolster his squad and the 'Spend, Spend, Spend' philosophy, so beloved of Sir David Murray in the early 1990s, ensured that his life, if not exactly a bed of roses, was hardly a duvet of nettles either.

Matters were a whole lot different when he arrived back at Ibrox in 2007 and, regardless of the tranche of trophies and enhanced season-ticket revenues which should have eased Rangers' spiralling financial woes, Smith knew, from the start of the 2008-09 campaign onwards, that the club was veering down a blind alley to Skid Row. Even amidst the heady scenes of triumphalism and appreciation of a job well done in wrapping up a League and Cup double in May 2009, there was no cash to purchase new players and, despite the paucity of resources being obvious to those inside the organisation, all the transfer movement was one way and that was out the exit door. Former captain, Barry Ferguson, renewed acquaintances with his old gaffer, Alex McLeish, at Birmingham City, Charlie Adam joined

Blackpool, Chris Burke hitched his wagon to Cardiff City, and Pedro Mendes headed back to Portugal. This, together with the loss in the previous 12 months of Carlos Cuellar and Alan Hutton (whose sales raked in nearly £17m between them), constituted a significant loss of talent for Rangers and, considering how much success that Smith enjoyed during the same period, begged the question: where was the Rangers money? It was an issue which overshadowed everything else during the 2009-10 season and yet, amidst a scenario of constant negative headlines and distracting talk about the threat of administration, the due diligence of would-be purchasers and the spectre of tax investigations, Smith elected to roll with the punches, put his head above the parapet to keep the fans in the picture – whereas the once-ubiquitous Murray suddenly decided that bullish talk didn't pay the bills – and was one of the few individuals to emerge with his reputation enhanced from the mess into which Rangers had stumbled.

Indeed, even as the storm clouds were gathering, the team began their defence of the SPL title in impressive fashion. Following their participation in the Emirates Cup, where they beat Manchester City in the pre-season slew of high-profile tournaments which fill space for satellite broadcasters, Rangers launched their league schedule with a convincing 4-1 victory over Falkirk, a match which featured the unusual phenomenon of a long-range wonder goal from Lee McCulloch! Across the city, Celtic, under their new manager, Tony Mowbray, made a similarly promising start with a comfortable victory at Pittodrie, but the contrasting temperaments, tactical strategies and man-management of these two Old Firm bosses was to diverge sharply over the coming months. Smith, a man with the requisite pragmatism to accept that he had to make the best of the talent at his disposal, worked minor miracles with modest resources, whereas Mowbray chopped and changed, never got the balance right between satisfying his supporters and stacking up sufficient points, and gradually wore the countenance of the wrong man in the wrong place.

Few predicted that his tenure would unravel as spectacularly as it did. For one thing, Celtic, at least in comparison to their Glasgow adversaries, were rolling in moolah. And yet, Smith and his ensemble kept grinding out results throughout August, even if the conspiracy theorists had a field day with the last-minute penalty decision which allowed Kris Boyd to secure a 2-1 win at Tynecastle, as the prelude to Hamilton being swatted aside 4-1 at Ibrox. All things considered, it was a creditable series of displays, but the gossip and rumour which had been sweeping the west of Scotland was finally confirmed on August 26 when Sir David Murray announced that he was to step down as chairman and as director of the club. Initially, the news that his successor, Alastair Johnston, was a fellow board member, seemed to suggest that nothing was seriously amiss, but even the combined efforts of Alastair Campbell and Malcolm Tucker couldn't have disguised the unhealthy state of Rangers' finances. 'There was no pressure from outside sources to step down. All the pressure came from myself,' said Murray. 'The club is in a good position and the balance sheet is okay. After 20 years, it was time to step down and it is a good time to go, there are no outside factors.' With hindsight, these remarks sound utterly ridiculous and many of us queried the apparent gap between the spin which was woven and the stark reality. But, for a few weeks at least, Rangers kept a lid on the full extent of the problems behind the scenes. That, however, coincided with a difficult period for Rangers in plain sight, as they toiled to maintain their early league momentum.

The consequence was a string of draws against Motherwell, Kilmarnock and Aberdeen, which allowed Celtic to establish a four-point advantage at the helm. In the second of these fixtures, Smith lost the rag at Rugby Park, and was eventually handed a four-match ban for adopting a 'threatening and aggressive' attitude. He accepted his punishment – there was nothing else for it in the circumstances – but the manager found himself under increasing pressure, both at home and in the UEFA Champions League, where the fleeting promise of a 1-1 draw in Stuttgart, with Madjid

Bougherra scoring a deserved second-half equaliser, was dissipated by a subsequent sequence of embarrassing defeats which were the low point of Smith and Rangers' season. At first glance, being drawn in the same group as Stuttgart, Sevilla and the little-known Romanian side, Unirea Urziceni, hinted at the genuine possibility of progress to the lucrative knock-out stages of the tournament for the Scots. Yet, in the event, these litany of matches offered a resounding confirmation that Smith was only being honest when he stated, in a post-match interview, that his side risked getting into trouble if they started playing football. *He* knew what he meant. *We* knew what he meant. But, of course, in the Glasgow aquarium, this was manna from heaven for opposition supporters, who couldn't suppress their glee as Rangers were thrashed 4-1 at Ibrox by Sevilla – which was, perhaps, almost forgivable – and then crashed to the same scoreline at home to Unirea – which most certainly was not. Around this juncture, the creased lines on Smith's forehead testified to his knowledge of the near panic which was happening in the boardroom, but he stuck to the party line and copped the flak with the phlegmatic demeanour of somebody who had been through plenty of turbulent times before, and wasn't surprised by anything.

He and his club were also bolstered by the psychological fillip of winning the first Old Firm derby of the season at the beginning of October when Rangers edged a typically fractious encounter by 2-1 at Ibrox. As usual, in a campaign which was surrounded by so many conspiracy theories that it owed more to *The X Files* than a sporting competition, there were loud complaints from the vanquished side about dodgy refereeing decisions. But, in the aftermath, the victory testified to the continuing ability of Smith to work wonders with a patched-up squad. In the absence of such luminaries as Bougherra, McCulloch and Kevin Thomson, and with Smith losing a further two players to injury during the first half, he could surely have been forgiven for cursing his ill fortune and seeking a more tranquil job, such as bringing peace to the Middle East. But instead, and despite having to watch from the stands, his enforced selection of Northern Ireland internationalist, Andrew Little, at right back for his first start – and who only lasted 13 minutes before retiring with an injury – while Sasa Papac partnered David Weir in the centre of defence, worked a lot more effectively than the Celtic duo, Stephen McManus and Glenn Loovens, whose perfectly-timed 'After You Claude' routines allowed Kenny Miller to break the deadlock in the eighth minute, prior to the same player doubling the hosts' cushion during a frenetic first half. Granted, Shaun Maloney had a strong appeal for a penalty turned down, which was waved aside by referee, Craig Thomson, and although the visitors did eventually gain a spot kick, converted by Aiden McGeady, when Papac made a clumsy challenge on Zheng Zhi, just inside the box, they left Ibrox with indignation coursing through their veins. However, in the bigger picture, the contest provided a template of why Rangers would flourish at their rivals' expense as the SPL battle raged on. Because, while Celtic were ineffectual in defence and only fitfully threatening up front, Rangers stuck to a limited game plan which suited their personnel, at the same time as it blunted the menace of the majority of their rivals. It was a blunderbuss rather than a rapier approach, and was never likely to be confused with the Mona Lisa in the aesthetic stakes. But, ultimately, it suited Smith's side, they were comfortable with the system, and they gradually made it work to their advantage.

What they *couldn't* control was the maelstrom of speculation which plagued the club and eventually Smith, a man with the instincts of a supporter, who realised that Rangers had nothing to gain from the crippling uncertainty as to where the club was headed, decided that enough was enough. Thus it was that, in the aftermath of a hard-fought 1-1 draw with Hibs at Ibrox, he spoke out, directly, purposefully, unequivocally, about his understanding of the reality behind the PR facade which had been erected.

'It's obviously not a good situation. It's not a situation that any-body wants the club to be in. But it [Rangers FC] has been up for sale for a while. It's not the bank's fault. If the bank has to take over in the circumstances it has, they are not going to invest in a football club, are they? I think that Rangers have been honest about their situation. The players at the club have been up for sale since January [2009]. We haven't bought a player for what will be 18 months in the transfer window. So these circumstances have been there for quite a while now and – despite some headlines – I have never complained about it. I am not complaining now either, I am just saying that it is a fact of life. A lot of companies are struggling financially. When Sir David Murray stepped away from the club, I felt that was a bad thing for Rangers, because he has tried as hard as he could over 20 years to invest in the club. Now we don't have that. So the quicker that gets cleared up, the better it will be for Rangers. Hopefully, there will be a change sooner rather than later.'

There was no requirement for Smith to break his silence in this manner, but he went further over the next few days, insisting that his own future was irrelevant compared to the need for his club to extricate themselves from the mire. Other, more selfish characters would have whinged about the lack of a budget, or attempted to deflect responsibility for the morass onto other people, but Smith had reached the stage of his career where he felt a paternal affection for Rangers and their supporters. It was as well that he adopted this stance, given the lack of firm leadership from other quarters at Ibrox – there were no signs of an imminent buyer being found, although Dave King, the Johannesburg-based businessman with a deep affinity to all things Rangers, was continually mentioned in the media's coverage of the ongoing soap opera – but Smith's candour struck with a chord with many people, not least because it was so crystal-clear that he genuinely cared.

'I have a contract up until January [2010], but the club is going to change owners. It is up for sale at the moment, so it's going to happen. The new owner might not want me as manager. That's acceptable enough for me. My only situation at the moment is to try and do the best I can for Rangers while we are in this position. Will I be here until the summer? I don't know. The club may be bought over. Nobody knows. We said last January that the players were up for sale, so how can the manager then say that he is in a safe position when the club is in this situation. My contract expires in January, because I signed a three-year deal when I came in, simple as that. But it's not the be-all and end-all for me. The most important thing is the football club. If the people running the football club just now ask me to stay on, because they haven't got a buyer, I would consider that and try to do it. But if there is a new buyer, and they want somebody else to take charge, then I would be happy to go – as long as it is in the best interests of Rangers.'

Even as the stalemate dragged on, Smith's powers of persuasion and the respect he commanded for his frankness brought a tangible reward for his personnel on the pitch. Sometimes, when doom-laden headlines hang over a club, it can demoralise those in the eye of the storm. On other occasions, though, it can actually act as a galvanising force and the latter was true of Rangers. During November, there were a series of setbacks for the team, including Stuttgart's clinical 2-0 win at Ibrox and Aberdeen's 1-0 success in the Granite City. But, regardless of the obstacles placed in their path, and the fact they were in danger of slipping significantly behind Celtic, who themselves were hardly firing on all cylinders, the tougher the battle became, the more Smith relished the task and warmed to the challenge, whereas his opposite number, Mowbray, was already showing signs of cracking under the strain of a constant interaction with a meddlesome media.

In which light, December was the month when the SPL race was transformed by a magnificently pugnacious string of high-octane displays from Rangers. At the outset, some of their fans cast an anxious gaze over what appeared a gruelling fixture list – with seven matches to be played on either side of the Christmas break – but, fuelled by a fluid 4-4-2 formation and the growing stature of young Steven Davis, allied to the ageless exertions of David Weir in the rearguard, and the re-emergence of Kris Boyd into the sort of striker who walks onto the pitch knowing he will get chances and knowing he will take them, Rangers cranked up the gears and crackled with vim. After beating Falkirk and St Johnstone, Smith's team travelled to Tannadice to replay the match, which had been postponed at half-time, due to flooding on Tayside a month earlier, and chalked up another comprehensive victory with a brace of goals for Kenny Miller. Motherwell were then dismantled 6-1, in what proved to be Jim Gannon's final game in charge at Fir Park, and, despite conceding a goal inside 12 seconds from Anthony Stokes – a new SPL record – Rangers orchestrated a stunning recovery to secure a 4-1 triumph at Easter Road, as Miller once again sparked havoc. His strike partner, Boyd, then grabbed the headlines in the next fixture when he shattered Henrik Larsson's SPL record with all of five goals to his name during the 7-1 win over Dundee United, just days after Craig Levein had left the Tannadice organisation to become Scotland boss. It was a remarkable metamorphosis from the side who had seemed barely capable of stringing two passes together during the awful October sequence, and, perhaps unsurprisingly, Rangers suddenly leapt to the top of the SPL table and wore the air of champions-elect, rattling in goals for fun.

Smith knew that any such talk was premature, but nonetheless, it was difficult to dent the fans' enthusiasm after the next result – a 1-1 draw against Celtic at Parkhead on an afternoon when the visitors created only one meaningful chance and Lee McCulloch bulleted home the header, shortly after Scott McDonald seemed to have grabbed all three points for Mowbray, whose hang-dog expression, at the climax of a match which his side had dominated, spoke volumes about how the balance of power was shifting.

For neutrals, the outcome was something of a travesty. No matter. The fact that the tussle finished in a draw meant that Rangers continued to boast a seven-point advantage over their city rivals, albeit having played a game more. At times, they struggled to stem the Celtic flow, but here was fresh evidence that Smith was making the best of an average squad, that he had stiffened their sinews in situations where they might have crumbled under Le Guen, and that even when Boyd contributed little, or other luminaries such as Kenny Miller, Madjid Bougherra and Nacho Novo were missing for a variety of reasons, somebody such as McCulloch had the presence of mind to provide salvation.

Ultimately, as Smith, the veteran of scores of these Old Firm contests, could testify, substance matters a lot more than style on the ledger sheet. Yes, his personnel were buffeted, bothered and bewildered for much of the proceedings and yes, Kyle Lafferty was fortunate to remain on the field, following a dreadful tackle on Andreas Hinkel, while other referees might have allowed Marc-Antoine Fortune's disallowed goal to stand. And yet, exemplifying the grit which had steered them to a European final 20 months earlier, they found a means of clawing themselves out of trouble. That they should have done so principally through the labours of McCulloch, Sasa Papac, Allan McGregor and Davis was a reminder of how Smith had forged a team in his own image.

In public, he was still taking nothing for granted, even when his troops edged to an unconvincing win at Hamilton, as the prelude to Mowbray's team slipping further behind when they could only draw with Falkirk. After all, Rangers were where Celtic had been 12 months earlier.

'I don't think we are that far ahead in the league. It's a good headline to say that you are nine points in front, but Celtic still have a game in hand, so we would look at it as being six points in front. At this stage last season, Celtic were seven points ahead of us, so it doesn't mean that much at this stage of the year.

'However, our players deserve a great deal of credit for the way they have handled things. It's not easy when you are involved in Champions League games and you are not doing well, it's not easy to keep a level of consistency going. In December, we played exceptionally well, but unfortunately since then, we have had a whole list of injuries and suspensions, and that has disrupted us a little. I don't think there is any doubt about that. There has been a bit of inconsistency in our team right from the very start of the season, in terms of performance, so any lead that we have in the championship at the moment is welcome. But it's welcome in the knowledge that we still have an awful lot to do.'

All the same, January was a pivotal month in the SPL joust. As everybody expected, Rangers had no money to spend during the transfer window and Smith was forced to persevere with the personnel at his disposal. What few people anticipated, though, was that Mowbray would adopt something close to a scorched-earth policy by getting rid of most of his defenders, while recruiting a fresh batch of players, including Robbie Keane, on loan from Tottenham Hotspur, for wages of between £60,000 and £70,000 a week. At best, it was a high-risk strategy, based on the assumption that all the new arrivals would click instantly. At worst, it smacked of desperation, of flinging some pearls out with the dross, and the policy duly returned to haunt him when Keane and Co made their debut against Kilmarnock at Rugby Park – and the hosts eagerly tore up the script with a 1-0 win, which was one of the last defining acts of Mowbray's ill-starred Celtic reign.

The end was in sight, but there was still an Old Firm derby at the end of February which offered the Parkhead men an opportunity to claw back some of the mounting deficit. This was a fixture they absolutely had to win, and yet there was a strange dearth of conviction about their endeavours. This being a Glasgow derby, it was probably inevitable that controversy once again reared its head – such as when referee, Dougie McDonald, sent off Scott Brown for an alleged head-butt on Kyle Lafferty, while refusing to enforce similar action against Madjid Bougherra after the defender, already on a yellow card, had blundered into a couple of challenges – but the bottom line was that, irrespective of the rights or wrongs of the above calls, McDonald wasn't the biggest culprit in Celtic's last-gasp defeat when they fell victim to Maurice Edu's injury-time goal. On the contrary, while Rangers bristled with industry and commitment at the back and in mid-field, before eventually ensuring that they moved 10 points clear of their rivals (with a match in hand), there was a lack of cutting edge or even fight from the visitors. At the death, Smith spoke admiringly of his team's energy. It was not a word which could have been applied to the losers in this instance. Their former hero, Charlie Nicholas, was scathing in his assessment of his former club's display, asserting that their high-profile players 'hadn't turned up' and that their defeat was due to their own deficiencies rather than any mistakes by the referee. It was a refreshing voice of logic in a tide of paranoia.

The crux of the matter was that Rangers knew how to win, even when below their best, or in the direst of straits. Smith had instilled that relentless mentality in his squad and there was never a more revealing demonstration of his motivational powers than when Rangers pitched up at Hampden Park in March for the CIS Cup Insurance final against St Mirren. On paper, it looked a fairly straightforward assignment for the Ibrox side, but although history will relate that they ended up lifting the trophy, the bare statistics highlight nothing of what was a superbly pulsating piece of theatre by the denouement.

In essence, if winning ugly is the mark of champions, then Rangers were giants of European football on this evidence. Here, as so often before in the past three years, they were generally outplayed, on their uppers and toiling to break down their rivals, to the extent that it was frequently difficult to guess which of the teams was in relegation trouble. As Gus MacPherson's ensemble cranked up the momentum and carved out a barrage of chances through David Barron, Michael Higdon, Billy Mehmet and Steven Thomson, it appeared to be only a question of when, not if, the underdogs took the lead, particularly when Kevin Thomson was red-carded early in the second period, as Rangers strove to regain the upper hand with an aggressive approach, which in itself was proof that they recognised that they were second best in most departments.

And yet, we had been in these scenarios so often before on Smith's watch. Even in advance of the contest, the canny manager was at pains to dampen talk of an Ibrox treble. He laughed off suggestions about statues being erected in his honour and talked up the threat posed by St Mirren. He knew that, especially in the absence of the injured Madjid Bougherra, and the fact that Steven Davis was struggling to shake off a virus, that MacPherson's troops could shed their inhibitions and forget about their relegation worries for a few days. Smith may have anticipated that there was no pressure on the Paisley club, but he surely couldn't have predicted that so many of his leading lights, men in the mould of Lee McCulloch, Kenny Miller and Kris Boyd, would find it so devilishly difficult to create any chances. Yet, as sometimes occurs when a side is reduced to 10 men, Rangers suddenly discovered fresh reserves of steel, vigour and *esprit des corps* and the balance of the battle began to shift. This wasn't the first occasion where they had lost the headstrong Thomson and prospered – he had been sent off against Hearts in the 2008-09 season, and Smith's men shrugged off that setback to engineer victory – and their fortitude as the climax beckoned was a reminder that, while there have been better, classier, Rangers ensembles in the chronicles, this current crop could never be accused of a lack of perspiration or endeavour when the going gets tough. What nearly did for them in the final quarter was a questionable decision by referee, Craig Thomson, to dish out a red card to youngster, Danny Wilson, as well, reducing them to nine men. It should have been St Mirren's Cup, and perhaps if they had been more pragmatic, and ushered the match into extra time, their numerical superiority would have made the difference. But, just when it appeared that Rangers were on the ropes, struggling for breath, and out of inspiration, they conjured up a magnificent goal for Kenny Miller, which was worthy of settling any showdown. Even their critics surely had to concede that these battling qualities, in the throes of adversity, were genuinely impressive. But whatever the verdicts, the bottom line was that another piece of silverware was bound for Ibrox and Smith's response was more like a teenager than somebody who had just turned 62.

However, their progress to further honours was hardly after the fashion of Usain Bolt. On the contrary, there were several stumbles in March and April which testified to the reality that several of Smith's squad were feeling the strain of what had been an arduous season. In the Scottish Cup, for example, the Ibrox side made terribly heavy weather of beating Hamilton, then were similarly unconvincing against St Mirren, and finally exited the competition at Tannadice in a replay, after establishing a 3-1 lead early in the second half of the first meeting of the sides in Glasgow. Perhaps more embarrassingly, Rangers then succumbed 4-1 in the SPL to St Johnstone at McDiarmid Park – the sort of midweek defeat which, in other circumstances, might have made Smith's life very difficult for the next few days – but Celtic had neither the wit nor resolve to capitalise on these failings. Instead, Mowbray's miserable stint as manger was terminated abruptly, after a 4-0 loss at St Mirren, and it has to be noted that all the early-season expectation and the prolonged huddles which greeted his appointment were the prelude to a calamitous campaign, which made Smith's job less treacherous than might have been the case. Indeed, I still maintain that if the roles had been reversed and Smith had been at Parkhead – a thought which would probably horrify him – that Celtic would have won the SPL. But it is all conjecture and, despite a few jitters, it was Rangers who strode over the finishing line in April.

Following victories against Hamilton and Aberdeen, they looked poised to seal their 53rd Scottish title at home against Hearts. However, a goalless draw with Dundee United kept the champagne on ice for another week and, as the Rangers fans waited, they searched for clues as to whether the club had found a new owner. Dave King's name was still mentioned regularly,

SilverSmith

while Andrew Ellis, a London-based property developer, received plenty of coverage over his plans for Ibrox if the terms were right. But so much of this was pure hot air and wishful thinking, as was to become clear in the coming weeks.

Mercifully, for those struggling to devise budgets and unearth future revenue streams off the pitch, Rangers were sufficiently in the groove to attract positive publicity where it mattered. A 2-0 victory over Hearts pushed Smith's team to within touching distance of the main prize and they travelled to Leith to tackle Hibernian on April 24. It was a trickier proposition than it might have been a couple of months earlier when John Hughes' side were in the midst of a dramatic collapse, which obliterated their excellent start to the campaign, but soon enough, all the talk about crisis at debt-ridden Rangers was drowned out in a cacophony of jubilation from the 1500-plus Ibrox aficionados, who had managed to secure tickets for the Easter Road match. Perhaps appropriately, their success owed more to athleticism and a clinical approach than artistry and class, and there was even a whiff of controversy over a disallowed penalty claim from Derek Riordan as the hosts sought to wipe out Kyle Lafferty's earlier goal. But Hughes was magnanimous in defeat, recognising that, over the course of the season, Rangers had been the club with the best claims to the title. Time after time, they had transcended whatever problems had cropped up, and in the likes of Davis, David Weir and Boyd, all of whom were among the nominees for Player of the Year, they boasted the sort of tough-as-teak individuals who could go the extra mile whenever they slipped into trouble.

None of it would have been possible without Smith's heroics since returning to Ibrox. He had inherited a poisoned chalice from Paul Le Guen, had subsequently found himself accused of encouraging 'anti-football', and, during the course of the 2009-10 season, regularly became embroiled in the kind of debates which were normally confined to the business pages. But, throughout it all, and regardless of having to sell players and being deprived of any money for new blood, Smith's resilience, stakhanovite work ethic and, perhaps most significantly, his undimmed love for Rangers had helped him steer a safe passage between Scylla and Charybdis. This was his ninth title success and, even as he celebrated in the aftermath of the Hibs win, admitted this was 'a wee bit special.' Later, once the Rangers contingent had caught their breath, he elaborated on the theme.

'We have got a good group of players, we just don't have a lot of them in terms of the size of group that is needed for a club like Rangers. That's what maybe separates this from a lot of the other championships I have been fortunate to win. It is a small group and it has maybe been a little bit against the odds. I've had to ask a lot of them this season and you could see, even today, that they have lost a little bit of the brightness which they had in the early part of the season. We've had to keep asking them to come back and play and they have done so. They have been fantastic. For the consistency they have achieved, they deserve enormous credit. When we have been under a little bit of pressure, we have usually managed to win through, because they have been such a resilient bunch.

'It's always a relief when you get the job done, maybe even more so in comparison to last season, when we had to come from behind. The crucial spell came in January when we survived an injury crisis to keep our challenge on track. This season, we had a lead and it seems for the last six weeks or so that everybody has been telling us we are going to win the championship, so it is always a great relief when you do so. It is always mentally tiring, but that goes with the territory. If you take up the job as a manager of an Old Firm team, then that is something you have to live with. It was my decision to come back in the first place and if it [the pressure] was that bad, I would have avoided it. I heard Sir Alex [Ferguson] say that there is pressure at this stage of the season, but he has shown he can handle it. If there is pressure on him, there is pressure on everyone.'

These words underlined the scale of what Smith had achieved and neither he, nor his second-in-command, Ally McCoist, were in any mood to listen to journalists, questioning the credentials and quality of their charges. 'I don't think anybody can say they did not deserve it. It is an argument that is put forward that nobody can substantiate,' countered McCoist. 'These boys have won six trophies in three seasons and reached a European final. You can't argue with this team and what they have achieved. You just can't. There might be talk that they are not as good as this team or that team. But I'll tell you what they are. They are the best that is going at the moment. They have proved that over a long period, they deserve their success, and are entitled to all the credit in the world.'

Unsurprisingly, given the exertions involved in their SPL success, Rangers struggled to maintain their focus in their remaining fixtures, with their prime objective already fulfilled. They beat Dundee United 2-1 at Tannadice with goals from Kris Boyd and Nacho Novo, both of whom had already announced their intention to leave Ibrox in the summer, and although Smith was fulsome in his tributes, he was surely entitled to wonder where he would find players to fill their boots. Next up was the last Old Firm derby at Parkhead where Smith's side lost 2-1 against a fired-up Celtic ensemble, who were determined to gain their maiden win of the campaign in these contests, with their manager-in-waiting, Neil Lennon, doing a decent impersonation of a carrot on fire on the sidelines. Even here, with nothing but pride at stake, the visiting supporters screamed in anguish at being denied what they considered a stonewall penalty, but it was time to lay the conspiracies to rest for a few weeks. Even when Motherwell scored twice in the last few minutes of the climactic fixture of the calendar, thus earning a creditable 3-3 draw at Ibrox, only a few days after rallying from a 6-2 deficit to gain a 6-6 share of the points with Hibs, these felt like the last acts in a play which had finished its run elsewhere.

In the wings, meanwhile, there was news, but whether it was

advantageous to Rangers was questionable. Sir David Murray revealed in May that the club was no longer on the market, an announcement which was greeted with scepticism in some quarters, if only because so few people were convinced that any of the alleged bids on the table from King, or Ellis, or some unnamed Arab consortium, carried genuine substance in the first place. Once one delved beneath the spin, which was initially applied to the story, the conclusion was clear. Rangers, for all their international reputation, their crop of recent trophies, and the sterling work carried out by Smith and his lieutenants, McCoist and Kenny McDowall, had been unable to persuade anybody to buy them. In short, there were still financial problems at this Scottish institution which required urgent attention. And with clubs in England and in Europe hovering around the likes of Madjid Bougherra, Danny Wilson, Kris Boyd and Steve Davis, one was left wondering whether the labours of Smith and his team had not, in fact, papered over an even worse situation at Rangers than had been reported. It was hardly the news to shift season tickets for 2010-11.

Nonetheless, if there was one quality that the Ibrox faithful could rely on in their club's pursuit of fresh plaudits, it was the dedication of the man at the tiller. Other, more selfish, individuals would have strolled away from Rangers, satisfied with the job they had done, and bolstered by a hefty cheque in their back pockets. But Smith recognised that with the club in flux, and no immediate sign of order being restored amid the confusion, it was no time to hand over the reins to an untested management team. In essence, he accepted responsibility for another twelve months, even though he knew they were going to be tough.

Mind you, if he could have had any inkling of the avalanche of aggravation and adverse circumstances which lay in store as he prepared for his last crusade, even the redoubtable Smith might have needed a quiet lie-down. There are graceful exits and then there are tumultuous departures, and his farewell fitted squarely into the latter category.

CHAPTER TWENTY

A Season in Need of an ASBO

❖

'All credit to my players, they have been brilliant'

The old joke goes that somebody went along to a fight and an ice-hockey match broke out. But that pretty accurately summed up the whole of the 2010-11 season in Scottish football. When referees weren't going on strike, or having their private emails aired in the press, Rangers were being investigated by UEFA for the sectarian behaviour of a section of their supporters, a Celtic follower was going to jail for racially abusing El Hadji Diouf, or Neil Lennon was being sent bullets and bombs through the post, even as Scotland's politicians decided that religious bigotry was once again an issue worth addressing. At times, the football seemed almost incidental, like the commercial breaks in the midst of a programme schedule of X-rated material. And Walter Smith summed up the reaction of many of his confrères when he eventually declared he was 'scunnered' by it all.

It was an appropriate response from somebody who had always recognised that football wasn't that important in the grand scheme of things, but Smith's words reverberated all the more strongly because they arrived towards the conclusion of a deluge of disgraceful tableaux, in and around the SPL. The veteran manager stayed out of the mêlées in various dug-outs, whether it was Lennon and Ally McCoist having to be separated at the climax of an acrimonious Old Firm derby, or Lennon being attacked by a so-called Hearts fan during Celtic's otherwise comfortable 3-0 victory at Tynecastle in May. But he couldn't escape the fall-out from the threats which were made to Lennon, even as police intercepted a number of suspect packages with postmarks in Ayrshire which were despatched to prominent Celtic aficionados. This was explosive stuff, in every sense. And the more that senior law officers, statesmen such as the First Minister, Alex Salmond, and Scotland's fourth estate highlighted the prejudice and ignorance which still surrounded the Old Firm – and other SPL clubs – the more Smith appeared to grow weary talking about attitudes which he believed were growing obsolete in the modern world.

In several respects, his reaction was understandable. After all, here was a man who had long harboured the conviction that the Old Firm were institutions worth cherishing, given their joint contribution to Scottish sport. Smith, too, had been amongst the throng at Ibrox when 66 fans lost their lives in 1971 and the disaster, briefly, brought both sides together. Surely, or so he argued, it wasn't asking too much that supporters rooted for their own team, rather than provoking and punching the living day-lights out of the other lot. As for the notion of any Scot in 2011 thinking there was any defence for bringing bullets and bombs into the beautiful game . . . well, it was ludicrous, wasn't it? But the trouble was that Smith's decency merely amplified the noxious actions of those who used football as an excuse to continue the battle they and their ancestors had waged since 1690.

The sectarianism separating the two clubs has always been part and parcel of what the two clubs were, in a situation which is just life in the west of Scotland. We have handled that aspect, maybe to our detriment, by ignoring the majority of it, and just getting on with it. But when we have reached the stage, as we have now, when it goes further than that, with threats to people's lives, then I question whether it is all worthwhile.

It is just a football match, after all, between two great football clubs. But it is degenerating into something far worse than just the sectarian aspect, or sectarian singing, and, in my own mind, it is just totally unacceptable. I am not quite sure why it has degenerated into the levels it has at the moment. We don't really know where this is going to go, do we? And whether it is going to continue to deteriorate. Being a football manager, I am not bright enough to know where it is going. But something terrible has happened this week. Is that not bad enough? How much worse can it get?

If it is a problem which rests with the two football clubs alone, then I am sure that they will try and adjust. But I think we have got to say that it rests with society and the way life has been led in the west of Scotland for a great number of years. What we are talking about here isn't just the traditional aspects of sectarian singing and chanting which go on during a game, or calling one manager one thing or another. This [the sending of bombs] is taking it into a far more serious realm than I can ever remember.

It [the bigotry issue] has always been there and we just carried on with it, because it was part and parcel of our lives where we were brought up. The football definitely brings it into people's consciousness. But we also have to try and eradicate the problem in west of Scotland society. It is such a pity, because Rangers and Celtic are two great, traditional football clubs. We should be concentrating on that and I feel that Scotland is fortunate to have them. In many ways, we have two clubs we should be proud of as a country, but that is a very difficult statement to make in the current circumstances.

This was Smith at his most reflective. He even admitted, as another absorbing season reached a dramatic climax, that part of the thrill of the Old Firm rivalry had dissipated, which probably wasn't surprising, considering how far he had moved 'off message' from the normal routine of a football manager. At the outset of his final campaign in charge, he looked enthused and motivated by being drawn against Manchester United – which pitted him against his fellow Govan warrior, Sir Alex Ferguson – in Group C of the Champions League, alongside Valencia and the unheralded Turkish club, Bursaspor. And, to Smith's credit, he invariably transcended the myriad difficulties surrounding the club, whether it involved talk of UEFA sanctions, or legal battles with HMRC over Rangers' tax dealings, or even the protracted story of Craig Whyte's takeover from Sir David Murray.

The latter saga was one of the most tedious affairs it would be possible to imagine – and reminded many of us why the business pages of newspapers are best reserved for cat litter – but it offered fresh evidence of Smith's unerring ability to stare adversity straight in the eye. More than a decade earlier, when he first departed Ibrox, he left without a trophy to his name, and that experience had clearly left its mark. It wouldn't happen again if he could help it and thus, even with a hard-working and tenacious, but limited, squad Rangers launched the defence of their domestic title, boosted by the philosophy that they would never fall short through a dearth of effort. Time and time again, as the season progressed, they were on the ropes, similar to Ali against Foreman, apparently on the verge of hitting the deck, but there was a stubborn refusal to be knocked out, whether at home or in Europe. It might not have provided a feast of aesthetic beauty – and critics had a field day with the 'Park the Bus' tactics of the Ibrox personnel when they travelled to Old Trafford, for instance. Yet, in the opening half of the campaign, Smith regularly used a 5-4-1 formation with notable success and even though Manchester United fielded a weakened side against the Scots at Old Trafford, the latter's 0-0 draw was a victory for pragmatism and demonstrated that artisans could mingle with artists and thrive.

During these early weeks of August and September, Rangers hit the ground running quicker than many observers had predicted, even as Celtic crashed out of Europe, and the contrast between the two managers offered a fascinating counterpoint. Smith, no shrinking violet when he needed to morph into a Terminator – as Chick Young had discovered! – had gradually mellowed in middle age, and developed a capacity for patience, born from the experience of fielding hundreds of half-witted leading questions, and he steadfastly stuck by his sedulous squad, constantly extolling the virtues of such uncomplicated characters as David Weir, Sasa Papac, Lee McCulloch and Kirk Broadfoot. He had invested shrewdly, too, with the signing for £4m of the Croatian striker, Nikica Jelavič from Rapid Vienna, and subsequently benefited from the steady improvement of the triumvirate of Stevens, Messrs Davis, Naismith and Whittaker.

Lennon, in contrast, was a coiled spring of restless energy, a chap who seemed addicted to controversy and clamour, and while nothing could possibly justify the firestorm which rained down on him later in the title battle, somebody at Parkhead should possibly have reminded the Irishman that he was no longer employed in the playground, but was earning his money for what he achieved in a managerial capacity. Too frequently, he blurred the distinction, and inflamed situations where he should have risen above the baiting of Neanderthals in the stands. That is easier said that done, perhaps, but the comparison between Smith, the grey-haired sage of Ibrox, who had pretty much seen everything in his career, and Lennon, a human flame-thrower with a disinclination to countenance a backward step, was illuminating. What was also interesting was that the two men enjoyed a healthy relationship, away from the theatre of conflict. They could quibble and bicker over refereeing decisions, but they both appreciated that everybody makes mistakes and nobody was immune from fallacy. Sadly, for the greater good of the Scottish game, that harmony was ignored by their more rabid supporters.

Yet there was little hint of the madness in store when Rangers made a creditable start in their Champions League crusade. In the previous season, they had been embarrassed in the competition, prompting Smith's cautious strategy, but there was nothing to be ashamed of in their haul of five points from their opening three matches in Europe. Even Wayne Rooney's much-publicised return to the United ranks failed to inspire Ferguson's troops, as they were held at bay on their own patch. Next up, the Ibrox men secured a 1-0 success over Bursaspor in Glasgow, courtesy of Naismith's predatory instincts, and the winning margin, in what was Rangers' first victory in the Champions League since they had beaten Lyon away from home in 2007, might have been more comfortable if Naismith and Kenny Miller had latched onto excellent opportunities. When the Scots then gained a 1-1 draw with Valencia, with Maurice Edu scoring at both ends, the more optimistic home fans even began to talk about qualification for the last 16. Smith, notably, refused to join them. He knew the strengths and limitations of his squad and was not inclined to waste breath on any cheap triumphalist nonsense.

He was correct to strike this tone, not least because the Scots had squandered a string of fine chances in that last contest. When his team resumed hostilities with the Spanish club, they were made to pay for these transgressions as Valencia ran out 3-0 victors, assisted by a brace of goals from Roberto Soldado, before Tino Costa applied the coup de grace in the closing stages. Even during this fixture, Rangers never stopped creating openings, with Naismith twice hitting the woodwork, and their obdurate qualities were to the fore again in the rematch with Manchester United, with Ferguson's men managing nothing beyond a Wayne Rooney penalty. But by now, Smith's side were scrapping for a Europa League place after Christmas and there was no disgrace in that ambition, given the number of players they had lost in the preceding two seasons. Their Champions League campaign climaxed with a 1-1 draw against Bursaspor, with Sercan Yildirim cancelling out Miller's cracking early goal, but Rangers' haul of six points from six games could and probably should have been better. Nonetheless, Smith was realistic in his objectives and, in any case, there were other matters to attend to, whether in the increasing interest being shown in the club by the venture capitalist Craig Whyte, or the serious injury suffered by Jelavič, who had displayed myriad signs of promise, including scoring the winning goal in his side's 3-2 win over Aberdeen at Pittodrie – a match where they had trailed 2-0 at one stage, but had buckled down to launching another revival.

As the nights lengthened and the Rangers takeover talk intensified, Smith was allowed a brief reprieve from his day-to-day pressures in the middle of November when he spoke at the Scottish Football Hall of Fame dinner, where he collected his prize from one of his former captains, Richard Gough, and revealed that he wasn't actually retiring from football altogether at the end of the 2010-11 season. Few should have been surprised by this news, nor the modesty which Smith exhibited in swiftly distancing himself from comparisons with Jock Stein and Sir Alex Ferguson – 'I wouldn't put myself up with these two managers. They are in a league of their own' – but Smith was typically honest in explaining why he had remained at Rangers and what his future might entail.

> Everyone says I'm retiring, but I'm actually leaving Rangers. I still hope I'll be able to do one or two things [in football]. Maybe not as a manager, but I hope to be involved with something. I saw it [returning to Ibrox] as a short-term job to help recover the period Rangers were going through. The financial problems were kicking in and Sir David Murray asked me to come back. With that in mind, I had appointed younger staff in Ally McCoist and Kenny McDowall who would be prepared to take over in a short period. Things have worked out okay and the two of them, more than anyone else, have encouraged me to stay on longer. But I have to be fair to them. That is one of the aspects of leaving. The other is, the last time I was here, I maybe stayed a bit too long.

These remarks highlighted Smith's self-effacing nature. It was left to other people to argue that, but for his return to Ibrox and the fashion in which he had immediately orchestrated a significant improvement from the underwhelming team which had lurched towards the abyss under Le Guen, Rangers might have plunged into administration in 2008 or 2009. Indeed, as the months passed and 2010 approached its conclusion, Smith increasingly became the pulse and the heart-beat of the decent aspects of Rangers FC and the majority of their followers. When Scotland's leading referees took industrial action, prompting the recruitment of foreign officials by the SPL, Smith publicly aired his reservations over the fact that he might be involved in strike-breaking. When Ibrox supporters sought details on what exactly was happening in the Whyte takeover saga – and even as the club's vetting committee procrastinated and raised concerns over his bid – the manager was as candid as he could be in the circumstances and made it clear he thought his ally, McCoist, would face 'a hell of a job' without substantial new investment.

Meanwhile, with blizzards wrecking the fixture schedule in November and December, Smith simply had to knuckle down and persuade his charges to keep raising their standards and aim for new targets in the war on two fronts. In the Europa League, Rangers were initially pitted against Sporting Lisbon, with the first leg at Ibrox, and their hopes were dealt a blow when substitute, Matias Fernández, cancelled out Steven Whittaker's earlier goal as the sides drew 1-1 in Glasgow. It was a situation which required the Scots to score at least once in Portugal, and they hadn't exactly been finding the net with any regularity during their recent Continental excursions. Yet, as it transpired, the visitors served up a performance which was a microcosm of their season: rugged, uncompromising and full of lung-bursting application from start to finish. They grabbed the initiative when their controversial new recruit, El Hadji Diouf, produced a storming header early in the first half, but were then rocked by a brace of goals from the hosts through (former Ranger) Pedro Mendes and Yannick Djalo, the latter of whom pounced on his opponents' poor defending. With the match almost finished, and Rangers 3-2 behind on aggregate, their cause looked fairly dismal, but suddenly, against the odds, Maurice Edu slid in to finish off a sniff of a chance, Rangers were level at 2-2, and they had progressed to the next round of the competition on the away-goals rule.

That propelled them into the next round and a joust with PSV

Eindhoven, but, if truth be told, this was a period when Rangers began to wheeze, both on domestic duty, and further afield. They had lost the services of Kenny Miller, who had been flogged on to Bursaspor for relative buttons – his sale for £400,000 was a reminder of the straitened circumstances in which the club was operating – and the Scots were eventually edged out 1-0 by their Dutch opponents, after the teams drew 0-0 in the Netherlands. This meant Rangers needed to be bold and show some genuine attacking intent from the outset, but instead, they were strangely timorous throughout the first half and trailed to a goal from Jeremain Lens after 15 minutes. It was a pallid, listless first-half display, but they improved after the interval, with a Naismith header hitting the bar, and the officials failing to spot the hand of PSV's Atiba Hutchinson stopping an Edu effort on the line. But, in the event, there were to be no reprieves on this occasion, and Rangers bowed out of Europe.

All the same, Smith was seething at the decision which went against his side, and vented his anger. 'I don't know how many officials we have got on the pitch, but they all missed it. It would have changed the game. It would have reduced PSV to ten men and given us a chance to apply more pressure.' But he was honest enough to acknowledge that his team hadn't been up to scratch in the opening period. 'We were a bit disappointed with the way we started and I didn't feel we played well at all in the first half.' The only consolation for Smith and his injury-hit squad, was that they could now focus all their attentions on vying with Celtic and the pursuit of their third league title in a row.

Some might wonder why I have left it until this stage to start discussing the ramifications of the anything-but-magnificent seven Old Firm fixtures which took place through the course of the 2010-11 campaign. Certainly, they were memorable affairs, though usually for the wrong reasons, but a more convincing explanation might be that, for all their sound and fury, sectarian bile, lurid front-page headlines and 'Why Oh Why' public breast-beating, they didn't actually resolve any major arguments in the chase for the SPL. In bare statistical terms, Celtic won three of the derbies and eliminated their traditional rivals from the Scottish Cup, whilst Rangers triumphed in two, and claimed the CIS Insurance Cup in the latter, with the other couple of matches ending in stalemate. But, while Celtic were undeniably the superior force in the majority of these contests, Smith and his confrères clung on to their coat-tails, and did just enough to prevent the Lennon bandwagon from gathering any sustained momentum as the season unfolded.

Inevitably, refereeing disputes were at the centre of much of the righteous indignation on both sides of the Glasgow divide and the tone was set during their first meeting at Parkhead in October. Rangers ended up as deserving 3-1 victors, despite Gary Hooper breaking the deadlock, by replying with a Glenn Loovens own goal and a brace from Kenny Miller, but these minor details were largely ignored the following morning. Instead, Lennon was incensed by the failure of the young whistler, Willie Collum, to send off Lee McCulloch after the Rangers man dragged back Georgios Samaras when already on a booking – just one of a spate of contentious incidents which eventually cranked up sufficient levels of detestation between the Old Firm's worst elements that they should have been served with an ASBO for disturbing the peace in their homeland. Smith, for his part, believed that Celtic's inordinate focus on Collum in the build-up to the contest had placed an undue amount of attention on his shoulders. Both managers had a point – and Collum also awarded a softish penalty to Rangers when Kirk Broadfoot collapsed in the box – but the fact is that there might have been more sympathy for Lennon if he had bothered to recognise that Anthony Stokes was fortunate to stay on the pitch for a horrible tackle on Sasa Papac in the very first minute of the fractious tussle.

But no, there wasn't a word. On the contrary, Lennon snarled his frustration and annoyance, which simply made Smith's responses sound doubly statesmanlike by comparison. 'There was unfair pressure on Willie Collum, there's no doubt about that,' he declared. 'That is two out of the last three Old Firm games in which the referee has been placed under unfair pressure before the start of the match, so we have got to stop and have a look at what is happening, instead of blaming officials. If you sit down and look at it, the better team wins an Old Firm game the majority of times.'

For a brief few weeks, Rangers held sway, despite the weather interrupting their programme, but one couldn't argue with the improvement in Celtic from the squad which had lurched into a series of setbacks under the hapless Tony Mowbray the previous year. Their newly discovered cutting edge and desire were amply illustrated when the traditional rivals met again on 2 January at Ibrox, where the minute's silence to commemorate the fortieth anniversary of the Ibrox Disaster was the prelude to Lennon's side serving up an ominous confirmation of their growing power. The hosts began brightly, but their initial menace soon fizzled out and it was Celtic who increasingly put their opponents under the cosh, to the stage where there was no element of surprise when the ubiquitous Samaras rounded Allan McGregor – who had dashed out of his area like Usain Bolt in an Olympic final – to open the scoring in the sixty-second minute. The Greek striker then doubled his tally eight minutes later when he was felled by Madjid Bougherra inside the penalty area, prior to despatching his effort past McGregor with consummate ease.

For Rangers aficionados, this was a sobering afternoon at the climax of the Yuletide celebrations, in what subsequently developed into an underwhelming January. They only trailed Lennon's men by four points, and had two games in hand, but the metaphorical alarm bells sounded around Ibrox, as if delivering the message to the fans that this was scarcely going to be another stroll to the title. If anything, with Miller departing and Diouf arriving, even as Craig Whyte's takeover bid dragged on interminably, there was a sense of stagnation lurking beneath the surface at the club. Smith coaxed, cajoled and concentrated the minds of his players, but he was dealing with limited resources and the danger was that even he would be unable to paper over the cracks in the façade.

If anything, the next SPL meeting, on 20 February, was even more depressing for Rangers and their adherents, because this was an afternoon where not even the most die-hard Ibrox fan could gloss over the deficiencies in Smith's defence, while they were swept aside 3-0 at Parkhead. David Weir had shown plenty of tigerish qualities in retaining his place at the heart of the rearguard after entering his fifth decade, but, in this instance, his diminishing pace was cruelly exposed on several occasions by Gary Hooper, who snaffled the opening goal in the seventeenth minute, as the entrée to the main course of finishing off Emilio Izaguirre's coruscating attack, eleven minutes later, to present Celtic with an advantage which they never threatened to relinquish. The visitors were rarely in the mix, both ponderous and out of sorts, and with Kris Commons wrapping up the spoils in the second period, Lennon's team moved eight points clear at the summit of the SPL, and the bookmakers installed them as favourites for the SPL crown.

Smith, understandably, was left vexed and anxious by the defeat, but the veteran manager refused to betray panic, admitting simply that his side's form was a concern.

> We are better than we showed, but give credit to Celtic, they capitalised on our errors and deserved to win. We never really started the game at all. Our defending was poor, our possession was poor and it was as poor a performance as we have had against Celtic since I came back. I don't think you can say our team lacks belief or character, but we didn't look as though we had the necessary edge and that was a worrying factor for us. Everybody looks at the Old Firm games, but I don't think we have been playing that well since the turn of the year. We have been patchy with our form and we are going to have to search for something that will give us a lift in the remaining part of the season.

That quest unearthed two or three saviours whose form was decisive over the next few tumultuous months. The key factor was the fashion in which Jelavič, who returned from injury at the end of January, struck such a rich vein of form that it both diminished the impact of Miller's exit, and enhanced the confidence of those around him, including Kyle Lafferty. With Allan McGregor in indomitable form at the rear and Naismith producing a string of excellent displays, Smith had several reasons to be cheerful as the weeks elapsed. But it was Jelavič who kept popping up with vital goals, whether in his hat-trick against Motherwell or the contributions against Hamilton and Aberdeen, which broke the deadlock and turned one point into three, who was the MVP when it mattered.

There was nothing, though, that he or anybody else in Smith's ranks could do to prevent Celtic from knocking their Old Firm opponents out of the Scottish Cup in the replay at Parkhead at the beginning of March. The combatants had drawn 2-2 when they first squared up at Ibrox, with a goal from youngster Jamie Ness, and a Whittaker penalty being cancelled out by Kris Commons and Scott Brown. In truth, Celtic managed to maintain their recent stranglehold in the derbies, to the extent that they were hardly discomfited by the first-half dismissal of their goalkeeper, Fraser Forster. By the end, Rangers were down to ten as well, with Naismith red-carded for simulation. And thus the stalemate meant the sides would have to do it all again more than three weeks later.

In the interim period, we have already discussed how Lennon's ensemble dismantled Smith's team 3-0 on 20 February. But, mercifully for the Ibrox club, Celtic moved from hitting the heights to plumbing the depths in the space of a week as they slumped to a 2-0 loss at Motherwell, with John Sutton scoring a brace for the Steelmen. The balance in the SPL race had shifted again, this time in Rangers' favour, and that incessant ebb and flow continued for the remainder of the league campaign. But first there were to be two very different Old Firm stories from their Cup assignations. The second saga was glorious, at least from Smith's point of view. The first, ah yes, the first contained sufficient dysfunctional behaviour to keep Jeremy Kyle in employment for a decade.

There is little to be gained from regurgitating the litany of violence, playground histrionics and pathetic posturing which scarred the Scottish Cup replay. Suffice it to conclude that Celtic merited their win, courtesy of Mark Wilson's goal. As the atmosphere worsened and Rangers strove in vain for sparks of inspiration, they were gradually reduced to 10, with Steven Whittaker's dismissal, then nine and eight, with the red cards handed out to Bougherra and Diouf. Both players could consider themselves fortunate not to earn greater punishment, with the former doing his best to grab the card out of the referee's hand, whilst Diouf, a chap whose CV testifies to his reputation as a ticking time bomb of insanity, might have been arrested after ignoring police instructions not to walk towards the crowd and flinging his jersey into the throng. This would have been bad enough from infants, but Lennon and McCoist had to be dragged away from each other at the final whistle, and there was sufficient trouble inside and outside the stadium and, further afield across Lanarkshire, Ayrshire and West Lothian, for the First Minister, Alex Salmond, to convene an urgent summit. It was ugly stuff, a sorry reminder of the tribal hostilities which still fester in the fastnesses of west and central Scotland, and Smith shook his head when asked about it a few days later. You could almost hear the thought: 'Why the hell did I choose to hang around in this cesspit?'

It might be worth mentioning a couple of factors. Firstly, the Old Firm met four times between 2 January and 2 March, with Celtic winning three times and drawing once, with an aggregate score of 8-2 in their favour. In these circumstances, and regardless of whatever McCoist said to Lennon at the finish – it was along the lines of 'Don't you ever f***ing speak to my players like that again!' – there was no need for the Celtic manager to blow a gasket: if anything, he would have made his counterpart look stupid if he had simply laughed in his face and disappeared into the tunnel rather than losing his rag. But these were the actions of somebody who was still kicking every ball on the pitch, and reacting instinctively to insults without clicking his brain into gear. As for McCoist, it wasn't any excuse that he later declared he and Lennon had quickly patched up their quarrel and shared a glass of wine together once the dust had settled. So what! The spectacle of two intelligent men at each other's throats sent out entirely the wrong message to the idiots amongst their supporters and was the catalyst for heaven knows how many bar-room brawls and battered wives in Glasgow later that evening.

In short, these were depressing times for Scottish football and the prospect of another Old Firm clash – they had both eased through to the CIS Cup final at Hampden Park on 20 March – must have been about as welcome to Strathclyde Police and the region's various accident and emergency departments as the arrival of Jeremy Clarkson at a Green Party conference would be. But, on the other hand, this contest offered Smith, one of the few characters to emerge with his dignity intact amid the madness, one last opportunity to strut his stuff at the national stadium where he had enjoyed so much success during the previous twenty-plus years in the management game. In the build-up, he looked relieved to be talking about football again for a few days, rather than agonising over his homeland's social ills, and although Celtic were installed as favourites, Smith utterly relished these challenges and it was hardly a surprise when Rangers switched from a defensive formation to one which raced out of the blocks and took the attack to their rivals.

The consequence was an absorbing tussle, with lashings of commitment, but one which didn't spill over into bampot territory. Instead, there was plenty of positive action from both teams, albeit with the now-inevitable refereeing dispute when Rangers were twice denied valid penalty claims by Craig Thomson. The first of these provoked the most argument when Thomas Rogne seemed to foul Jelavič inside the penalty box and, initially at least, Thomson pointed to the spot. But thereafter, while surrounded by Celtic players, the official changed his mind and booked the Rangers striker for diving.

It was a contentious judgment and Smith later made his objections clear.

It's dangerous for a referee to do that. If it had happened in the other box . . . I don't know. I've said before that Celtic mounted a campaign at the beginning of the season, but if you are good enough, you will win, despite a refereeing decision. I felt aggrieved that Jelavič was booked, because the referee's first reaction was he had been fouled.

Nonetheless, Rangers gained the upper hand over their city rivals with a vengeance as the battle raged on. They seized the lead with a superb 20-yard shot from Steven Davis and, although Joe Ledley headed Celtic level, the Ibrox men kept streaming forward, as if collectively determined to ensure that their manager would collect his twentieth prize. Smith had been forced to pick a makeshift combination, one in which the versatile Naismith turned out in his eighth different position in the campaign and where Maurice Edu was at full-back. But there was no halting their relentless march and, when the contest advanced into extra time, it was fitting that Jelavič applied the coup de grâce for his club, as the prelude to Smith's men celebrating a merited success. Indeed, twelve months after their nine men had somehow prevailed over St Mirren in the same competition, there was ample proof of the remarkable esprit de corps which Smith had instilled in his squad.

It's a good victory, a terrific win. I thought the team played exceptionally well and I know that I am a bit biased, but we deserved to win the game. I've always been proud of this group of players. They are a great group to work with, they work incredibly hard and I am delighted for every one of them. The most important thing was that we won and anything else that surrounds it doesn't really matter from my point of view.

This was Smith's way of reminding people that he was unconcerned with personal glory, but, in his heart, there must have been a huge sense of relief that he wasn't going to depart Rangers for a second time without leaving anything in the trophy cabinet. By the stage that the season progressed into April, the SPL title race remained in the balance, whilst Craig Whyte continued to press forward with his Rangers takeover, even as some board members resurrected the implausible notion that the South African-based Dave King might ride to the rescue with an alternative bid. In this climate, it would have been easy for Smith and his personnel to be distracted by events outwith their control, and their title prospects received a jolt when they were beaten 3-2 at home by Dundee United. It meant that when the final Old Firm match of the season arrived on 24 April, Rangers really needed a victory at Ibrox to guarantee that their fate would be in their own hands. Celtic, in contrast, could afford a draw, as long as they could win their remaining matches, and they had shown plenty of indications they could achieve that aim.

Predictably, therefore, given the backdrop and threats which had been made against Lennon's well-being, this was no Easter Sunday gathering for those of a sensitive disposition. There were rancorous moments and further contentious decisions from Craig Thomson, who awarded a late penalty to Celtic when Davis made minimal contact with Anthony Stokes, but Allan McGregor saved Samaras' effort magnificently and despite all the grisly endeavour and enterprise on show, it finished up as much ado about nothing-nothing. At the death, however, Lennon couldn't resist sprinting on to the pitch with his hands mockingly cupped behind his ears in the direction of the massed ranks of Rangers supporters, which was bad enough, but worse still, the Celtic manager then refused to discuss his behaviour at the post-match press conference, giving the withering rejoinder: 'Don't ask me about it and don't write about it.' Was it 'humour'? Of course not!

Smith, meanwhile, knew that his side remained a point in front, but that Celtic had the benefit of a game in hand, and he was fractious in the aftermath, as if to reinforce the message that he hadn't suddenly metamorphosed into kindly Uncle Walter, with pipe and slippers and a bag of boiled sweets for the children. On the contrary, Smith could still seethe when he needed to and bristled with frustration. 'It wasn't a penalty, but then Celtic's whole campaign has been about asking for decisions,' he fumed. 'Over the whole of the season, all we've heard is that Celtic don't get penalty kicks – well, they got one today. In fact, they tried to get another, but neither to me were penalties.'

Naturally, Lennon thought differently and dragged up decisions from the first Old Firm game six months earlier, which had already attracted more than enough Collum inches. But the equation was simple enough. Rangers had to get the better of Motherwell, Hearts, Dundee United and Kilmarnock and hope that Celtic came a cropper during their run-in against Dundee United, Inverness Caley Thistle, Kilmarnock, Hearts and Motherwell. There wasn't an excessive amount of optimism among Ibrox fans that Lennon's side would buckle under the pressure, but there again, few people on either side of the Old Firm divide could have grasped at that juncture the importance of McGregor's penalty save. If it had gone in, there would surely have been no way back for Smith.

But it didn't, and one of the wonderful aspects of sport is how it can make asses of the wisest of pundits on a regular basis. As the countdown commenced to what eventually turned into another 'Helicopter Sunday', Rangers and Celtic initially traded blows as if the rest of their SPL rivals were mere cannon-fodder. Motherwell were the first to suffer, Stuart McCall's men being unceremoniously trounced 5-0 at Fir Park with goals from Lafferty, Davis, Jelavič and a Naismith brace. Then Lennon's team demolished Dundee United 4-1 at Parkhead on Mayday, with Hooper, Beram Kayal, Commons and Daryl Murphy scoring in what was an untroubled march to victory. At this stage, it was difficult to envisage another twist, and despite their past travails against Inverness, one couldn't imagine Terry Butcher's team springing an upset on a glorious evening in the Highlands when the so-called 'experts' were unanimous in their forecasts of a Celtic triumph.

More fool them. And more power to those who savour Caley's rise to the SPL.

Quite simply, this was the evening when the princes strolled onto centre stage and were trampled into the dust. In advance, Butcher had warned his players that if they repeated their mediocre performance against Aberdeen from the previous weekend, they might well get beaten 10-0. Yet, from the outset, the hosts paraded their defiance, their commitment – and no little skill – in taking the fight to their opponents. They went in front, through an own goal from Charlie Mulgrew, but any hint of surprise had barely registered before Commons snaffled the equaliser two minutes later and it appeared that normal service would be restored during the remainder of the proceedings. Yet that assumption ignored the pride, passion and panache of the Inverness ensemble, several of whom were playing for their futures after being informed by their straight-talking manager that they wouldn't be offered a new contract for the 2011-12 campaign.

And lo, they emerged in the second period and blew away Lennon's team. Grant Munro conjured up a magnificent goal to send his side back in front, then, in the sixty-second minute, a volley from Shane Sutherland struck the post and rolled into the Celtic net. Suddenly, a shock of seismic proportions was on the cards and Smith and Rangers, who had themselves surrendered four points to the same Inverness during the championship season, were rooting for one of their former heroes, Butcher. It was tense, it was fraught and Celtic reduced the deficit with a Commons penalty deep into added time. But there was no way back and that reverse gifted the initiative back to Rangers at a stroke.

The psychological effects of that outcome could hardly have been more resounding. Yet, with hindsight, Celtic could have surrendered another couple of goals and had no genuine complaints. Almost to a man, with the exception of Commons, they had been posted missing when presented with an opportunity to move two points clear of their Old Firm opponents. It was a hammer blow and the shell-shocked Lennon made no excuses.

Or at least, he didn't immediately. But in the build-up to the next round of matches there was a new controversy, amid a slew of the kind of Old Firm conspiracy theories which test the patience of the majority of rational folk. On Friday at Lennoxtown, Lennon was asked if he believed Rangers' three remaining opponents were capable of stunning Smith's side as Inverness had done to Celtic, and replied: 'I would like to think so. I don't think it is too much to ask. But you all heard David Goodwillie's comments last week [the Dundee United player had stated he wanted Rangers to win the SPL, so that the Tannadice side would qualify for Europe]. I know what he meant, but it tells a story. I'd like to think there is the same professional pride [in United] as Inverness showed the other night. Put it this way, I will be watching the games with interest. I like to think that Dundee United will be as professional as they can be and put on a game [at Ibrox].'

This was hardly the stuff of Kennedy assassinations or faked moon landings, but, given the febrile atmosphere which surrounded the title race, Lennon might have been more sensible to keep his own counsel and concede that, if Samaras had converted the penalty at Ibrox and his side had performed to their usual standard against Caley, they would have been at least two and possibly four points clear of their Old Firm rivals. His alternative strategy – which amounted to an insinuation over the attitude of fellow professionals – was always likely to be the catalyst for a fresh storm of abuse and, sadly, so it transpired.

Certainly, Walter Smith was scornful of the notion that opponents might roll over meekly and hand gifts to Rangers. He might have added that such a notion was the last thing Scottish football required, as authorities strove to deal with letter bombs, bullets and death threats, but chose instead to assert his belief that the title would need to be earned and that he was actually surprised his side had advanced to the top of the pile.

In my experience, that is not how it works in football. You show a lack of respect by even suggesting it. Moreover, in Scotland, I think you always see a good level of commitment from players and teams. I knew, coming into these games, that people would say: 'You'll win this game, that game, you'll win them all.' But, if you look back over the season, there have been points dropped in the games after the split. As soon as the split occurs, and the fixtures come out, some people say, 'Motherwell won't try or this team won't try.' But, in my experience, that doesn't happen. I always think that the managers get a good level of commitment from their players, so if you do manage to win the title in the latter stages of the season, you have got to play well to do it.

I didn't think we would get to this position [of his team's one-point lead], but we're in it. We've been there and won it in the last couple of seasons, so, hopefully, we can repeat that again. We've had the league, given it up, had the league again, and given it up again. In January, when we lost Kenny Miller and when Nikica Jelavič still wasn't back fit, I thought it would be very difficult to have the consistency to win a championship this season. But all credit to my players, they have been brilliant. We have been steadier, recently, and that is the most important thing going into these three matches.

Rangers had also capitalised from the final completion of the takeover by Craig Whyte in one of the pivotal weeks of the whole campaign. And their next mission was against a Hearts side which had lost much of the momentum and positivity which they had generated earlier in the season. Indeed, though at one stage the Tynecastle men were close to catching the Old Firm, they now trailed the Glasgow giants by more than 25 points, reflecting the miserable slump in their fortunes since the end of February. Nor was their cause helped when their maverick owner, Vladimir Romanov, interfered anew in matters of team selection, forcing Jim Jefferies to leave out Marius Zaliukas when the player was already on the bus to Ibrox. The subsequent explanation for this withdrawal – that Romanov feared the player would have been sent off by referee, Iain Brines – was a major slice of hogwash, but it amply demonstrated the difficult circumstances in which the Hearts management were having to operate while their campaign imploded.

Perhaps predictably, there was precious little indication of the vim and vigour which Hearts had exhibited before Christmas. Instead, it was Smith's warriors who grabbed the initiative and never looked like relinquishing it, especially once the ever-dangerous Jelavič sent the hosts in front in the twenty-third minute. By this stage Ibrox was a raucous arena, and the fans' elation increased when their heroes added another brace of goals from Kyle Lafferty and Steven Davis before the interval, ensuring that maximum points were in the bag before the half-time team talk. When the action resumed, Hearts' problems intensified with the ordering-off of Eggert Johnson and the visitors' misery was complete when Ryan Stevenson put through his own goal in the eighty-fourth minute to cement a 4-0 victory which was every bit as emphatic as that capsule review might suggest. If this display had followed several outstanding performances from Hearts, it might have looked a bit suspicious. But the reality was that the Gorgie side had never recovered from being trounced by the same scoreline at Parkhead, so it was simply another dud afternoon and one which exposed the gulf between the Old Firm and the rest of the chasing pack.

The following day there was a similar comfort to Celtic's 2-0 win over Kilmarnock, once they had broken the deadlock through Scott Brown on the verge of the interval. Until that stage, the Rugby Park collective had defended stoutly and they couldn't be accused of any lack of effort, but victory was secured with a marvellous goal from Kris Commons in the sixty-eighth minute and the status quo remained as the SPL entered its final week.

At this juncture, Smith was a mass of contradictions. One could detect his pride in confounding the club's critics, but he was undoubtedly growing brassed off with how every press conference was turning into a seminar on sociology and sectarianism, and whereas twenty years earlier his delight in managing Rangers had been all-consuming, some of the joy had clearly gone out of the whole business for him. In the approach to his last match at Ibrox – against Dundee United – there was a flood of lachrymose tributes and sentimental paeans in his honour, but Smith refused to be distracted by such concerns. And if he said it once, he said it a hundred times: namely, that this wasn't the end of his involvement in football, but merely the conclusion to his tenure at Govan. In short, it wasn't a moment for premature obituaries when there were battles still to be won.

That largely explained Smith's refusal to wallow in nostalgia, or parade his emotions for the benefit of the media. Instead, his countenance was a mixture of relief and defiance as he contemplated the imminent passing of the torch to Ally McCoist and spoke again of his admiration for the fashion in which his squad had rallied in adversity and made his task easier than it might otherwise have been in his last season at the helm.

This time it was my decision to go. It wasn't my decision alone to leave the last time [in 1998]. Sir David [Murray] always sacks you quite nicely. Back then, I didn't think I would ever be back at Rangers. If you get the opportunity to manage here, you are lucky. If you get two, you try to make the most of the second time. Obviously, with some decisions you make, there is a tinge of regret, but I don't see it as a sentimental thing. Overall, I have enjoyed what I have done, but I'm stepping away from it now. It's not a big thing. But I still consider it a big thing to be the manager of Rangers. You still get that buzz when you are standing in the dugout watching the game. So I'll miss that more than anything else. As I say, my leaving Rangers doesn't really matter. Whatever I feel, or whatever I've got, it matters not. Tomorrow night at Ibrox [against Dundee United] is the most important thing, because the whole club is focused on winning.

In the closing stages of a campaign which had frequently brought out the worst instincts in significant sections of Scottish society, it surely wasn't asking too much for Smith's exploits to be accorded their due recognition, whatever materialised between the Old Firm behemoths. But that wasn't how the script unfolded and maybe, given the backdrop, nobody should have been surprised that the festering tide of acrimony continued all the way to the finishing line. And beyond!

CHAPTER TWENTY ONE

Goodbye to All That

'It was a nice reception, but the time is right to go'

Even as a young man, Walter Smith was never one of life's Flash Harrys, somebody who sought special attention, or strove to hog the limelight from his peers. He was happier in a tracksuit, on the training pitch with his players, than taking centre stage and being asked to talk about himself. In which light, as Smith drew near to his final curtain at Ibrox, and the tributes began to appear, in honour of the myriad trophies he had collected since he first joined Graeme Souness at his favourite club, it was noticeable that he looked ever so slightly embarrassed by the fuss which everybody was making about his exploits.

From his perspective, it was far more important that Rangers completed the task of wrapping up their third consecutive SPL title than that he should engage in self-indulgent trips down Memory Lane. Yet, as Smith arrived at Ibrox on a rain-lashed evening in early May for his last home match in charge of his team, against Dundee United, it was difficult not to focus on the remarkable achievements he had orchestrated since he had left Tannadice for Glasgow 25 years earlier. There was the silverware, of course, the raft of league crowns and Cup prizes, but there was also a widespread feeling that Smith had transcended a string of problems which would have floored lesser individuals since returning to the Govan-based organisation. And, whether Smith liked it or not, there was no escaping the adulation of the fans, and the approbation of even those who had voiced disapproval of his tactics or team selections in previous months and years. Quite simply, he had rescued Rangers, extricated them from the mire, and saved them from the spectre of administration or worse. These were no mean feats – the opposite in fact – and thus the massed ranks of red, blue and white duly turned up to pay homage to their hero.

In these circumstances there might have been a frisson of anxiety that football would come second to fond farewells, but Rangers soon settled any misgivings on that score with a wonderfully compelling and coruscating performance, particularly during the first 45 minutes, when they ran United ragged. This was one of their most impressive qualities in the closing chapters of the season; there was no initial sparring or recourse to patient approach play, but instead a ruthless ability to go for the jugular and hit opponents where it hurt. Nikica Jelavič, who had turned into a talismanic figure and one of Smith's shrewdest acquisitions, was once again in the thick of his side's fiercest attacks and broke the deadlock with his eighteenth goal of the campaign, latching on to Steven Whittaker's cross and heading past the despairing Dusan Pernis. Then, as the atmosphere grew increasingly raucous, and the visitors were caged deep in their own territory, Steven Naismith surged forward, laid the ball off to Kyle Lafferty at the edge of the penalty box, and the Northern Irishman beat Pernis again with a well-directed shot into the right corner of the net.

Thereafter, Lafferty might have added to his tally in the second period whilst the likes of Craig Conway, Scott Robertson and Jon Daly created decent opportunities, as Peter Houston's personnel provided sterner opposition the longer that the contest progressed. Yet there was never any genuine threat to Rangers' hegemony and eventually, when the contest ended, nothing, not even the heavens emptying their load on the stadium, could dampen the fervour of the supporters, who cheered themselves hoarse, and especially when Smith and his family returned to the pitch for a lap of honour. It was a slightly surreal scene; that of the modest fellow embracing the cacophony of applause even as he and his grandchildren were soaked in the process. And Smith knew that the victory guaranteed nothing in the overall picture. Yes, it amplified the pressure on Celtic ahead of their Wednesday evening visit to face Hearts, but the SPL title still had to be won and there was every prospect of it only being decided on 'Helicopter Sunday'.

Nonetheless, he wouldn't have been human if there hadn't been a tear or two amid this tumultuous reception and perhaps it was fortunate that the rain fell when it did. Afterwards, as he spoke about his feelings, Smith seemed to recognise that he had finally gained the respect and unanimous backing of the fans, and his gratitude was plain.

This was a good win for us. Dundee United have been awkward opponents for us and I think we played exceptionally well before half-time. Our aim was to get into a position where we wanted to win our final three games – now we've won two of them. On Sunday, we can now clinch the championship [against Kilmarnock], so I hope that we can close it out. It was a nice reception I received and I thank everyone for that. For so many people to stay behind and applaud at the end was very nice. It's nice, if you are a manager, to get a reception like that. If you are leaving a club, you normally get the sack – you get thrown out. So when you get an opportunity to get applause like that, then, of course, you get a wee bit emotional. But the time is right to go. There is a change of ownership at the club and a change of manager. So I'll let them get on with it.

If Smith was basking in a radiant glow, Neil Lennon was continuing to discover that there are no hiding places in Scottish football, not even in his own dug-out. The following evening Celtic, who travelled to Edinburgh conscious that defeat would hand the title to their Old Firm rivals, were efficiency personified in disposing of Hearts 3-0, with the host's David Obua being sent off early in the proceedings, but only after Gary Hooper had pushed his team in front in the twelfth minute. The prolific striker doubled his tally in the second half – and Kris Commons wrapped matters up with a third goal – but the headlines were dominated not by the quality of Celtic's football, but the moronic behaviour of a Hearts supporter who managed to run on to the pitch and attack Lennon before being hauled to the ground and dragged away unceremoniously.

It was a scary moment all the same, and the incident prompted fevered questions as to the paucity of the Edinburgh club's security operation, although they responded with the counter-argument that it is very difficult for anybody to prevent these sort of situations if one solitary miscreant is hell-bent on sparking trouble. Sadly, though, there were subsequent scuffles between Celtic supporters and the police and, by the conclusion, the atmosphere was as sour as a month-old bottle of milk. Nobody, least of all Rangers or Smith, condoned this harassment of Lennon, and the more so because it provided fresh ammunition for some journalists – especially those with a rugby background – to claim that Scottish football was a hotbed of bigotry, violence and troglodyte behaviour.

Such a generalisation was nonsense, but rather than focusing on the last act in a pulsating championship battle, there were instead detailed reports of a beefed-up police presence in Glasgow for the SPL climax, while a variety of pundits debated whether Lennon would carry on at Celtic, when he was faced with an apparently incessant amount of hostile attacks on his person and intrusions on his privacy. Smith subsequently confessed that he wouldn't have hung around if he had been in Lennon's shoes. 'Nothing is worth that, just for a game of football. If any [suspicious] packages had been directed at me, then I wouldn't have been in the [Rangers] job any longer,' he declared. 'I know Neil said he wouldn't let bomb threats drive him out, but they would have driven me out. I have no time for the sectarian aspect which attaches itself to the Old Firm and neither do my Catholic friends. I think that if Tommy Burns had still been alive, he would have been horrified by some of the things which have gone on this season.' It was a welcome note of sanity in a climate of hysteria and, once again, Smith had demonstrated that it was possible to be a fervent Rangers supporter without hating Celtic and their fans.

Yet, not without due cause, the Ibrox boss was counting down the days until he could settle into a more tranquil pursuit, such as a white-water rafting assignment in America! There was one last round of media duties and press interviews for him to carry out and the tone of these mostly reflected both Smith's desire to escape the Old Firm pressure cooker and his understated pride at what he and his players had achieved, in fraught circumstances, since he had walked back into Ibrox Stadium in January 2007 after quitting Scotland and accepting responsibility for digging the club out of a serious hole.

It had been four years of constant pressure. There had been plenty of highs, such as coming close to winning four trophies in 2008, including reaching a European final, and the thrill derived from securing back-to-back league titles and seeing off the challenge of Gordon Strachan and Tony Mowbray in the process. But there were also lows, such as the riots in Manchester, the club's dire financial position, and the actions of some of their so-called supporters in dragging Rangers into disrepute with the panjandrums of UEFA and the police and politicians in their homeland. You didn't have to be a genius to comprehend that Smith would be well rid of that litany of woes, but he was too much in love with the Ibrox way of life not to be thankful for the chance to serve them well.

Managing Everton had been a difficult time for me and I never envisaged that, when I came back to Rangers, it would be as successful as it has been. When I got sacked at Everton the experience was not a good one, but I learned a lot while I was there and it helped me when I came back to Rangers in terms of handling certain aspects [of the job]. I do think the level of success we have had has kept the club going. I don't think administration was ever a real danger, but maybe if we hadn't won and generated the type of money we did from the likes of Alan Hutton and Carlos Cuellar, as well as the cash that we got from the Champions League, then there might have been a bigger problem. But, because of that success, I don't think there was a real danger of it.

We may have been short of iconic figures that Rangers teams have had, down through history, and in recent seasons, we have had former players saying that we were a poor Rangers team. So I don't think this team has received the credit for their abilities. If they do manage to win on Sunday, three league championships in a row would be quite an achievement. Not a lot of the players who have played for Rangers have managed to do that. They have worked under very difficult circumstances. The club has been up for sale, the contracts of team mates and others have been allowed to expire and they have gone, yet those who have stayed have retained a terrific level of professionalism.

Some of the boys who are here got new deals at the last minute. So it has hardly been a great environment, and it is quite remarkable we have got to this situation. They have seen some guys leave [such as Kenny Miller] and that can knock the stuffing out of a team, but they have shown real resilience. As a manager, you just couldn't ask for a better bunch of players to work with. I enjoyed that tribute at the end of the [Dundee United] game on Tuesday night, but that is it for me, I have had my time in the sun. If we do win the title at Kilmarnock on Sunday – and I do stress if – then it will be the players' turn to take the plaudits. They will really have deserved it.

These words reflected Smith's long-cherished philosophy of placing team success significantly beyond individual glory. It was left to others in the business to dole out lavish amounts of praise, as the 63 year-old prepared to depart his beloved Ibrox. His former confrère, Graeme Souness, declared, 'Walter has established himself as one of the finest managers Scotland has ever produced.' Craig Brown added: 'He is not just a football manager, but a human being of outstanding calibre.' Colin Calderwood, the Hibs boss, asserted: 'It's the dignity and the character of the man that stands out to everyone.' And McCoist, the fellow charged with following in his footsteps, remarked: 'I have been privileged to learn from one of the greatest managers in world football.'

Given these encomia, it would have been a terrible anticlimax if Rangers had suffered a last-ditch collapse at Rugby Park. But, in truth, such was the momentum they had cranked up whilst disposing of Motherwell, Hearts and Dundee United with an 11-0 aggregate score that there was never any genuine possibility Kilmarnock might emerge as party-poopers. Indeed, the visitors roared out of the blocks with sufficient purpose and potent striking power that the match – and the SPL title – were both effectively wrapped up in the space of seven minutes. It was a tremendous blitzkrieg from Smith's troops, who went ahead in the first minute through Kyle Lafferty, then continued their charge with further goals from Steven Naismith and Lafferty, as the travelling fans were allowed to begin their celebrations before the game had barely started. In Glasgow, meanwhile, Celtic were tackling Motherwell, and eventually trounced the Steelmen 4-0, with goals from Hooper, Samaras, Shaun Maloney and Paddy McCourt. But it was all rendered academic by the efficiency and expertise with which Rangers seized their opportunities and when they went 5-0 ahead in the fifty-third minute, with further strikes from Jelavič and the completion of Lafferty's hat-trick, there were a few supporters who wondered whether the Ibrox men might surpass the 9-0 spanking which Celtic had inflicted on Aberdeen earlier in the campaign. But they had done enough, more than enough, and Smith looked on them with the beatific smile of a master who had taught his pupils well.

It left them a single point clear of Celtic – 93 to 92 – and meant that Smith had gained his tenth Scottish championship: a tally which brooked no argument over his motivational qualities, tactical acumen, and – in Jelavič and Lafferty – savvy in the transfer market. Given the tide of goodwill which was sweeping around him and his collective on that merry day in mid May, it would have been easy for the manager to have soaked up the adulation, hoisted the SPL trophy high, and then strolled off into the sunset. But, befitting his determination not to leave his old comrade, McCoist, in the firing line, the man of the hour chose to use his valediction to call on Craig Whyte to invest properly in the future. It was a bold gambit, but nobody had more knowledge of the issue than Smith.

> The new owner is aware that this club needs quite a large level of investment in the team. He's also aware that if Rangers don't get that, they will not continue with the success they have had. Historically, if you look at Rangers over the last twenty years, they have needed a fairly large investment in the team to boost them. When the team has not had that, it has not been successful. The team now needs this boost. I think [Whyte] would be blind if he didn't realise that. Unless there is a significant investment, Rangers will stagnate. This team can't continue to do what they have been doing.

And so it continued, this bold declaration of intent. Next on the agenda, Smith discussed his admiration for Jelavič, and expressed his hope that the new Rangers regime would cling onto the Croat, despite interest being expressed in acquiring his services from the likes of Manchester United, who were rumoured to be preparing a £13m bid.

> You can see the difference Jelavič makes to the team when he's fit and I don't think that he will leave this. I don't think it would be the brightest thing for the new owner to sell one of our best players – especially when everyone is expecting him to spend money. Since Jelavič has come back from injury, we have been a different team, attacking-wise. At the start of the season, we were only just getting him bedded into the team, but since he has come back, we've had a

better knowledge of how he plays and what he does. He has been terrific for us – the focal point of everything we have been doing.

From Smith's perspective, the shackles were off. He was quitting Rangers in any case, so he might as well depart with a call to arms and speak as a fan might speak. In his previous spell at Rangers, he had looked worn down, knackered even, at the close of his tenure, but there was nary a hint of combat fatigue in this instance. On the contrary, it was evident he wished to unburden himself of the stress which had accumulated whilst he was being interrogated by the media during a veritable string of stramashes in the preceding twelve months. Thus, although Neil Lennon responded to Rangers' SPL victory with warm and sincere praise for his counterpart – 'He is one of the best managers in Scottish football and he's a really decent guy. If I had to lose to anyone, it would be to Walter' – there were some sharp words from Smith in the ensuing 24 hours, as he spelled out his anger at how Celtic had conducted themselves throughout the campaign.

With hindsight, this was one outburst too many, but it was as if Smith, having savoured his last hurrah prior to setting off for five days of white-water rafting in Idaho in aid of the Rangers Charity Foundation, had sat down and trawled over the spate of political battles, resignations at the SFA, internal wrangles within Ibrox, and the regular threats to Lennon's safety, and decided that he couldn't depart without taking a swipe at the people he considered to be primarily responsible for the brouhaha of bampottery.

After the season we have had, I am ready to get out of here, out of Scotland. It has been a fraught year for everybody. I don't think there is any doubt about that. The season got off to a bad start when Celtic put up a challenge to referees and to everybody else. That got the season off to a bad start and it all went downhill after that. From my own point of view, I hope everybody will realise that people who work in Scottish football – referees included – are always under terrific scrutiny. It was an unfair circumstance the referees were placed in and I just hope now that everybody gets on with it. And I hope Celtic realise that if their team is good enough, they will win. If they are not good enough, they'll not win – and they can't look at anybody else, whether it is referees or any other influence. I don't say that in any smug way. I just felt it set the tone for what has been a poor season for our country, in terms of publicity.

It seems as though I have spent a season answering questions about everything except football. When it gets to this stage, it seems that all of the focus has been deflected away from what it should have been on, which is football players, what they do, who wins, who loses. We've not been talking about that this year and it has been very frustrating.

Smith finished with the revelation that he had no intention of overstaying his welcome at Ibrox or seeking a sinecure at the club. On the contrary, whilst wishing the best to his successor, McCoist, it was pretty obvious that Smith believed it would be in Rangers' best interests if he didn't accept some honorary role upstairs in Govan. Instead, his conversation centred on his ambition to enjoy an element of winding down into retirement.

I will now go to watch Rangers as a fan, but it's not right for me to be hanging around when there are new people there. Everybody keeps asking me what I am going to do. I don't know, but if I wanted to stay in football, I would have stayed here. I am leaving to go and, hopefully, enjoy myself a wee bit. I will be back at Rangers, but only as a supporter. I will be buying season tickets – four of them actually. So, I will be investing in the team. If I can, I will also buy a couple of tickets for the members' suite. But other than that, you might see me at Dumbarton or Forfar.

Yet, predictably, it was his attack on Celtic which commanded banner headlines and drew a furious reaction from Lennon, whose team were in the midst of preparing for the Scottish Cup final with Motherwell, which they subsequently won 3-0. Indeed, such was the intensity of the Celtic manager's response that it was difficult not to imagine that relations between the pair of them had grown strained in the previous months. As men, as human beings, they could sympathise with the pressure that the other was under in the Old Firm goldfish bowl. But as totemic figures for their clubs, there was nothing to suggest either was ready to join the diplomatic corps when it came to allocating blame and, especially not over the issue of how the former referee, Dougie McDonald, had admitted to lying about the circumstances of a penalty decision in a match against Dundee United, back in October. (McDonald later resigned, sparking a chain of events which eventually led to a referees' strike and the subsequent exit of Hugh Dallas from his post at the SFA.)

I didn't think a lot [of Smith's comments], but I was disappointed by them. He could have spoken to me about it first. He had plenty of opportunities to do that. I didn't think there was any real need for it either. I think he's wrong, he's totally wrong. Listen, I went into a referee's room and the guy didn't tell me the truth. Then his assistant came out two days later and blew the whistle on him. I didn't, our club didn't. They did. Then there were the cover-ups and non-truths. It led me to think: 'Well, I'm not the first Celtic manager not to be told the truth.' You know, I wasn't even going to go into the room that day. It was the SPL match delegate who told me just to go in and get clarification on it. Our club was just looking for transparency. I don't think that's a lot to ask for. I mean, you are being lied to. It's not even a major lie, but it just grew and grew and grew into something which they created themselves. If I see unfairness or something I don't think is right, then I'll speak up about it. I don't see anything wrong with that. If any other manager wants to do it for his club, then I don't see anything wrong with that either. If I get criticised for it, fine. You get criticised for doing things as the Celtic manager anyway. You're damned if you do and damned if you don't.

This was a kerfuffle from the kindergarten and Smith might have been better taking the plaudits and leaving Scotland's football fraternity to make up their own minds. Because the truth is that there are few subjects more tedious than Old Firm bosses moaning about decisions going against them. Yet this battle of words shouldn't be allowed to disguise the scale of Smith's achievement in steering Rangers to another prosperous season when there were so many obstacles which might have derailed his team's progress.

In the end, the argument boiled down to whether you believed Rangers or Celtic were the better football team. Under Smith's stewardship, a squad lacking in depth won the SPL and the CIS Insurance Cup, despite suffering a series of disappointments in the Old Firm derbies as the winter marched on. He splashed out big bucks – for a Scottish club – on Jelavič, and his judgement was vindicated in a precious crop of goals as the campaign reached its climax. He showed faith in individuals such as Lafferty, Naismith and Whittaker and they came up trumps as well. And there were heroics when it mattered from the likes of Allan McGregor, David Weir, Madjid Bougherra and Steven Davis. The latter wasn't as influential as he had been in the previous season, but he rose to the challenge when it was most required and, if Craig Whyte has any sense, the spine of the future Rangers team will be built around him and Jelavič, both of whom will probably attract a growing amount of attention from England in the next transfer window.

In any case, there is no need to justify Smith's place in the pantheon of Scottish managers, not when the greatest there has ever been, Sir Alex Ferguson, is still hoovering up titles and pursuing European glory at Manchester United in his seventieth year and watching the feats of his Glaswegian comrade, Smith, with conspicuous pride. Forget, if you can, the tantrums and teddies-out-of-prams routines which disfigured the 2010-11 season to a significant extent and consider what Ferguson made of his compatriot's efforts.

Rangers are a huge club. The problem is that the fans expect success every year. More than 40,000 of them turn out at home games and still expect to see quality players in the mould of Jim

Baxter. It's amazing Walter has been able to handle that, despite the lack of investment. I recently offered him a couple of players on loan and he couldn't afford to pay their wages. He has given everything to the club and is going out at the very top. It's the same as what I told our keeper, Edwin van der Saar – make sure you go out at the top.

What he has achieved this time, in his second spell, is better than the Nine-in-a-Row success. And to do it this year, taking everything he has had to deal with, away from football, into account . . . well, I can't speak highly enough about him.

Walter is a good man. He has always stuck by his own principles and has always worked hard. He's a good thinker, a cautious thinker. He will obviously be a loss to Rangers, because it is nothing short of amazing what he has achieved there.

Once the dust has settled, that is how posterity will remember Smith, irrespective of what he chooses to do in the future. Ferguson famously retired prematurely and was bored to tears, whereupon he came back to Old Trafford and has now made the Red Devils the most successful club in the history of English football. One suspects that, following a few months away from the game, Smith might similarly be afflicted with the urge to find a new challenge, even if it is unlikely to be at the highest level. But who knows? After all, nobody would have offered you odds on his returning to his old stomping ground at Ibrox five years ago and yet he has steered his employers into a bright new dawn.

I like to think that will be his lasting legacy to McCoist and Craig Whyte and their lieutenants in the years ahead; the stability he brought, amid chaos, the success in the teeth of adversity, and the fact that, for the most part, he was a pillar of dignity and sound commonsense when so many others in his homeland were crying 'Foul', passing the buck, or shrieking Cassandra-style messages of doom and gloom.

Because, ultimately, Smith might be a sexagenarian, but he isn't some old fogey with antediluvian attitudes. He has changed things and done it his way at Rangers, whether telling his own fans that they risked grievous consequences if they didn't bid farewell to 1690 and all the accompanying baggage of tribalism, or spreading the gospel to the wider Scottish football community that change is required, and that we should be worried about how attendances are falling at nearly every club in the country.

Nobody's perfect, of course, and perhaps Smith could have exited Rangers more gracefully than by deciding to fling a few unnecessary thunderbolts at his Old Firm opponents. But in the bigger picture, this redoubtable fellow has thrived under scrutiny and being presented with fresh problems to solve at Ibrox, the place where he and his grandfather thrilled to the sight of blue-clad warriors giving their all for what they sincerely believed to be the greatest football club in the world.

And, as Walter Smith will tell those who care to listen, Rangers remain just that.

Afterword

❖

The news cycle tends to follow a predictable pattern whenever a famous name dies in the world of sport, arts or show business.

There will be initial lamentations and lavish tributes, accompanied by a lachrymose response from their former friends and colleagues, even as the public reacts to the news with different messages on social media.

But then, in many cases, even as the plaudits are still being dispensed, there will be the arrival of the contrarians who do their best to pour cold water on the commemorations.

The type of people who can 'exclusively reveal' that, behind the scenes, the man or woman who has just passed wasn't as nice or as generous as their image might have suggested. Occasionally, this sheds light and raises eyebrows. Sometimes, it even sparks a reappraisal of starry reputations.But, more often than not, it leaves one asking the question, if this is what you truly believe and you had any evidence to back it up that a person's behaviour was unacceptable, why didn't you write about it while they were still alive?

Thankfully, there was none of this with Walter Smith, a man whose demise was the catalyst for countless tributes which offered a unanimous reminder that, with this redoubtable customer, what you saw was what you got.

Scottish football, from the smallest Highland League organisation to the Premier League hierarchy, joined in a rare show of solidarity, praising Smith's qualities. Many English Premiership clubs followed in their footsteps, led by Everton, Manchester United and there were also affectionate tributes from such esteemed people as Manchester City manager, Pep Guardiola, who said:

'I was very aware of Walter's impressive management career before I came to the Premier League. But through his role as technical consultant for the League Managers Association, I have had the opportunity over the past five years to get to know him and see what a humble, insightful and very genuine man he was.

'I always enjoyed spending time with Walter and we had been planning to have dinner together again. I feel very fortunate to have had the chance to get to know him and I send my deepest condolences to Walter's wife Ethel, his sons Neil and Steven, his grandchildren and all of his family who have lost a very special man.'

Even as these paeans were being sung, the conversation started as to the best way to honour Smith's memory, with the usual discussions about the creation of statues or monuments to pay enduring homage to his memory.

Ally McCoist even called for the whole of the Ibrox area to be renamed 'Smithsville', as he delivered another touching tribute to Smith, an idea was greeted positively by significant numbers of the club's supporters.

Yet somehow, such ostentatious proposals seemed at odds with the very down-to-earth and practical, pragmatic man who achieved so much in football without ever showing any semblance of look-at-me prima donna-ism.

On the contrary, Smith never forgot his early years, growing up in a working-class family in the 1950s and studying at

Coatbridge Technical College, even as he was playing football with Chapelhall Youth Club in Lanarkshire.

His parents had encouraged him to learn a trade and, as always, he listened to them, aware of the treacherous and transient nature of pursuing ambitions in a world where you are only one crunching tackle away from the scrapheap.

Which is why, even when he was signed by Dundee United as a teenager in 1966, he was an apprentice electrician, who spent his days working with Loudon Brothers, the machine tool makers in Glasgow. This was simply common sense in his opinion. If the door was shut in his face in football, he would have an alternative vocation to help him earn a living.

His life, of course, veered off into a completely different direction, but Smith was reluctant to embrace any notion he was a stellar figure in his sphere, even after decades of winning prizes and cups at Rangers and with Scotland.

He could be as passionate as anybody in the frenzy of victory – and there were plenty of these throughout his career – but he had no interest in celebrity for its own sake or, heaven forfend, letting *Hello* magazine or any other publication into the Smith household. His private life was just that and his love for his family was one of the enduring cornerstones of his life.

Therefore, we should probably just be glad we have so many memories in print and on film of his triumphs and joyful moments, along with – and he regretted his grandchildren asking, 'Why are you swearing at that man on the TV?' – the infamous occasion when he tore strips off the BBC's Chick Young.

After all, his success coincided with the arrival of satellite TV, multi-channel broadcasting and YouTube. If you want to watch his Ibrox side from the 1990s or the 2000s in action, with Brian Laudrup, Michael Mols and Paul Gascoigne in their pomp, the pictures are there at the click of a few buttons. Similarly, if you wish to hear his own tributes to such people as Tommy Burns, Jim Baxter and Sandy Jardine, they are easily accessible.

Invariably, he didn't want a fuss made of his own endeavours, preferring to let the spotlight shine on his players, but they loved him and, almost without exception, lined up to salute him when he handed over the management reins to his confrere McCoist a decade ago.

As it transpired – and Smith had predicted as much – Rangers were forced to suffer all manner of privations and embarrassments after his departure, including liquidation and demotion to the bottom of the Scottish football league. They eventually regrouped and rebounded back into the top flight, eventually winning the title in 2021, but it was a painful process and a reminder that no organisation has a God-given right to behave as if the normal rules don't apply to them.

Smith knew that and was sounding the alarm bells as he left the dug-out while financial journalists were poring over the Ibrox balance sheets and discovering discrepancies. There was nothing he could do about that but, let's be clear. it's almost impossible to imagine that Rangers would have won three consecutive league titles in 2009, 2010 and 2011 without him at the helm.

So those championships are a fitting testimony to his powers. So too the memory of that remarkable victory over France in 2006 when Scotland were under the cosh during a first half as their opponents, replete with world-class talents such as Thierry Henry, Patrick Vieira, Franck Ribery and David Trezeguet, oozed menace and class.

Yet, by the skin of their teeth and the sheer force of their belief, they weathered the storm and Hampden resembled a revivalist rally when Gary Caldwell scored the only goal of the match in the 67th minute.

Once again, the glorious images are available to anybody who desires a shot in the arm. Caldwell himself became friends with Smith and was among the many people to recall his old gaffer with fondness in the days after his death.

Speaking to the *Sun*, Caldwell recalled:

'I think we always had a connection because of that goal I scored against France. Don't get me wrong, I know he was the type of man who made everyone feel special, but it was a moment that bonded us.

'That goal was a big one for both of us and, when we met each other, someone would always mention it. I would thank him for playing me and for giving me that opportunity and he would thank me for scoring the goal.

'But I'll never forget the one team meeting we had that week. He got us all together and spoke for about two-and-a-half hours, and he went through absolutely everything he planned to do and how he was going to do it.

'Remember, at that time, we were rock bottom. We weren't in a good place as a team and things weren't looking particularly promising. But Walter addressed everything and we all sat there hanging on absolutely every word.

'One of the things he spoke about was how important it was that we had a good relationship with the media. He told a story about how he had two framed newspaper headlines, one basically saying that he was the best manager in the world and the other saying he was the worst.

'He said if we did everything he planned, we would get the supporters with us and it would galvanise the entire country. And he was right.

'Honestly, I have never been so captivated by someone or believed in someone so much. We all walked out of that room looking at each other, utterly convinced this man was going to take us where we wanted to go.'

It is eloquent testimony to the influence of this canny operator and the way in which he used psychology and his man-management skills to galvanise and inspire his team, regardless of how the odds were stacked against him.

Nobody left his presence without a lesson, even if it was a dig in the ribs. No wonder that many players began talking about him as 'Sir Walter' even though he had never actually been knighted.

But, in so many other respects, he was both blessed and a blessing to his country. And if he considered himself fortunate to take charge of the club he loved, so many of us felt lucky that he made such an impression on our lives.

He didn't search for accolades, but he merited them in any case.

So RIP Walter Smith. And night, night, sir!

INDEX